HANDEL'S MESSIAH

THE LONDON CHORAL SOCIETY

JOHN TOBIN is well known internationally as a musicologist and conductor specialising in performances of 18th century works according to the conventions and style of that period. His performances with the London Choral Society of his own edition of the *Messiah* and Bach's *St. Matthew Passion* at the Royal Festival Hall have become annual events.

Mr. Tobin became a Licentiate of the Royal Academy of Music before he was fifteen and a Fellow of the Royal College of Organists when he was nineteen. He was Director of the Liverpool Repertory Opera in 1923; conductor of the British National Opera Company in 1927; Director of Music at Toynbee Hall in 1930; conductor of the Liverpool Philharmonic in 1940; and has been conductor of the London Choral Society since 1946.

TOBIN, John. Handel's Messiah; a Critical Account of the Manuscript Sources and Printed Editions. St. Martin's, 1970 (c1969). 279p il tab bibl 69-13491. 29.50

Lucid, terse, eminently readable, this 15-year investigation of *Messiah* MSS. and early printed editions is important for conductors, music historians, performers. Musical influences of the Italian cantata, German passion, baroque traditions of ornamentation, figured bass, and — significantly — chamber music quality, plus Italian vowel elision contribute to an understanding of Handel's intentions. Appendices provide valuable tables of MSS. and edition variants, figurings, metronome and speed ratings and musical examples of variant versions for recitatives, solos and choruses in the Autograph score, the Tenbury-Dublin, Hamburg, and RM 18.e.2 MS. copies and the Randall and Abell printed score. Selective bibliography; index. Handsome format, clear printing. Tobin's *Handel at Work* (CHOICE, Sept. 1964) represents "Handel's first, second, and third thoughts as disclosed in his many alterations in the Autograph Manuscripts of *Messiah*." (W. C. Smith) For the creation of a definitive, Urtext edition, Tobin has chosen to rely mainly on primary and early secondary sources. See also H. Watkins Shaw's *A Textual and Historical Companion to Handel's Messiah* (1965) — investigations for the preparation of his full and

Continued

TOBIN

organ-vocal scores, with particular acknowledgement to Jens Peter Larsen's "highly technical and comprehensive study," *Handel's Messiah; Origins, Composition, Sources* (1957).

GEORG FRIEDRICH HÄNDEL.

Geb. 23. Februar 1685. Gest. 14. April 1759.

HANDEL'S MESSIAH

A Critical Account of the Manuscript Sources and Printed Editions

by

JOHN TOBIN

ST. MARTIN'S PRESS · NEW YORK

Contents

Preface

THE origins of this research was a performance; a performance in scale and style such as the composer himself would accept. For while the establishment of a definitive text is of great importance, it is of no less importance that the music be brought to life in performance in the style for which it was conceived.

For many years musicians have had misgivings about the mammoth performances of Handel's music, a vogue which was established by the 1784 Commemoration Festival in Westminster Abbey. But only of late has it been realized that performances in which the overweighting of the orchestra by the chorus completely obscures the texture, the distinctive timbre of high trumpets, reeds, and strings is lost, the quality and function of the harpsichord is ignored, and the singers studiously avoid the addition of *appoggiaturas*, graces, and cadenzas to the vocal line, that such performances are completely alien to Handel's conception. Of course, music that is born of inspiration wedded to high craftsmanship will communicate its vitality even when mispresented, but this is no justification for the continuance of a false tradition.

When it was suggested that I should conduct the London Choral Society in a performance of *Messiah* I decided that research was the first essential and that it should be undertaken not only as a musicologist in search of a definitive text but as a musician in search of meaning. The two objectives, however, were often complementary each to the other. For instance, in the air 'If God be for us' Handel wrote

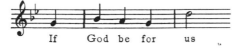

and not the sing-song

that has been printed for long years. This was an exciting discovery on both counts. And again the passage from the chorus 'For unto us' usually printed and sung

was written by Handel

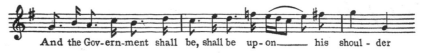

And the Gov-ern-ment shall be, shall be up-on⎯⎯⎯ his shoul-der

This search led first to the British Museum, to which any serious Handelian the world over must go; we in Britain are fortunate in that most of the surviving Handel autographs are housed in the music room there. All told they consist of ninety-seven volumes, of which thirty-seven are operas and twenty-three oratorios, including the Autograph of *Messiah*. Then to the library of St. Michael's College, Tenbury Wells, Worcestershire, where the copy from which, it is reasonably assumed, Handel conducted the first performance is housed. Thereafter to whatever museum, college library, or private collection possessed any primary copies or secondary copies of importance.

The search was revealing and seemingly unending. Fresh facts and unknown sources would unexpectedly discover themselves; a letter from the late Robert Sterndale Bennett disclosing his possession of an eighteenth-century copy containing a number of unusual features; a request from Trinity College Dublin to examine a recently acquired and hitherto unknown *Messiah* manuscript which turned out to be an eighteenth-century copy throwing fresh light upon a previously obscure point; and in Halle-Saale, Handel's birth-place, where, while looking through a pile of second-hand vocal scores, I came across a copy of the Schwenke-Klopstock-Ebeling edition published in Hamburg, 1809, in which, printed between the air 'He was despised' and the chorus 'Surely he has borne our griefs', I found an *accompagnato* for bass voice to the words 'Darum, das seine Seele gearbeitet hat, wird er seine Luft sehen, und die Fülle haben'. Authentic or not, it is of interest in that it forms a modulatory link the obvious purpose of which was to soften the impact of the F minor chorus immediately following upon the E♭ major aria. It raised an interesting question, for Handel more often modulated by the interval of a third to the chromatic mediant or chromatic submediant harmony. Did he intend the violent modulation from E♭ major to F minor, or has this *accompagnato* some significance?

The study of each succeeding copy threw fresh light upon those previously studied, sometimes confirming and sometimes questioning previous conclusions. The collation of the manuscripts covered the text; notes; clefs; signatures; tempo and general dynamic indications; instrumental phrasing and syllable slurs; ornaments; Handel's own alterations disclosing his first, second, and third thoughts; the difference between his sign for the extension of a syllable over several notes and that for the repetition of a complete sentence; *ripieno* and *tutti* indications; close scrutiny of all thumb-smudges and ink-blots; marginal notes giving the singers' names and key transpositions; and alterations in the distribution of the syllables in order to emphasize the *Affekt*. Then came the collation of the first printed *Messiah* music with other eighteenth-century editions and the pertinent nineteenth-century editions, together with the word-books of the early performances, in order to gain some idea, if not of which alternative settings Handel himself performed, at least of which settings were generally sung.

The research led to a detailed examination of the performing conventions of the period: the understood *forte* of the opening bars of any music, whatever its form or style, unless otherwise indicated; the double dotting of the dotted groups where justified by the *Affekt;* the free use of the trill to increase the tension in the line of a sustained note, or to add point to the following unadorned note, the copious use of various ornaments to underline salient notes, or intensify the sense of rhythmic progression in voice, orchestra, opera, and oratorio alike; the invariable ornamentation of cadences, particularly at the ends of sections, by a free cadenza, and this in sacred as well as secular music (the contemporary objections to the cadenza sometimes quoted were not against the cadenza *per se* but against its misplacing or its unsuitable style); the copious use of *appoggiaturas*, not only at the middle and final cadences but throughout the recitative wherever it serves the *Affekt*, i.e. wherever it adds a salient note to the salient word—further, not only in *recitative* but also in the *air;* the gracing of the *da capo* (it was a contemporary opinion that a singer who could not vary the repetition for the better was no great master); the castrati in relation to vocal timbre, for not only did Handel compose certain solos expressly to be sung by male alto but he wrote the alto chorus parts with this timbre in mind—hence the undue sepulchral quality of this part when sung only by female contraltos; and the function of the harpsichord for over two centuries as the core of the instrumental sound—so thoroughly summed up by F. T. Arnold in his invaluable book *The Art of Accompaniment from a Thorough-Bass.*

Evidence particularly relevant to the foregoing points is to be found:

(a) in Handel's own Autographs and the quite extensive ornamentation added by him to some manuscript copies in the Fitzwilliam Museum Collection, and

(b) in Tosi's *Opinioni de' Cantori antichi e moderni o sieno Osservazioni sopra il canto figurato.* This book was first published in Italy in 1723, translated into English by Galliard and published in London in 1743 and later translated into German by Agricola and published in Berlin in 1757.

The early research resulted in the performance by the London Choral Society on 18th March 1950, in St. Paul's Cathedral, London, to some six thousand people, when the oratorio was presented swept free of textual errors, garnished by the conventions of eighteenth-century performance, and in the chamber music style which was an essential part of Handel's conception of the work. Since then the Society has given some thirty such performances and at long last the style is being adopted by other groups and conductors. The author hopes that his attempt to set forth all the cruxes in the very complicated source-history of one of the world's accepted masterpieces of music and to solve the problems of performance may result in such performances being the rule, not the exception. For only when the oratorio is performed with regard for the performing conventions of the period does it sound as Handel meant it to sound. The *appoggiatura*-ed recitative, the melismatic treatment of the long sustained note, the gracing of the vocal line, the decoration of the *da capo*, and the cadential cadenza—all these are essential if the music is to spring to life. It is true that the majority of artists today are unaccustomed to the technical and stylistic demands of baroque music. But technique grows with demand and style with experience.

JOHN TOBIN

1 The Source Manuscripts

THE AUTOGRAPH SCORE

A VOLUME in the Royal Music Collection of Handel autographs in the British Museum, R.M. 20 f 2, obl. 4to. The paper measures 29·4 x 23·6 cms. The volume consists of 138 folios and one blank sheet and one other upon which is written a note regarding the bars missing from the overture and 'Comfort ye'. The collection was presented in the latter part of the eighteenth century to King George III by John Christopher Smith in appreciation of the continuance of his royal pension. It was deposited on loan in the British Museum by King George V in 1911, and in 1957 it was presented as an outright gift to the Trustees of the Museum by Her Majesty Queen Elizabeth II.

The pages containing the last 61 bars of the Overture and the first 13 bars of 'Comfort ye' are missing. These bars are not to be found anywhere in Handel's hand.

On folio 1 recto Handel wrote 'angefangen den 22 August 1741' and on folio 130 verso 'S.D.G. Fine dell' Oratorio G. F. Handel. Septemb^r 12. 1741. Ausgefüllet den 14 dieses'.

Begun on 22nd August 1741, and finished by 14th September 1741, the score contains a complete setting of Jennens's text. In spite of the many statements to the contrary the scoring, in relation to eighteenth century continuo-orchestration, is complete.

It is of supreme interest as the source of the alto-duet and chorus setting of 'How beautiful are the feet', the arioso setting of 'But lo, the angel of the Lord' composed for Mrs. Clive, the setting of 'But who may abide' throughout in $\frac{3}{8}$, and the $\frac{12}{8}$ setting of 'Rejoice greatly', as well as the non-autograph setting of 'Their sound is gone out' as a tenor arioso.

At various points throughout the manuscript Handel has written fifteen still legible marginal entries concerning seven singers; from this we learn, amongst other things, that the soprano Signora Avolio sang the tenor *accompagnato* 'Thy rebuke' as on another occasion her fellow soprano Frasi was to sing the opening tenor arioso 'Comfort ye'.

As the only complete score of *Messiah* in Handel's autograph this manuscript is of prime importance.

THE TENBURY–DUBLIN COPY

This copy is in the library of St. Michael's College, Tenbury, Worcestershire, England: MSS. 346 and 347. It consists of two volumes, oblong folio. The original leather covers have been pasted inside the present covers. The paper measures 23 x 29 cms.

The volumes came into the possession of the Ottley family. They were presented by Captain Ottley to Sir Frederick Gore-Ouseley. He, in turn, presented them, as part of his collection, to St. Michael's College Library.

The copy was made by Smith the elder. Although mainly in the hand of Smith it contains the Guadagni setting of 'But who may abide' with the change into common time at the words 'For He is like a refiner's fire', and the $\frac{4}{4}$ setting of 'Rejoice greatly' (both of which are generally sung today), the alternative recitative ending for 'Why do the nations', and the orchestral *ripieno* instructions. All of these are in Handel's own hand.

It contains also the non-autograph alternative setting as a *secco* recitative of 'Thou shalt break them', the pencilled cadenza for 'Every valley', and the transposition down into F major for contralto of the first stanza of the original setting (in B♭ major for soprano) of 'He shall feed His flock'.

This copy also clarifies Handel's almost illegible alterations in the Autograph score in the first bars of 'Thus saith the Lord'; a clear copy on a separate half-sheet of Handel's alteration to recitative is inserted over the previously copied arioso beginning.

The volume also contains ninety-nine marginal entries made by Handel himself of singers' names referring to twenty-three or possibly twenty-five artists; two entries are now illegible.

Because of these additions and clarifications there has grown a tendency to regard this copy as sacrosanct and to invest the non-autograph alterations in notes, time-values, and word arrangements contained therein with an authority overriding that of the Autograph itself; Chrysander with less reason regarded the Hamburg score in the same way. In the absence of definite evidence as to by whom and at what date they were made, all non-autograph alterations must be seriously questioned irrespective of the copy in which they occur.

Nevertheless this copy is of very great importance because of its contents alone. Further, although references to this copy as the score from which Handel conducted the first performance are for the sake of exactness usually qualified by the words 'said to be', the great number of marginal entries indicates that this was the score Handel used in his own performances, and the inclusion of the name of the bass singer, Mason, who sang in the first performance of the oratorio in 1742, points to its probable use at that performance.

THE FOUNDLING COPY

This copy is in the archives of the Thomas Coram Foundation, formerly the Foundling Hospital, London. There are three volumes, oblong quarto, bound in leather. Volume I, 89 folios; volume II, 114 folios; volume III, 53 folios. The paper measures 24 x 30 cms. The copyist in the course of the manuscript refers to each of the three sections of the oratorio as a Part, but on the front covers in gilt lettering in an ornamental gilt panel the part is described as an Act. On the inside cover of each of these volumes in exquisite penmanship is written:

CODICIL to the Will
of
GEORGE FREDERICK HANDEL Esqre
I give a fair Copy of the score and all the parts of my oratorio called
the Messiah to the
FOUNDLING HOSPITAL
Proved at London the 26th April 1760 by Amyand Esq
the Executor in the first codicil, with power
reserved to Johanna Frederica Floercken, Wife
of Floercken, the Niece and Executrix named in
the will when she shall apply for the same.

This bequest was duly executed by John Christopher Smith according to the following extract from the Minutes of the Hospital dated 13th June 1759:

> 'Mr. Smith attended the Committee and delivered to them a copy of the score of the music for the oratorio called *Messiah* left to this hospital by George Frederick Handel Esq.'

None of the volumes appears to have been used. The condition of the paper is as new. There are no marginal entries as in the Autograph, Dublin, and Hamburg manuscripts. The contents of the score differ from those of the solo part-books; 'Behold and see' and 'He was cut off', although written in the score for tenor, are not included in the 'Tenore Principale' part-book. There is a difference also in the order of contents; the order in the score is normal but in both the 'cello parts the chorus 'For unto us' is immediately followed by the air 'If God is for us'. The fact that, again in both parts, the air is copied a second time in its normal situation before 'Worthy is the Lamb' does not correct the error. Nor does the correspondence in the key of the transposed arias as between the score and the orchestral parts give the score any authority.

The Foundling score was certainly not a working copy. It is noteworthy for the following reasons: 'But who may abide' is in the Guadagni setting but is here in the soprano C clef and transposed up into A minor. The Pastoral Symphony is without a middle section; it consists of only 11 bars. 'Glory to God' has *Basso tutti* against the continuo stave in the first bar in spite of the tenor C clef and of the fact that the same music in bar 10 is marked 'Violonc'. 'Rejoice greatly' is the later setting in $\frac{4}{4}$. 'He shall feed his flock' is the first setting as an all-soprano air in B♭ major, although the score is a late copy; further, the copyist began to write the entry of the voice in the second stanza a bar too soon, a mistake that he thought to rectify by omitting a bar of the preceding *ritornello*. 'Thou art gone up on high' is in the Guadagni coloratura setting, but is here in the soprano C clef and is transposed up into G minor. 'Why do the nations' is the shortened version consisting of the first 38 bars of the air terminated by the recitative from the Tenbury–Dublin copy.

3

The manuscript contains an interesting and clear indication of the conventional use of the oboe, for, although there are no oboe parts in the score (apart from the independent parts written by Handel in the chorus 'Their sound is gone out'), the copyist in just two choruses, 'Hallelujah' and 'Worthy is the Lamb', has added to the two violin staves the indication 'e H'.

OTHER FOUNDLING MANUSCRIPTS

The Foundling *Messiah* manuscripts also include a set of orchestral parts, a set of chorus part-books, and a set of solo part-books.

The orchestral parts are in fifteen books; each book being numbered:

No.	1	Violin Primo	No.	8	Violoncello
,,	2	Violin Concertino	,,	9	Viola
,,	3	Violin Primo	,,	10	Viola
,,	4	Violin II° Concertino	,,	11	Bassoon
,,	5	Violin II°	,,	12	Bassoon
,,	6	Violin II°	,,	13	Hautbois Secondo
,,	7	Violoncello	,,	14	Hautbois Primo

No. 15   Trumpet and Kettledrums

The vocal material is in thirteen books:

No.	16	Basso Principale	No.	22	Principal Alto
,,	17	Basso	,,	23	Alto
,,	18	Basso	,,	24	Alto
,,	19	Tenor Principale	,,	25	Canto Primo
,,	20	Tenor	,,	26	Canto Primo
,,	21	Tenor	,,	27	Canto Secondo

No. 28   Second Soprano [*sic*]

Of these, nine are chorus part-books and four (Nos. 16, 19, 22 and 28) are solo part-books.   One solo part-book is missing; it was customary to divide the soprano solos in *Messiah* between two soloists, and there is only one soprano solo part-book.   The books provide authoritative evidence regarding Handel's own performances, for they bear the names of the singers who took part in the 1754 performance in the Chapel of the Foundling Hospital.   They are:

No. 28	Second Soprano [*sic*]	Sigra. Passerini
No. 22	Principal Alto	Sigra. Galli
No. 19	Tenore Principale	Mr. Beard
No. 16	Basso Principale	Mr. Wass

The other soprano who sang in the 1754 performance was Frasi.   As Passerini's book only contains the solos 'But who may abide' (in the Guadagni setting and transposed up into A minor), 'Thou art gone up on high' (in the Guadagni setting and transposed up into G minor), and 'If God is for us', it would seem that Frasi sang all the soprano solos with the exception of 'If God is for us', probably also the tenor recitative and air 'He was cut off', and 'But

Thou didst not leave His soul in Hell' (as they are not contained in the Tenore Principale part-book; at this point in that book occur the words 'Recit and Aria tacet'), and possibly 'Thy rebuke' and 'Behold and see' (for although contained in the tenor book, they are written in the soprano C clef).

Obviously the soloists also sang in the choruses, acting as leaders of their respective choral voices, for each solo part-book contains the vocal lines of all the choruses in the appropriate clef together with promptings such as *Volti e segue il coro; Segue il coro presto; Segue il coro subito*. This gives meaning to the *tutti* written by Handel himself in the Autograph score against the opening vocal subject of the choruses 'And the glory', 'And He shall purify', 'O Thou that tellest', and 'He trusted in God'; against the soprano and tenor entries in 'His yoke is easy'; and against the entry in all four voices in 'For unto us'. It would seem that in general the first vocal entry, wherever the voice was unaccompanied or where the subject was coloratura in style, was sung by the soloist(s)—the choral *concertino*. The *tutti* in the *Messiah* Autograph would seem to be specific warnings of exceptions to this convention.

THE HAMBURG COPY

This is sometimes called the Schoelcher copy. It forms part of the Schoelcher Collection in the Staats und Universitäts bibliothek, Hamburg. Shelf Mark M.A/ 1030:1, formerly 221. It consists of three volumes, bound in leather, corresponding to the three parts of the oratorio. The paper generally measures 29·2 x 23·1 cms. The manuscript is noteworthy; first, for a copy of the air 'He was despised' transposed a fifth higher into B♭ major for soprano, written in the soprano C clef (an ungrateful *tessitura* for this air): this is followed by a copy in the original key, E♭ major. Secondly, for evidence that 'He shall feed His flock' in the alto-soprano version was sung at some performance by two male singers. To the left of the top margin of this air is written 'Sig^r Tenducci' and to the right 'Guadagni'.

Thirdly, for evidence that at some time during the period the score was in use the airs 'But who may abide' (in both the original key and the transpostion) and 'He was despised' (in the soprano transposition only) were not sung. The pages containing these numbers are folded down the centre and heavily creased. Fourthly, for fourteen marginal entries. Three concerned the enigmatical contralto 'Sig^{ra}' Moser, who sang 'But who may abide' (though her name was later crossed out and replaced by that of Guadagni), the first stanza of 'He shall feed His flock' and 'He was despised'; and one concerned 'Mrs. Frasi', who sang 'Comfort ye'. Other names noted are Miss Brent and Mrs. Pinto (formerly Sig^{ra} Sibilla). At least two other entries are indecipherable. Fifthly, for containing only the shortened form with the recitative ending of the air 'Why do the nations'. Sixthly, for the fact that the chorus 'Glory to God' has neither *Disparte* nor *Lontano e un poco piano* either at the head of the score or between the two trumpet parts. Seventhly, for copies in the hand of both the Smiths, the elder and the younger. The volume is mainly in the hand of Smith the elder. But the transposed version of 'But who may abide', in folios 21–26, was written by Smith the younger. This is immediately followed by the same air in the original key written by Smith the elder. As the transposed version ends on folio 26 verso and that in the original key begins on folio 27 recto it is easy to compare the two handwritings. Lastly, for one of the two fair copies that I have found in the manuscripts of the so-called duet version of 'He shall feed His flock'.

The transpositions of the airs 'But who may abide' and 'He was despised' are later additions, for the paper of the folios concerned, volume I folios 22–26 and volume II folios 5–8, is smaller than the rest, measuring 28·6 x 22·9 cms.

The copy was clearly used in performance, but because of its many copyist's errors, because of some of the singers' names inscribed in the margins, and because it contains only the makeshift version of 'Why do the nations' it cannot be regarded as either reliable or representative of Handel's own practice.

THE GRANVILLE COPY

This copy is among the Egerton Manuscripts in the Manuscript Room of the British Museum, shelf mark Eg. 2937. It is one of thirty-seven volumes, bound in leather; the paper measures 37 x 27·7 cms., folio. The hand is that of the elder Smith. It was made for Handel's friend Bernard Granville (1709–1775) of Calwick Abbey, Staffordshire, who was brother to Mrs. Delaney, a fervent admirer and friend of Handel. The collection came into the possession of the British Museum in 1916.

It is of interest to note among the contents that the Pastoral Symphony is complete with the middle section; 'And lo' appears as an arioso only; 'He shall feed His flock' is in the all-soprano version; 'How beautiful are the feet' is in the alto-duet and chorus setting only, followed by 'Their sound is gone out' in the tenor arioso setting only.

As one of the earliest copies, *circa* 1744, the manuscript is of great interest.

This collection is in the possession of the Manchester Public Libraries. The *Messiah* section of this collection is unique as it contains score, solo vocal part-books, orchestral parts, and word-books. For years we have referred to the Foundling orchestral parts as the only known set of eighteenth-century orchestral parts. This statement in future will need to be qualified.

The score is worthy of note; first, for the considerable figuring against the basso-continuo; the air 'The people that walked in darkness' is even more copiously figured than in the Jennens harpsichord part. Secondly, as the possible source of the incorrect tie between the first two vocal notes in 'He shall feed His flock' as generally sung today. The copyist wrote:

He   shall   feed   his   flock

Note both tie and syllable slur.

Thirdly, for the numerous alterations (even though non-autograph)[1] in words and word distribution in the air 'I know that my Redeemer liveth'.

Lastly, for Handel's original word distribution in 'If God be for us'.

The word-book is of the performance immediately before Handel's death:

Printed for J. Watts: And Sold by B. Dod at the Bible and Key in Ave-Mary-Lane near Stationers' Hall 1759.

'But who may abide' is described, as in the Dublin 1742 word-book, as a recitative.

The orchestral material consists of violin primo, violin secundo, viola and 'cello. There are four solo voice part-books: canto primo, alto primo, tenor primo and basso primo. As the alto book does not contain 'He was despised' and as each of the other books at this point has 'Song tacit' it could be that at the performance for which these part-books were written this air was sung by the second soprano soloist in the transposed version from the Hamburg–Schoelcher score.

THE MARSH–MATTHEWS COPY

The copy in the Archbishop Marsh Library, Dublin, Ireland, made by one John Matthews, a lay vicar in the cathedrals of Winchester, Salisbury, and Durham, is the source of the setting of 'But who may abide' as a recitative, which was sung in place of the air at the first performance. This is not to be found in autograph in any manuscript. The manuscript throws light upon the *da capo* printed in the 1742 and 1745 Dublin word-books at the end of 'How beautiful are the feet' in the alto-duet and chorus setting (see Alternative Settings, p. 48). It is also of interest as it includes oboe staves. Mr. Watkins Shaw, in his article in *Music and Letters* on 'The John Matthews Manuscript of *Messiah*', calls attention for the first time in print to many interesting details in the writing for oboe in this copy.

[1] Identified by Professor Larsen, from a facsimile, as in the hand of Jennens, the librettist.

THE TOWNLEY HALL COPY

This is in the library of Trinity College, Dublin, Ireland. Formerly in the possession of the Townley-Balfour family, of Townley Hall, Drogheda, County Louth, Ireland, it came into the possession of Trinity College Library in June, 1960. The shelf mark is D.5.20. The volume is folio, bound in suede and measures 33 x 24 cms. The contents are especially noteworthy for the additional evidence regarding the use of the all-alto solo version of 'He shall feed His flock' and of the truncated version with the recitative ending of 'Why do the nations'.

THE MANN 'DUBLIN' COPY

In the Rowe Music Library, King's College, Cambridge. It was presented to Dr. A. H. Mann on 1st January, 1895, in Dublin. Mann dated the copy as 1780–90. The shelf mark, formerly Mn.17.25, is now Rw.MS.200. It is of interest because it contains oboe staves and because the air 'He shall feed His flock' is in the all-alto solo version only.

THE BRITISH MUSEUM RM 18.e.2 and RM 18.b.10 COPIES

The copy presented to King George III by Smith (RM 18.e.2) and an early copy (RM 18.b.10), although of value as evidence, do not add anything new to our knowledge.

THE BARRETT-LENNARD COPY

This copy is in the Fitzwilliam Museum, Cambridge. A volume in the collection presented to the museum by Francis Barrett-Lennard in 1902, it contains additional figuring and copious ornamentation in pencil in the choruses as well as the airs. Mr. C. L. Cudworth of Cambridge University dates the ornamentation, on very clear evidence, as early nineteenth century.

THE ROWE COPY

This copy, in the Rowe Music Library, King's College, Cambridge, came from the Louis Thompson Rowe Collection. The shelf mark, formerly Rw.75.8, is now Rw.MS.8. It is dated down the spine 1761 and is of interest for evidence regarding the use of alternative settings.

THE GOLDSCHMIDT COPY

The Goldschmidt copy, now in the possession of an anonymous collector (anonymity was a condition of the sale when it was purchased some years ago by a New York bookseller from the 1946 Rosenbach catalogue, in which it was item No. 448) contains added ornamentation (non-autograph) for the *da capo* of 'He was despised' as well as altered word arrangements in 'I know that my Redeemer liveth'.

THE NEEDLER COPY

This copy is in the British Museum Manuscript Room, Additional MS. 5062.

THE BARCLAY SQUIRE AYLESFORD COPY

This copy is in the British Museum Manuscript Room, Additional MS. 39774, and, with the Needler Copy, is of interest in that the only settings in both of 'How beautiful' and 'Their sound is gone out' are the alto-duet and chorus and the tenor arioso respectively.

A CONTEMPORARY EIGHTEENTH-CENTURY MANUSCRIPT HARPSICHORD PART

In the British Museum. Royal Music Library, shelf mark RM 19.d.1. This is in the hand of Jennens, the librettist of *Messiah*. It contains copious figuring and elaborate ornamentation. The copy is incomplete as it finishes with 'Glory to God'.

THE GERALD COKE COPY

This copy is in the Gerald Coke Collection, Jenkyn Place, Bentley, Hampshire, England. There are three volumes, oblong folio, bound in leather, measuring 24.5 x 30 cms.

It is noteworthy for its contents: 'And [*sic*] lo!' is in the arioso setting only. 'Rejoice greatly' is in the original $\frac{12}{8}$ setting only, but in a shortened version. 'He shall feed His Flock' is in the original setting as an air for soprano, preceded by the recitative in the soprano clef, at the soprano pitch. 'He was despised' has added ornamentation in the voice part. 'How beautiful are the feet' is in the alto-duet and chorus setting only, and is followed by 'Their sound is gone out' in the tenor arioso setting only.

The manuscript is also of interest because 'Why do the nations', following after the particular settings of the previous two numbers, is in the unshortened form; while the basso continuo in the air of 'O Thou that tellest' is unfigured, it is figured in the chorus; and 'The trumpet shall sound' has one word only as an indication of style—*pomposo*—Handel's further explanatory *ma non allegro* is omitted.

THE STERNDALE BENNETT COPY

This is in the possession of Mrs. Robert Sterndale Bennett, of 8 Eastgate, Tenterden, England. There is one folio volume, bound in leather, which measures 27.5 x 42 cms. It was presented to Sir William Sterndale Bennett (Professor of Music in the University of Cambridge, Principal of the Royal Academy of Music, and a close friend of Mendelssohn) 'by his friend and lover of his genius Edward Clare'.

The manuscript is noteworthy, first, for the copyist's use of the violin clef (𝄞) generally discarded after the seventeenth century. This, of course, was only for the violin parts, except in one case—the arioso 'But lo!' in which he wrote the voice part in the violin clef, in error. Secondly, because pages 31 and 32 are in Smith's handwriting. It should be further noted that these two pages are the only pages in which the later form of the G clef occurs.

Thirdly, for its contents, in which 'But who may abide' is in the original setting for bass. 'But lo!' is in the setting as arioso only. 'Rejoice greatly' is in the original $\frac{12}{8}$ setting, unshortened and with a full *da capo*. 'He shall feed His flock' is in the original setting as an air for soprano, preceded by the recitative in the soprano clef, at the soprano pitch. 'Thou art gone up on high' is in the soprano setting (described by Chrysander as contralto, see page 25). 'How beautiful are the feet' is in the alto-duet and chorus setting only, and is followed by 'Their sound is gone out' in the tenor arioso setting, only. It should also be noted that the copyist writes tympano for timpani and, in the Pastoral Symphony, violetta for viola.

2 *The Printed Editions*

IN the two hundred years since Handel's death *Messiah* music has been published in very many editions and various forms and formats:

'Songs in *Messiah* an Oratorio set to musick by Mr Handel';

'*MESSIAH* an Oratorio in Score. As it was originally performed composed by Mr HANDEL. To which are added His additional Alterations';

'The Overture, Songs and Recitatives in the *Messiah* a sacred Oratorio';

'*The Messiah* an oratorio composed by Mr Handel for the Voice, Harpsichord, and Violin with the Chorusses in score';

'Handel's Hallelujah in the *Messiah* and Grand Coronation Anthem to which are prefixed two new fugues';

'Ten Grand Choruses from Mr Handel's oratorio of the *Messiah*';

'Six Overtures fitted to the Harpsichord or Spinnet' (*Messiah* is here 'The Sacred Oratorio');

'Sonatas or Chamber Aires for a German Flute, Violin or Harpsichord being the most celebrated Songs and Ariets collected out of the late Oratorios and Operas compos'd by Mr Handel';

'A fourth set of Favourite Bass Songs. . . . . These Songs are proper for two Violoncello';

'The sublime Oratorio of the *Messiah* . . . with the Choruses in Score';

'The best edition of the best musical work at a price to suit everyone Combining unprecedented cheapness with superior arrangement and splendid embellishments' (Edited by Dr John Clarke of Cambridge);

' "Comfort ye my People" as sung by Mr HARRISON, in the *MESSIAH*';

'The complete Oratorio arranged for piano solo' (Czerny);

'A selection for Cornopean'; 'for two concertinas';

'3 Stücke aus Händel's *Messias* in Form einer Sonate zusammengestellt';

'Potpourri';

'Fantasia on Subjects from Handel's *Messiah*' (Dupuis);

'Auszug der Vorzüglichsten Arien Duette und Chore aus G. F. Händels *Messias* . . .';

'*The Messiah*, An oratorio in complete score Composed by G. F. Handel, First performed in the year 1741 [*sic*], with all his subsequent alterations and additions. Appended to which in a distinct form are the accompaniments for wind instruments added by W. A. Mozart';
and other editions of the full score with which I will deal later, as well as numerous editions of the vocal score.

In spite of this body of work there was urgent need for a new edition, for the errors in print (even as late as the full score issued by Fischer, New York, in 1950) and the misinterpretations of eighteenth-century performing conventions are many.

The task of editing *Messiah* is onerous because the Autograph in places is indistinct or almost illegible, the composer's intentions not always clear, his alterations often difficult to decipher. Smith himself in several places misinterpreted the Autograph, and his team of copyists repeated his misinterpretations; Handel, like many another composer, thought one thing and inadvertently wrote another; some of the important primary and secondary manuscript copies have been altered not only by an obvious crossing-out and superimposing of the alteration but also by knife-erasure and rewriting so that the alteration is likely to remain unperceived except under microscopic examination. In some cases no form of scientific examination can disclose when or by whom the alterations were made. In the course of the years the MSS. have been rebound. During rebinding not only were the edges of the pages trimmed (so removing what might have been valuable evidence in the form of marginal notes) but quite possibly an air or chorus was removed or another inserted. There is, in fact, evidence of this mis-binding in the Tenbury–Dublin copy. In that manuscript the chorus setting of 'Their sound is gone out' is bound *in the middle of* the G minor soprano setting of 'How beautiful'. The twenty-fifth bar of the air (i.e. the fourth bar of the eleven-bar middle or contrast section) which completes the verso of one folio is immediately followed by the chorus. And after this chorus, which ends the recto of a folio the verso of which is blank, the remaining bars of the air are to be found beginning a fresh folio. A somewhat similar mis-binding is to be found in the Aylesford copy in the Newman Flower collection. In this the sequence is 'Let us break their bonds', bars 1 to 47; 'Hallelujah' chorus, bar 7 (beat 3) to 47; 'Let us break their bonds', the remaining bars—48 to 62; 'He that dwelleth in Heaven'; 'Thou shalt break them'; 'Hallelujah', bars 1–7 (beat 2) immediately followed by bars 47 (beat 3) to the end. It follows that the presence or absence of any one setting in any one MS. is, in itself, insufficient evidence for any definite conclusion. The Tenbury–Dublin copy, a working copy (the many notes in Handel's own hand indicate that it was used by him) and generally considered to be the copy from which he conducted the first performance, contains 'How beautiful' only in the setting as an air for soprano in G minor. Yet there is almost incontestable evidence that the alto-duet and chorus setting was sung at that performance. Again, the manuscript of this duet and chorus setting is not to be found in the Tenbury–Dublin conducting copy but in the appendix to the Autograph score. The evidence is further confused because of the multiplicity of contemporary manuscripts and of early printed editions; because editors in the past have pinned their faith to a particular manuscript (Rimbault to the Smith copies and Chrysander to the Schoelcher–Hamburg copy); because for two hundred years edition after edition of the full score, almost without exception, has repeated some, in most cases all, of Smith's errors: Walsh in 1749, Randall and Abell in 1767, Wright in 1785, Arnold in 1789, Preston in 1807, Bland and Weller in 1813, Addison in 1831, John Bishop and Sir Henry Bishop in 1841 *et seq.*, Vincent Novello in 1846, Rimbault for the English Handel Society in 1850, Chrysander Handelgesellschaft in 1901, Prout–Novello in 1901, Schering–Peter in 1939, Fischer (New York) in 1950. One example will suffice. In 'The trumpet shall sound' Handel brought in the second violin and viola (after a rest of six beats) on the third beat of bar 112. Smith, writing the Tenbury–Dublin copy, wrote the entry on the third beat of the following bar, 113 (altering the rest to nine beats), and from Walsh in 1749 onward this error has been repeated in print (with further alterations of the notes by the different editors in endeavours to correct the resulting obviously incorrect harmony) by, to name only the principal editions, Randall and Abell, Arnold, Rimbault, Chrysander, Prout, and the edition issued by Fischer of New York in 1950 as the full score to be used with the scholarly Coopersmith vocal score.

This confusion has been aggravated by the failure of editors to distinguish between a definitive *Urtext* edition and an exact reproduction of the Autograph score in type. The latter, with its reproduction of Handel's errors of commission and omission and with no explanation of the performing conventions of the period, is of little use either to scholar or performer. Even the scholarly Schering full score in the accompanied recitative 'Thus saith the Lord' reproduces Handel's fortuitous mixture of conventional note-values in bars 1, 5, 7, 8, 9, 25, and 27, and actual (i.e. performing) note-values in bar 3, without any indication that in all these bars the first struck note of beat 3 is to be played as a semi-quaver, not a quaver as printed, and that this is not a matter of editorial interpretation but the unquestionable application of a convention which every eighteenth-century musician would here observe.

The true purpose of research is not merely to place yet another definitive and *Urtext publication* upon library shelves, not merely to disclose the many textual inaccuracies that through repetition have become accepted, but rather to produce a definitive and *Urtext edition*. Definitive, in that it contains all the music of the work extant in the composer's own hand, together with any non-autograph settings of whose authenticity there is satisfactory evidence; *Urtext*, in that all the composer wrote is so printed that it is clearly to be seen; and an edition which, being faithful not merely to the composer's text but also to his intentions, will enable whoever may be so inclined, scholarship apart, to perform the composer's work as the composer himself would have wished to hear it, with the forces and balance and in the style of his period. Such an edition is of necessity an interpretation, but an interpretation in the light of scholarship and with all that is editorial made obvious by the use of a special editorial type.

In the course of my research I have collated not only all the available principal and secondary *Messiah* manuscripts of importance, but also all the full scores, most of the vocal scores, and much other *Messiah* music published during some two hundred years.

THE EARLY EDITIONS

The printed music of *Messiah* was issued in four main forms:

1. The airs and recitatives with the Overture and Pastoral Symphony.
2. The same as the above, but with the addition of the choruses in score.
3. The choruses only.
4. The full score.

The airs and recitatives were first engraved in 1749 for Walsh as 'Songs in *MESSIAH* an ORATORIO Set to Music by Mr. HANDEL'.[1] Later editions were published as 'The Songs', etc. All the vocal music was printed on two staves. The lower contained the single-line basso-continuo only, and the upper the voice-part with words, plus any possible instrumental cues in the *ritornelli*. Only the Overture and Pastoral Symphony were printed with a four-stave layout, the basso-continuo stave representing violoncello, contrabass or *fagotto*, and being figured for the keyboard continuo player. Not all publishers printed figurings; e.g. Harrison & Cluse published an edition in 1798 without a single figuring. Some, on the other hand, added figuring where none was intended, e.g. Harrison & Co., issued an edition in 1784 in which the bass of the two *grave* sections of the sequence 'Since by Man came death' is figured, so erroneously implying an accompaniment, for although Handel troubled to figure even *bassetti* basses when he desired a continuo accompaniment, in these choruses not merely did he not figure but he filled the continuo stave with rests.

The second form, apart from the choruses, is generally similar to No. 1, except that whereas in that style of publication the only indication of the orchestral matter is a violin cue in a *ritornello*, in No. 2 the orchestral parts are shown in reduced close-score. Not in every case, however; e.g. the fully scored *accompagnato*, 'All they that see Him' is here given in two single lines only, one containing the first violin-cum-voice, the other the basso-continuo. The choruses are laid out on four staves.

The early issues of choruses from the oratorios were arrangements for organ or harpsichord. The early 'SIX / GRAND CHORUSSES [sic] / From Mr Handel's / ORATORIOS / Adopted for the / ORGAN or HARPSI-CHORD / By / Mr Hook. Price 6d / LONDON / Printed for Wm. Randall Successor to the late Mr J Walsh in Catherine Street in the Strand', contains three choruses from *Judas Maccabeus* and three from *Messiah*. The three from *Messiah* are 'He trusted in God', 'Surely He hath born [sic] our griefs' (the latter including 'And with His stripes' and 'All We like sheep'; in the early editions these three were always listed under the one title, the source, *Messiah*, being printed only against 'Surely He hath born our griefs') and 'And He shall purify'.

[1] The earliest known general issue of *Songs in Messiah* is 1763, but the plates were first prepared in 1749; therefore, for the purpose of scholastic argument, I refer to the earliest extant printed *Messiah* music as the 1749 edition.

Another publication is 'Ten / GRAND CHORUSSES / From Mr Handel's / ORATORIO / OF THE / MESSIAH / Adapted for the / ORGAN or HARPSICHORD / AND VOICE / Book 2nd Price 3/6d / LONDON / Printed by THOMAS PRESTON 97 STRAND / of whom may be had / Most of the favorite Songs, &c in the several Oratorios, 50L pr. Cent cheaper than at any other place . . ' The words 'AND VOICE' are very thick and black and would appear to be an addition. In spite of this addition the publication is a two-stave lay out, a sort of 'piano-conductor' copy. The various contrapuntal entries are indicated by *Treble, Contra, Tenor* or *Bass;* the words of the momentarily predominant voice are printed between the staves; in *divisions* of secondary importance the notes are printed in small size; the left hand is generally in single notes or octaves; even in a passage where there is only the soprano against the basso-continuo (e.g. bars 1–7 of 'His yoke is easy') there is no attempt to *realize* the harmony. The engraving is cramped in comparison with the Randall publication.

There is yet another interesting issue of the choruses, printed by Rt. Birchall at 133 New Bond Street and edited by Dr. Crotch. Crotch was born in 1775 and died in 1847. He was organist of Christ Church, Oxford, in 1790, when he was fifteen, and professor of music in the University in 1797, when he was only twenty-two. This publication is a keyboard arrangement of the Overture, Pastoral Symphony, and complete choruses. It contains much ornamentation—trills, turns, long and short appoggiaturas—and indicates the

arpeggiation of chords by pyramidal forms of differing sizes △ △ △

when the pianoforte is used; the arrangement is advertised as for organ or pianoforte, not harpsichord. And, especially noteworthy, the tempo of each movement is given as for a hanging pendulum (a piece of string with a weight attached) in inches; e.g. 'Surely He hath borne our griefs' is given as ♪=26 inches, while 'All we like sheep' is given as ♪=6 inches.

Before discussing the full scores there is one other early publication to which I would refer. This is

SIX Overtures
fitted to the
HARPSICHORD or SPINET
VIZ.

Samson	Deidamia
The Sacred Oratorio	Hymen
Saul	Pernasso in Festa

Compos'd by
Mr. HANDEL
Being all proper Pieces for the Improvement
of the Hand on the Harpsichord or Spinet
Eighth Collection
London. Printed for J. Walsh in Catherine Street in $\frac{e}{y}$ Strand

The *Messiah* Overture occupies pages 173 to 175. It is numbered XLIII. The first section is described as *grave* but the fugue is without the usual *allegro moderato* indication. The arrangement is exceedingly thin. There is very little attempt to give any indication of the inner parts. Except for the opening and closing bar the left hand is in single notes. Many bars consist merely of a single line of notes in each hand. The ornamentation consists of sixteen *trs* and one 'mordent'. Ten of the sixteen trills and the mordent are in the twelve bars of the *grave*, the remaining six being spread over the eighty-nine bars of the *allegro*. The positioning of the ornaments is of interest:

FULL SCORES

The first known full score is the one first issued by Randall and Abell in 1767. But there exists a score which bears a Walsh imprint. This is from an edition issued by J. Alfred Novello in 1850, the advertisement of which reads:

Full Scores of Handel's Works, printed from the original plates engraved by Mr Walsh (and his successors) and which were corrected by Mr

Handel himself and published in his lifetime, being the only five works which have been preserved Viz:—

    I.   The *Messiah* in full score, with the appendix.

   II.   *Judas Maccabeus*, full score.

 III.   *Acis & Galatea*, full score.

 IV.   The Coronation Anthem 'Zadock the Priest' in full score.

  V.   The Dettingen Te Deum.

            Known as Walsh's Edition, 5 Vols.

            J. Alfred Novello London 1850.

The Walsh title-page reproduced by Novello suggests that the Randall and Abell 1767 edition is not the first edition of the full score, that Walsh himself published a full score. However, that most knowledgeable of Handelians, Mr. William C. Smith, declares that this Walsh title-page is not genuine— that originally the plate used was a Randall and Abell plate, but that prior to the Novello 'Walsh' publication Randall and Abell's name was removed and Walsh's name substituted. Examination of the volume discloses that 'Comfort ye', 'But who may abide', 'But lo', 'He was despised', 'Thou art gone up on high' (soprano setting), 'How beautiful' (soprano G minor air), 'Thou shalt break them', 'If God be for us', and 'O Death' (in the appendix) are printed from plates used by Randall. They have *Messiah* in the top margin of the first page and 'W.R.' in the bottom margin of the last page of each of these numbers. 'He shall feed His flock', 'But thou didst not leave' and 'I know that my Redeemer liveth' have *Messiah* but not 'W.R.' Further, the index page is from the plates used by Preston in 1807. It differs from the Randall and Abell index as follows: It is without the note, 'The songs marked thus (†) were set after the original Performance a Second Time and are inserted in the Appendix'; the type is much smaller; the page is divided vertically by a plain *rule* instead of an ornamental printer's *flower;* it does not use the conjunction 'and' either by word or sign except in one instance: 'Sym^y. & Rec^e.'; it uses 'song' instead of 'air'; 'Valley' is printed 'Valey'; the three parts of the Passion choral trilogy are listed separately instead of under the one title 'Surely he hath borne our griefs'. Further, the index and the contents of the Novello–Walsh-cum-Preston publication do not agree. 'But who may abide' in the body of the score is described in the index as 'Rec^e.' although the version printed is the bass air, and in the index to the appendix it is again listed as 'Rec^e.' although the version printed in the appendix is the Guadagni air; 'But [sic] lo' is described as 'Rec^e. Accom^d' although the version printed is the soprano arioso; the $\frac{4}{4}$ 'Rejoice greatly' is not listed in the Appendix although the setting is actually printed; 'Thou art gone up on high' in the body of the score is listed in the index as 'Rec^e.' although the version is the soprano air, and in the index to the appendix it is again listed as 'Rec^e.' although the version printed is the Guadagni air.

We can, therefore, dismiss the Novello–Walsh publication and its part-parent, the Preston edition, from serious consideration. But before doing so it is worth while to inquire into the description of 'Thou art gone up on high' in the Preston index as a recitative.

Both 'Thou art gone up on high' and 'But who may abide' were generally described as recitatives in *Messiah* word-books for a quarter of a century (only in one word-book—that of the Academy of Ancient Music issued in 1744— are they described as 'songs'). This might be regarded as the careless repetition of a printer's error, but is it likely over such a period of time? Handel, when he first composed the oratorio, set both these texts as 'airs'. There is no proof that he at any time set them as recitatives. However, Arnold in his edition *circa* 1787, over the 'Contents' at the end of the volume (page 219) printed a recitative setting of 'But who may abide', with the heading: 'N.B. This Recit. was originally performed in Ireland'. And this same setting is to be found in manuscript in the Marsh–Matthews copy dated 1761 with the note: 'N.B. If the foregoing Song is to be left out, as it was in the performance at Dublin, sing this Recitative upon the very same words.'

The evidence of Marsh–Matthews and Arnold may be considered as reasonably conclusive that 'But who may abide' existed from early days as a recitative and was so sung in Dublin at the first performance. Therefore, with the exception of the performances in which Guadagni sang, this recitative may well still have been sung. But while this recitative is to be found both in print and in manuscript (although not in Handel's autograph) there is not any trace of a recitative setting of 'Thou art gone up on high', and yet, as we have seen, its description as such persisted in the word-books and is to be found in the Preston index. On the other hand, Arnold did print the 'But who may abide' recitative. If such a setting of 'Thou art gone up on high' existed would he not have printed that also? It could have been that there was not space for it. The position in the Arnold score of the 'But who may abide' recitative (occupying the top quarter of the Contents page, immediately following the 'Amen' chorus, with the word 'Contents' engraved in large capitals part-way down the page) shows that its inclusion was an afterthought. There certainly was not room for another afterthought. So the possibility remains that 'Thou art gone up on high' in the form of a recitative did exist and may yet be discovered in some as yet unknown manuscript.

Of the eighteenth-century full scores there remain only Randall and Abell (the first printed full score) 1767, H. Wright, 1785, and Arnold, 1787. The Randall and Abell and the Wright are almost alike, the variations being slight, such for example as the design of the printer's flower and the sign for the conjunction. The lay-out, pagination, and contents are alike, and the actual contents of each publication agree with its index.

However, the contents of the early editions and the contents of the Autograph do not agree, and from this arises a matter for speculation; it concerns the setting of the text 'And lo!' Handel twice set this text, first as an accompanied recitative and later as an arioso (in the latter setting he wrote 'But lo!')

I have used the words 'first' and 'later' purposely, for in the Autograph the verso of one folio contains the last few bars of the Pastoral Symphony, the *secco* recitative 'There were shepherds' and the accompanied recitative 'And lo!', followed on the recto of the next folio by the *secco* recitative 'And the Angel said unto them' and the accompanied recitative 'And suddenly'; there is not an inch of wasted space. The sheet containing the arioso setting (inserted between the above verso and recto) is an obvious addition to the manuscript; the verso of this sheet is empty save for the final seven bars, which take up only the top two of the ten staves. At the head of this arioso is written the name of the actress-singer Mrs. Clive, and it is generally assumed that Handel wrote it expressly for her. As far as we know, Mrs. Clive sang only in the 1743 performance.

When first setting the section of text between the Pastoral Symphony and the chorus 'Glory to God', Handel clearly had decided upon the plan of *secco—accompagnato—secco—accompagnato*, using the *accompagnato* to express the heightening of emotion within the recitative, c.f. in *Alexander Balus* the recitative beginning 'Yes he was false' that precedes Ptolemy's aria 'O Sword and thou all daring hand' or, in *Esther*, the recitative beginning 'How have our sins provoked the Lord' that precedes the chorus 'Ye sons of Israel mourn'. In view of this one might reasonably suppose that with the disappearance of Mrs. Clive from the *Messiah* cast Handel would discard the arioso and revert to his first and logical plan. Yet six years later in the first printed *Messiah* music it is not the *accompagnato* but the arioso that is included. (As it is commonly supposed that Smith must have had something to do with this publication—at the least to have advised regarding the contents—it should here be remembered that the Smith Tenbury–Dublin copy contains only the *accompagnato*.) Twenty years later still Randall and Abell included both the arioso and the *accompagnato* in the full score. They were, however, unquestionably in error in printing the *accompagnato* in the Appendix (so declaring it to be an alternative) and giving pride of place in the body of the volume to the arioso. This idea persisted till the middle of the following century, for Edward Rimbault, in the preface to the edition which he edited in 1850 for the English Handel Society, writing of 'And lo!' comments 'which Handel *originally set*[1] as a short air'. Still, the error had some justification, for the arioso is the only setting to be found in the Smith British Museum R.M. 18.b.10, Egerton, Mann 'Dublin', Townley, and Gerald Coke manuscripts. It is also to be found, together with the *accompagnato*, in the Autograph, Needler, Barrett-Lennard, and Marsh–Matthews manuscripts. Further, it was printed by Randall and Abell 1767, by Arnold *circa* 1787, and by Clarke in various editions between 1809 and 1835. Therefore, Mrs. Clive and 1743 notwithstanding, it would appear that the arioso continued to be sung privately if not publicly for some years, possibly for the first quarter of the nineteenth century, but not later publicly. For in the edition published by Goulding and D'Almaine

---

[1] The author's italics.

in 1831, against the arioso the following statement is printed: 'N.B. This is usually omitted.'

An analysis of the editions from Randall and Abell to Rimbault is informative regarding the particular versions of the alternative settings that were sung and the general performing practice. In the following notes the editions will be dealt with separately, although not exhaustively as that would involve much repetition, but everything that is unusual or otherwise of interest will be noted.   First let us look at the four full scores: Randall and Abell 1767, Arnold 1789, D'Almaine 1831, and Rimbault for the English Handel Society 1850.   (The Bland and Weller *circa* 1813 is not discussed as it is identical in contents, pagination, and lay-out, even to the numbers of bars to a page, with the Preston, although the engraving is different in note- and letter-size and the placing of the basso-continuo figuring differs.)

The Randall and Abell full score is virtually complete, for it contains, either in the body of the volume or in the Appendix:

'But who may abide' in the all-$\frac{3}{8}$ bass air, and the Guadagni $\frac{3}{8}$-C settings;

'And lo!' in the recitative *accompagnato* and the arioso ('But [*sic*] lo') settings;

'Rejoice greatly' in the $\frac{4}{4}$ and the $\frac{12}{8}$ settings;

'He shall feed His flock' in the all-soprano air and the 'duet' settings;

'Thou art gone up on high' in the soprano (rising to f$^{\prime\prime}$), the Guadagni, and the bass settings;

The 'How beautiful' and 'Their sound is gone out' sequence in the soprano G minor *da capo* air, the first section of the G minor air followed by the E♭ chorus, the alto C minor air followed by the tenor arioso, and the alto-duet and chorus settings;

'O Death where is thy sting' in both the complete and the shortened version.

The only numbers missing are the recitative setting of 'But who may abide', the alto transposition of 'Then shall the eyes of the blind' (to precede the duet version of 'He shall feed His flock') and the shortened version of 'Why do the nations' with the recitative ending.   I leave out of consideration the non-autograph recitative version of 'Thou shalt break them' as, apart from being pencilled in the Tenbury–Dublin manuscript, there is no evidence to support its use.

The Arnold score lacks only the alto transposition of 'Then shall the eyes of the blind'.   It is the first attempt at the production of a score which is both authentic and performing.   In other works Handel gave quite explicit instrumental indications.   E.g., against the obbligato stave he wrote variously *violini tutti*, *unisoni*, *tutti unisoni* indicating violins or violins and oboes.   And against the basso-continuo stave he wrote *piano senza viola*, *forte colla viola*, *violoncelli*, *viola e violoncello senza contra basso*, *bassi pizzicato senza cembalo*.   But in the Autograph of *Messiah* he wrote scarcely any such indications.   Arnold, in his edition of *Messiah*, interprets Handel's intentions in accordance with the practice of the period. He indicates the use of violins in unison (not solo) in *obbligato* airs. He indicates the varied treatment of the basso-continuo by the use of *bassi* in airs, *tutti bassi* (indicating wind and strings) in choruses, *violonc* in high passages in airs, and in choruses when the bass is not singing, *Org. e. Violonc* where only the alto and tenor are singing, *Org.* where only the soprano is singing, *organo e tutti bassi* in such numbers as 'Worthy is the Lamb'. Arnold also makes clear Handel's dynamic intentions; e.g. at the beginning of 'Glory to God' he adds *forte*. (Later editors, either unmindful of eighteenth-century performing conventions or misunderstanding Handel's *Da lontano e un poco piano* written between the trumpet staves, have here indicated *piano*). Arnold also provides the evidence of the conventional use of oboes. In the orchestral lay-out of 'And the Glory', first and second oboes are named and bracketed respectively with first and second violins. This is merely a general indication that oboes are to be used. It does not mean that the oboes double the violins throughout. The Mann 'Dublin' and Marsh–Matthews manuscripts—also the Foundling contemporary orchestral parts and Handel's own scoring for oboes in 'Their sound is gone out'—show the oboe as a composite part, here doubling the voices, there doubling the strings. Indeed, Arnold indicates this, for, while after 'And the Glory' oboes are not mentioned at the beginning of the score of any number, Arnold indicates the use of oboes with the voices, e.g. over the first entry of the sopranos in 'For unto us a Child is born' is printed *Oboe 1° e 2° col Soprano*.

The D'Almaine full score (*circa* 1831) (copy in the British Museum, shelf mark Hirsch IV, 777) was issued in two volumes. The title-page of volume I bears the imprint 'D'Almaine & Co. Soho Square'. Opposite the title-page, below the engraving, is 'Published by Goulding & D'Almaine for Addison's edition of the *Messiah*'. At the end of the second part is a circular stamp: 'Printed by Goulding & Co Soho Sq: London'. Opposite the title-page of Volume I is the *Ecce Homo* engraving of Christ wearing the crown of thorns, 'on stone by L. Haghe. W. Day lithog 17 Gate St.' Opposite the title-page of the second volume is an engraving of the Hudson portrait of Handel engraved by M. Gauci. The edition was printed from plates engraved for separate issues of the airs. Each air bears a full title, together with the price (though sometimes the actual figure following the word 'price' is omitted). The basso-continuo is figured and there is an attempt to realize the bass. For example, in 'Every valley' the single bass notes in bars 16, 17, and 18 are printed as close-position triads. Mozart's additional orchestral accompaniments are included. The contents include all the alternative settings and versions with the exception of the alto transposition of the recitative 'Then shall the eyes of the blind' and the recitative setting of 'But who may abide', and with the addition of 'The trumpet shall sound', and 'If God be for us' 'as altered by Mozart'. Referring to the additional accompaniments to 'The trumpet shall sound', the editor writes that he 'hopes he will not be thought guilty of presumption for having introduced a few notes for the

B

Horns in those parts of the Air which Mozart had omitted altogether'. Of the alternative settings the following are stated to be the ones 'usually performed': the Guadagni setting of 'But who may abide', the *accompagnato* setting of 'And lo!,' the bass setting of 'Thou art gone up on high', the G minor setting of 'How beautiful are the feet' (the alto duet and chorus setting is 'usually omitted in performance'), the chorus setting of 'Their sound is gone out'—sung as 'semi-chorus and repeated in full chorus', the complete air 'Why do the nations' and the shortened version of 'O Death where is thy sting'.

It is noteworthy that although in other airs the editor has printed 'improved' word arrangements (including the following less than felicitous final vocal cadence in 'I know that my Redeemer liveth'),

he wisely ignores the alteration in 'If God be for us' printed in the 1749 edition of *Songs from Messiah* and prints Handel's original:

In view of the various imprints, three things will serve to identify the publication: First, the note in the tenor part, bar 102, of 'And with His stripes', lacks the necessary ♮. Secondly, the figuring ⁷₄ proper to that same bar is misplaced in the previous bar. Thirdly, a very unusual version of the voice part in bars 52 and 53 of the Guadagni setting of 'Thou art gone up on high'; in the Autograph the note b in both of these bars is flat. While reasonable doubt has been expressed about Handel's intention in bar 52, there is no doubt that in bar 53, the note is b♭. The D'Almaine score gives b♮ in both bars.

The Rimbault edition printed for the English Handel Society in 1850 was an attempt to produce a scholarly score. It was not a very successful attempt for, in addition to repeating over thirty errors, Rimbault omitted the alternative settings but included Mozart's additional accompaniments, the truncated 'The trumpet shall sound', and the mis-shapen 'If God be for us' with the drastically altered melody. All this in the name of the English Handel Society! That he should print this footnote to the original trumpet parts: 'Handel's original trumpet parts to be omitted in performance', is understandable in view of the changed use of the trumpet as a general-purpose middle-compass instrument and the consequent change in the rim and bowl of the mouthpiece and the bore of the instrument. But there is little justification for the footnote to 'Rejoice greatly': 'Handel's violin part to be omitted in performance', nor for that to the G minor soprano air 'How beautiful': 'The violin part to be omitted in performance, Mozart having given it to the flute'.

If Rimbault worked on the Autograph he misread it, for referring to 'And lo!' he writes 'which Handel *originally set*[1] as a short air'. Of the duet version of

---

[1] The author's italics.

'He shall feed His flock' he writes: 'The alteration is most unwarrantable and absurd.' He cannot have seen the interpolation of the alto transposition of the first stanza in the Tenbury–Dublin copy, containing the marginal note that in effect gives authority to the duet version. Rimbault would seem to have regarded the shortened version of 'Why do the nations' with the recitative ending as the original version, for of this air he writes: 'In its original state a mere sketch of what Handel afterwards filled up.' The facts are that the Autograph score contains the air complete in every way; while the recitative ending, to be introduced at bar 39 of the original air, was an afterthought on a separate sheet of manuscript to be found at the end of the Tenbury–Dublin copy. In the score Rimbault describes 'Thy rebuke', 'Behold and see', 'He was cut off' and 'But thou didst not leave' as for soprano. And yet he must have known that Handel composed them for tenor, for in the Preface he refers to the last two as usually 'now' soprano.

VOCAL SCORES

The earliest vocal scores, as we have seen, are of two forms. One contains only 'The overture, Airs, Duets, etc.'; the other is complete with recitatives and choruses, the latter being 'in score'.

Harrison and Co. issued one of the former, 'published as the Act directs May 27, 1786' and 'corrected by Dr Arnold', under the general title 'The Songs of Handel'. Except for an occasional short-score reduction of orchestral harmony this is a simple two-stave lay-out for voice and basso-continuo. Instrumental *obbligati* are shown only in *ritornelli*, never against the voice.

The contents include 'But who may abide' in the Guadagni setting; 'Thou art gone up on high', neither the original bass nor the Guadagni version which superseded it, but the soprano setting not extant in Autograph but to be found in manuscript in the Egerton copy, the Smith copy RM. 18.b.10 (with the voice part written in the soprano C clef) and printed in 'Songs' (1749) and in the body of the Randall and Abell score 1767; 'He was despised' and 'The trumpet shall sound', printed minus their middle sections; 'How beautiful', printed in full as a *da capo* air; 'Rejoice greatly', printed in the $\frac{4}{4}$ setting only; and 'Every valley' printed with one bar too many in the opening *ritornello*, the deletion in the Autograph score being unobserved.

The same publishers two years earlier had issued an edition of the second form—with the recitatives and choruses. Except for the choruses, which were in open score, this also was a two-stave lay-out. As in the 1786 publication the orchestral harmony here and there is reduced to short score, but only here and there. Unlike the 1786 publication, both 'He was despised' and 'The trumpet shall sound' are printed as *da capo* airs with their middle sections, although the *da capo* indication is omitted from the former air. But at the end of 'Why do the nations' a large D.C. is printed erroneously. The G minor soprano air 'How beautiful' being printed in full, there is not, of course, any setting of the text 'Their sound is gone out' following that air, the next number being 'Why do the nations'. This publication, however, has an appendix which contains just two numbers, the chorus setting of 'Their sound is gone out' and the alto-duet and chorus setting of 'How beautiful'.

Mention must be made of three publications issued by Walsh relating to *Messiah*. First, 'A / Fourth Set of / Favourite Bass Songs / Collected from the Late / ORATORIOS / Compos'd by Mr. HANDEL / These Songs are proper for two / Violoncello'. This contains the four bass airs and the *accompagnato* 'For behold, darkness' from *Messiah*. This publication, as the description 'proper for two Violoncello' indicates, is a simple two-stave lay-out.

'HANDEL'S Songs / Selected from His Oratorios / FOR THE / HARP-SICHORD, VOICE, HOBOY, or / GERMAN FLUTE / The Instrumental Parts to the above Songs may be had Separate to Compleat them for Concerts'. This publication is a simple two-stave lay-out, without any attempt at a reduction of the orchestral harmony. The five volumes contain nineteen numbers from *Messiah*. They include the *accompagnato* 'Thy rebuke', the duet 'O Death', and the arioso 'But lo!' The avoidance of any reference to *Messiah* is pointed. For example, the first volume contains eighty arias, two of which are from *Messiah*. In seventy-eight cases the title of the oratorio is given, but against the *Messiah* numbers the space is empty. 'O Thou that tellest' is printed as for counter-tenor at the octave above. 'Why do the nations' is marked *da capo* erroneously.

'Sonatas / or / Chamber Aires / for a / German Flute / Violin or Harpsichord / Being the most Celebrated Songs & / Ariets, Collected out of the late / Oratorios & Operas / Compos'd by / Mr Handel.' Only two of the volumes contain airs from *Messiah*: Volumes V and VII. Volume V contains eighty-nine items of which only one is from *Messiah*. On the Contents page this is given as 'He was despis'd . . . (No.) 398. *Messiah*'. But at the top of the air itself it is described as 'No. 398. Air by Mr Handel in the Sacred Oratorio', and over the opening bar, 'He was despised'. Volume VII includes some sixty-six items (including an occasional instrumental 'Symphony' or minuet and an odd vocal duet) of which nine are from *Messiah*. On the contents page the source is stated in each case as *Messiah*. In these volumes the numbering of each air is *seriatim* but not the pagination. The melodies are quite copiously ornamented.

A very interesting *Messiah* score 'carefully adapted to the VOICE AND ORGAN, the Choruses in Score' was published and edited by James Peck of No. 47 Lombard Street in 1813. The format is much the same as the Harrison and Co. 1784 publication. Except for the choruses, which are in open score, the lay-out is simply two single lines, the basso-continuo and the voice. The bass is figured throughout. Where Handel's choral bass differs from his continuo bass both are printed (on the same stave) but the continuo bass is given in notes of smaller size. The choral alto part is printed at the octave above, as for counter-tenor. Where *ritornelli* are printed they appear in notes of small size, and in order to differentiate completely between voice and instrument they are marked 'INS^t.' or 'IN^t.'

The lay-out in choruses is unusual. The top stave is the alto, below that is the tenor, next comes the soprano ('treble'), followed by the figured bass. In the preface the editor hopes that the edition 'will be found useful and convenient to singers and to players, for which purpose the treble part is set next the base contrary to the usual practice—but custom (the wise man's plague and the fool's idol) is here thought of less consequence than utility—for it can make no difference to the singer and must be of essential convenience to the organist, as it enables the player to have his hands always employed by the introduction of the leading parts when the treble is silent'. The preface also includes 'a few observations on the general manner of performing this oratorio' from which the following extracts are taken:

'Comfort ye' and 'Every valley' "were originally written in the tenor cliff and, of course, intended to be sung by a male voice, but it has been sung by Madame Mara and other great soprano voices."

'But who may abide' "is intended for an Alto voice, but it is frequently sung with great effect by Mr. Bartleman as a Base Air." Obviously the Guadagni setting.

'Then shall the eyes' "is written in the contra-tenor and is sung by an Alto or Mezzo Soprano as is the first part of the succeeding Air 'He shall feed His flock' and the second part thereof by a soprano primo." Handel, in fact, wrote the recitative in the soprano C clef. The alto transposition was the work of a copyist.

'He was despised' "is usually sung by an Alto or mezzo-soprano for which it is intended. I have heard the late Mr Harrison sing it as a Tenor in the key of B♭, but the accompaniments lose much of their effect." The transposition into B♭ is in the Hamburg–Schoelcher manuscript.

'Lift up your heads' "is now generally sung as a semi-chorus . . . but it does not appear to have been the author's intention." In the word-book in the Eindhoven collection at the Victoria and Albert Museum, London, GE 144, said to be of the 1743 performance but being without a printed date, this chorus is printed in seven sections described as: semi-chorus 'Lift up your heads'; semi-chorus 'Who is this King'; semi-chorus 'The Lord strong and mighty'; semi-chorus 'Lift up your heads'; semi-chorus 'Who is this King'; semi-chorus 'The Lord of Hosts'; chorus 'The Lord of Hosts'.

'Thou art gone up on high' is set "twice as a Tenor [*sic*] and also as a base (very nearly all alike) but as the air here given is now always used it has not been thought necessary to insert the others." Peck's tenor may mean counter-tenor, although his use of contra-tenor, alto and mezzo soprano in the reference to 'Then shall the eyes' suggests that by alto he means the male voice. The version of the air printed by Peck is neither the original bass nor the Guadagni but the non-autograph setting for soprano. It obviously was not intended to be sung by a male alto, for in addition to being written in the soprano C clef the compass rises to f^{11}.

Handel's 'Pifa' is described as 'Sinfonia Pastoralle', doubtless out of courtesy to its Italian origin.

The volume has an appendix which contains the duet-and-chorus setting of 'How beautiful are the feet' and the middle sections of 'He was despised' and of 'The trumpet shall sound', which, according to the editor, "are not used at the best Publick concerts".

This edition repeats the errors of all previous editions together with an odd misprint peculiar to itself, e.g. in the duet 'O Death where is thy sting' Handel's note c^1 in the alto to the word 'is' in bar 5 (of the shortened version) is given as d^1.

The Clementi Collard and Collard edition is printed from the same plates as the Peck edition. The title-page declares it to be 'Printed by Clementi Collard and Collard, 26 Cheapside', but on the final page is 'Peck engraved 1813'.

An edition on similar lines was 'Published and Sold by G. Walker at his Music Warehouse, No. 106 Great Portland Street' as 'The Sublime Oratorio of the *Messiah*'. It differs from the Peck in the following particulars: it has not an appendix, it includes the middle sections of 'He was despised' and 'The trumpet shall sound', 'Thou art gone up on high' is printed in the Guadagni setting, the sequence 'How beautiful are the feet' and 'Their sound is gone out' is given in two forms—(a) the G minor soprano air (the first section only) followed by the chorus setting of 'Their sound', and (b) the duet and chorus followed by the tenor arioso of 'Their sound'.

John Clarke-Whitfeld (1770–1836), otherwise 'Dr. John Clarke of Cambridge', Professor of Music in that University in 1821, edited vocal scores of the oratorio for a number of publishers including Jones and Co., T. E. Bates, and Button, Whittaker and Beadnell. The last of these announced him as editor of 'The Vocal Works composed by G. F. HANDEL'. The general title-page to the series bears an engraving by Henry Cooke of the Roubilliac statue. Then follows a page taken up with a dedication to the King by the publishers, dated 20th October 1809. The title-page to *Messiah* bears an engraving by Isaac Taylor of the painting by Carlo Dolci of Christ carrying the cross, with the superscription 'He was a man of sorrows'. An advertisement reads 'Best edition of the Best Musical Work at a price to suit every one. Published fortnightly price one shilling or complete bound in cloth Price 12s. Plate edition 21s. Under the immediate patronage of His Majesty. National Edition of Handel's Works. The *Messiah* by Dr. John Clarke of Cambridge combining unprecedented CHEAPNESS with SUPERIOR ARRANGEMENT and SPLENDID EMBELLISHMENTS No. 1 Price one shilling containing the whole of the words, with an interesting account of the Oratorio, Sixteen folio pages and Four Sheets of Music (equal to what is usually charged 4s.) on superior paper and printing and a splendid engraving from the celebrated picture of "St. Cecilia" by Raffaelle.'

The Button, Whittaker and Beadnell volume has an appendix. This includes 'But who may abide' in the original all-$\frac{3}{8}$ setting for bass, 'But lo!' in the arioso setting for soprano, 'Rejoice greatly' in the $\frac{12}{8}$ version, 'Thou art gone up on high' in the Guadagni and the soprano settings, 'How beautiful are the feet' in three forms—(a) the soprano G minor air complete with the middle section, (b) the alto-duet and chorus, and (c) the alto C minor air—'Their sound is gone out' as a tenor arioso, and the uncut version of 'O Death where is thy sting'. In the recitative that precedes 'O Death', Clarke provides an amusing deviation from Handel:

R. Cocks and Co., 6 New Burlington Street, London, founded in 1827, issued five editions of the vocal score between the years 1841 and 1857, all edited by John Bishop of Cheltenham. The 'Centenary' edition of 1841 and the 'People's' edition of 1855 were general-purpose publications, issued, in the words of the publishers, 'to meet the wishes of those who simply require the work as it is generally performed'. The contents are remarkable only in that, although 'But who may abide' is the later setting (the Guadagni), 'Thou art gone up on high' is the original bass setting, and although 'Thy rebuke hath broken his heart' and 'Behold and see' are described as for tenor, 'He was cut off' and 'But thou didst not leave' are described as for soprano. The 'Library' edition of 1852 and the 'Student's' edition of 1855 were, as their titles suggest, attempts to produce an authoritative and complete edition. They include an appendix which contains 'But who may abide' in the recitative and the original all-$\frac{3}{8}$ setting for bass; 'And [sic] lo!' as a soprano arioso; 'Rejoice greatly' in the $\frac{12}{8}$ setting complete; 'He shall feed His flock' in the original all-soprano setting; 'Thou art gone up on high' in the Guadagni and the soprano settings; 'How beautiful' in the alto C minor air and the alto-duet and chorus settings; 'Their sound is gone out' from the middle section of the original soprano setting of 'How beautiful' and as a tenor arioso; 'Why do the nations' in the shortened form with the recitative ending; 'O Death where is thy sting' in the first, i.e. the complete version, also 'The trumpet shall sound' and 'If God be for us' "as altered by Mozart". Both volumes contain a complete book of words, and the 'Student's' 1855 edition also contains a memoir of Handel and a reproduction of the Hudson portrait. The publishers also advertised separate vocal parts in folio, with the alto and tenor parts in the C clefs. The 'Festival' edition of 1857 was another general-purpose publication of no particular importance.

Sir Henry Bishop (1786–1855), Professor of Music in the University of Oxford, edited a vocal score 'Printed and published (for the Proprietors) by D'Almaine and Co., 20 Soho Square'. This also is of no particular importance.

Dr. George J. Elvey (1816–93), organist of the Chapel Royal, St. George's, Windsor, edited (*circa* 1854) a vocal score 'As performed by the London Sacred Harmonic Society'. (This was the society that published the facsimile of the Autograph score in 1868.) The contents follow the by now well-established plan, and include such settings as the Guadagni 'But who may abide'; the *accompagnato* 'And lo!'; the $\frac{4}{4}$ 'Rejoice greatly'; the 'duet' 'He shall feed His flock'; 'He was cut off' and 'But thou did'st not leave' as for soprano; 'Lift up your heads' as semi-chorus until bar 33 (at the beginning is 'Chorus', but at bar 33 is 'Full Chorus'); 'Their sound is gone out' to be sung first as a quartet and repeated as a chorus, and 'Why do the nations' as a *da capo* air.

A study of these various publications in relation to the use of alternative settings yields the following results:

'And lo!': *Accompagnato* or arioso?
Although Randall and Abell and Arnold erroneously gave pride of place to the arioso, and although the arioso was still printed in 1855 in R. Cocks's 'Student's' edition, this error was corrected in practically every other publication. Where, between 1809 and 1855, both settings were printed, the *accompagnato* setting was either printed in the body of the volume (and the arioso relegated to the appendix) or in order of printing it was placed first; see Button, Whittaker and Beadnell 1809, and R. Cock's 'Student's' edition 1855. Many editions included only the *accompagnato*—Harrison 1784, Peck 1813 and the many 'as it is generally sung' publications issued during the second quarter of the nineteenth century.

'Rejoice greatly': $\frac{12}{8}$ or $\frac{4}{4}$?
Randall and Abell naturally gave first choice to the $\frac{12}{8}$ setting, the only setting in the Autograph score, as did Wright, Arnold, Preston, Bland and Wellers, and Goulding and D'Almaine. But Harrison, 1784, and all the general-purpose publications of the first half of the nineteenth century printed only the $\frac{4}{4}$.

'Thou art gone up on high': Bass, soprano, or Guadagni?
This is the most interesting question of all. But first let me clarify my description of one setting as soprano. The three settings are generally referred to as one for bass and two for alto. Peck, in 1813, wrote: 'Set twice for Tenor and also as a Bass.' (I have suggested elsewhere that Peck's 'tenor' means counter-tenor, for one of these two settings was composed by Handel specially 'For Guadagni' the male alto, and more likely than not Peck would have known this.) The bass and the Guadagni settings are autograph, being contained respectively in the Autograph score and the Tenbury–Dublin manuscript. The third setting, non-autograph and one of Peck's 'tenor' settings, is described by Chrysander as for contralto. The facts regarding

this setting are:

(a) The earliest manuscript source is the copy of the score made by Smith *circa* 1744 for Handel's friend Bernard Granville;

(b) The voice part in that manuscript is written in the soprano C clef;

(c) The compass rises to f''.

The use of the soprano C clef does not necessarily rule out the male alto, but the tessitura and the sustained notes c'', d'' and e'' together with the use of f'', completely rule out this voice. That this setting was written for the female alto (i.e. Chrysander's contralto) is equally unlikely. The contralto, as distinct from the mezzo-soprano, like her so-called male counterpart the contra-alto[1], regards e'' as the general upward limit. For this reason, and to avoid confusion with the Guadagni setting and the more readily to distinguish between the alternatives, I refer to this setting as for soprano.

The choice between these three settings made by the various editors and publishers is somewhat puzzling. That the Guadagni is the superior few would question. In the Tenbury–Dublin manuscript I found a sheet of blue note paper on which is written: 'Thou art gone up on high: Handel seems to have preferred the variations rather than the bass form in the printed copies, as the C. Tenor and soprano resemble each other.' Mr. Watkins Shaw, the Hon. Librarian of St. Michael's, Tenbury, thinks the writing could be that of Capt. E. T. Ottley who presented the manuscript to Sir Frederick Gore-Ouseley. Yet only one general-purpose edition (i.e. printing a single editorial choice), Walker *circa* 1820, printed the Guadagni. Four other general-purpose editions issued between 1830 and 1850 printed the bass setting. Six of the more scholarly (the work of only two editors, John Clarke and John Bishop between *circa* 1809 and 1855) printed all three but gave first choice to the bass. Another six, issued between 1767 and *circa* 1831, printed all three but gave first choice to the soprano. Another two, Harrison, 1784, and Peck, 1813, printed only the soprano. Now, as the Randall and Abell full score derived from the early publication *Songs in Messiah*, it is understandable that Randall and Abell (followed by Wright and by Preston) should give as first choice the setting included in *Songs*. Obviously *Songs*, first prepared in 1749, could not include the setting composed for Guadagni, who had but recently arrived in England. One would, however, expect to find printed there the setting written by Handel in the Autograph score, i.e. the setting for bass. Instead of this, the setting is one not to be found in either the Autograph score or the Tenbury–Dublin manuscript, one that is not extant in autograph but only in the hand of a copyist—the soprano setting. Yet this setting must be considered equally with the other two as being authentic, for, although the least good of the three settings, it is unmistakably Handel. Further, it would scarcely have been written by Smith in the Egerton manuscript in 1744 and printed by Walsh in the 1749 edition of *Songs* had it not been authentic.

[1] In the manuscript in the British Museum, shelf mark RM 20.g.6, Folio 1, verso, Handel refers to 'Mr. Elford', a male alto, as 'Contra Alto'.

29

It remains a matter for speculation why the Guadagni setting, composed by Handel for a favourite singer, should have been ignored by Harrison in 1784, and, with the exception of the Walker, 1820, by all general-purpose publications of the first half of the nineteenth century.

'How beautiful are the feet': Soprano air, alto-duet and chorus, or alto air?

All editions from 1749 to 1855 gave the soprano air in G minor as the first choice (the earlier ones printing it in full as a *da capo* air, the later ones printing only the first section)—this, in spite of the fact that in Dublin for the first performance Handel chose the alto-duet and chorus setting.

The alto-duet and chorus setting was generally printed as second choice. Rimbault, however (printing only the soprano air in G minor—without the middle section) in his preface gave the order of composition as, 1. Alto duet and chorus; 2. Contralto air in C minor; 3. Soprano air in G minor.

The contralto air in C minor (non-autograph and printed with a written-out slide, *appoggiaturas* and *divisions*) was generally printed last. R. Cocks's Library edition printed it second, while both Harrison and Peck, as well as later nineteenth century general-purpose editions, ignored it.

'Their sound is gone out': Chorus or tenor arioso?

With the exception of Arnold, who placed the arioso first in order of printing, all the editions gave first choice to the chorus. As Harrison, except for the middle section of the soprano air 'How beautiful', prints only the chorus setting of this text, it would seem that when 'Their sound' was sung as a separate number it was customary, as early as 1784, to sing the chorus setting.

SOME CONCLUDING THOUGHTS

Alternative settings

Whether the particular versions were printed because they were the versions sung at that time, or were sung because they were the versions to be found in print in general-purpose editions, it is a reasonable presumption that they were the versions generally sung.

The da capo *air*

Of all the solo numbers in *Messiah* only two are *da capo* airs: 'He was despised' and 'The trumpet shall sound'. (Although the soprano air setting of 'How beautiful' was first composed as a *dal segno* air, the evidence suggests that Handel himself later deleted the middle section.) It is obvious, therefore, that this was not a mechanical act of composition; he intended them to be performed as *da capo* airs. When they are so performed in the style that was intended, with the *da capo* ornamentation that the *Affekt* demands, then the charge of monotony so often levelled against the *da capo* air is groundless. Nevertheless it has to be recorded that in one edition (Peck 1813) these airs were printed in the body of the volume minus their middle sections, the

middle sections being relegated to the appendix. In the same volume, however, the air 'Why do the nations' is marked 'D.C.' although not so intended
by Handel. It also is to be noted that the G minor soprano air 'How beautiful'
was printed as a *da capo* air in the editions of the eighteenth century and those
editions of the first half of the nineteenth century that aimed at being complete
—with two particular exceptions, Rimbault and the R. Cocks 'Library'
edition. But while Rimbault did not print the middle section Cocks did print
it separately in the appendix.

Ornamentation

With the exception of Arnold's, practically all the editions issued within a
hundred years of Handel's death contain the minimum of ornamentation—just
some instrumental trills on the penultimate note in transitional and final
cadences in addition to those ornaments written by Handel. There is almost
no additional vocal ornamentation.

The Randall and Abell full score issued in 1767, the first edition of the
complete oratorio (*Songs in Messiah*, although issued eighteen years earlier,
contains only the Overture, Pastoral Symphony, and airs—and for the most
part these plates were used when printing the score) reflects the Autograph.
The few editorial ornaments are outbalanced by the number of Handel's
trills which are omitted. Here are some of the omissions—the reference unless
otherwise stated is to the first violins or violins in unison, the bracketed figure
indicating the beat of the bar.

'Every valley,' bars 5 (3), 45 (2) and 63 (1st quaver).
'O Thou that tellest,' bars 11 (1) and 60 (1st quaver).
'The people that walked in darkness,' bar 8 (2): Handel's only trill in this air.
The Pastoral Symphony, bars 3 (1), 7 (1) second violin, 7 (3), and 11 (1).
'Rejoice greatly,' $\frac{4}{4}$ bar 41 (2).
'Behold the Lamb of God,' bars 2 (4), 3 (4) second violin, and 6 (4) first
and second violin.
'He was despised,' bar 2 (the 5th quaver) first and second violin: Handel's
only trill in this air.
'Thy rebuke hath broken His heart,' bar 7 (4) first and second violins:
Handel's only trill in this number.
'Lift up your heads,' bar 7 (1): Handel's only trill.
'I know that my Redeemer liveth,' bar 42 (1–2), the voice: Handel's only
vocal trill in this air.
'Thou art gone up on high', Guadagni, bar 115 (3–4), bass setting bar 72
(1–2).

The omissions in the printed score are, however, quite fortuitous, for in
many instances where a trill has been omitted in an opening *ritornello* it is
reinstated in the closing *ritornello*. The basic similarity between the Randall
and Abell score and the Autograph is further shown where Handel, in a fully
written-out closing *ritornello*, did not trouble to write any of the trills he had

written in the opening *ritornello;* in such cases (see the chorus 'Behold the Lamb of God') the closing *ritornello* in the printed score is similarly without a trill.

The editorial trills number thirty-five, but nineteen of these—all in the one air 'If God be for us'—are identically situated repetitions of a trill written by Handel. The remaining sixteen are mainly conventional cadential trills.

The almost complete lack of vocal ornamentation in the Autograph score is due, as students of the period know, to the fact that the technique of improvisation and ornamentation was part of the equipment of every singer, and therefore it was unnecessary for the composer to write other than the essential notes. But orchestral ornamentation was a different matter, for while the players would automatically ornament the supertonic or leading-note in cadential progressions it was necessary to write it in those cases where ornamentation was required during the course of a phrase in the *ritornello* of an air or during the accompaniment to a chorus. Hence the greater number of trills written by Handel in the orchestral staves. But even so, these are not the sum total but merely indications of what he expected throughout the air or chorus.

For example, in 'He was despised' Handel has given to the violins a distinctive figure of three notes consisting of a couplet of quavers preceded by a single quaver. This figure is repeated some twenty times during the air. Where it first occurs, in bar 2, he indicated a trill over the first note of the couplet in the first and second violins, i.e. the first quaver of beat 3. This is the only ornament he wrote in the air, but it cannot be argued seriously that he either wanted or expected just this one couplet to be so treated and the other nineteen to be played plain. This trill is not just a piece of conventional ornamentation, as it were a bit of plaster stuck on to the façade; it is an integral part of the figure, it is essential to the *Affekt*. When Handel wrote the one *tr* in bar 2 he was indicating ornamentation of the figure throughout the air.

Altogether Handel wrote 112 ornaments in the Autograph. Of these three are *appoggiaturas* and 109 are trills. Of these trills only seven are vocal, and of these one is choral. As with the instrumental ornamentation, so it is with the vocal ornamentation. No one can seriously contend that in the performances conducted by Handel the team of soloists contributed between them only six trills and one *appoggiatura*, or that the only choral trill sung during the whole of the oratorio was the solitary trill that Handel indicated over the choral bass note at the beginning of bar 43 of the 'Hallelujah' chorus. This argument also holds in relation to the orchestral accompaniments to the choruses. Out of nineteen choruses in the Autograph, only six have any ornamentation in the orchestral staves. In each of four of these Handel wrote only one trill: one in 'Lift up your heads', over the first violin, bar 7 (1); one in 'The Lord gave the Word', over the penultimate note of the final cadence in the first violin; one in 'Their sound is gone out', over the first violin, bar 22, the first note; and one in 'Hallelujah', bar 80 (3) in the first violin. In one other, 'Behold the Lamb of God', he wrote ten trills in the first six bars (three of these are against the chorus, not merely in *ritornelli*) and left the remaining twenty-six bars bare of ornamentation.   The inference surely is obvious.

One or two of the various editions under review added instrumental trills (other than cadential) and a few cadential trills for the voice.   Harrison and Cluse, in 1798, added trills to the *grave* of the Overture (on the third beat of bars 5, 7, 9, and 11), and cadential trills in the voice part of 'He was despised', 'But Thou did'st not leave', 'How beautiful are the feet' (soprano air), and 'Why do the nations'.

But while the scores of the oratorio contained little ornamentation, other publications of *Messiah* music contained a great deal.   Volume VII, part 4, of 'Sonatas or Chamber Aires for a German Flute, Violin or Harpsichord Being the most Celebrated Songs and Ariets collected out of all the late Oratorios and Operas composed by Mr HANDEL', issued by Walsh in 1757, contains 'How beautiful are the feet' in the following form:

Although Walker, in the score, had printed 'The Trumpet shall sound' without a single ornament, he issued it as a separate air with the following ornamentation in the opening *ritornello* as well as various ornaments in the voice part:

trum-pet shall sound _____ and the dead shall be rais'd

In view of the evidence of the Autograph alone, it is at the very least a reasonable supposition that in all eighteenth-century performances of *Messiah* both the vocal and the instrumental parts were enriched with considerable ornamentation.

This detailed analysis has been confined to English editions and limited roughly to the period of a century from the date of composition. During roughly the last quarter of the eighteenth century *Messiah* was performed in Germany. In, among other places, Hamburg, conducted by Michael Arne and with the English text; Hamburg again, conducted by C. P. E. Bach with the Klopstock-Ebeling German translation: and in Berlin conducted by Hiller with an Italian translation. The poets Goethe and Herder discussed and wrote extensively about the oratorio, indeed Herder made a most musical translation of the text into German. Kapellmeister Hiller was an ardent Handelian even though it would seem that his performances were as lacking in style as was his editing in taste. Baron van Swieten, with the laudable desire to present Handel in the best possible performance, mistakenly commissioned Mozart, in effect, to over-paint an already complete master-work.

All this activity naturally resulted in the publication of German editions in the early nineteenth century (Hiller's publication issued by Breitkopf in 1789 was not an edition of the score but only a selection) but discussion of them must be postponed to some other occasion.

3 The Alternative Settings

VARIOUS attempts have been made to prove which of Handel's different settings of the same words is the one he himself preferred. Some, it is obvious, were make-shifts: the pencilled-notes alteration in the alto-duet and chorus setting of 'How beautiful' which made it possible for the duet to be sung by a soprano and alto was most likely due to the lack on some occasion of a second counter-tenor: and the truncated version of 'Why do the nations', in which the last fifty-seven bars of the air are replaced by a recitative of only seven bars, to the lack of an adequate bass vocalist. But others were obviously completely new settings, even though the *motif* was not new. Such cases can scarcely be regarded as the result of expediency but rather of Handel's continuing dissatisfaction and his determination to compose something better. But second thoughts are not always best and where there are more than two settings the choice is increasingly difficult.

It is necessary to clarify what constitutes a different version. Statements such as 'The dozen versions of the "generally omitted" "Thou art gone up on high"[1]' are somewhat misleading. Handel did not write a dozen settings of any air in *Messiah*. An instruction in the margin for an air to be transposed for a particular singer, such as 'Mr. Norris F natural' or 'for Guadagni Ex C', even though in Handel's autograph, does not constitute a new setting. Only in one instance, 'He shall feed His flock', does a transposition in any way demand fresh consideration. Here the transposition is of one section of the air only, thus causing within the number a change of register and timbre. Apart from this one case transpositions will not be discussed in this chapter.

In the course of a search for Handel's own preferences, Professor J. P. Larsen in his book *Handel's Messiah* has gathered together a considerable body of evidence. He has made a paleographic study of the various manuscript scores of *Messiah*, first in order to determine which are genuine Smith copies (Smith the elder) and then to place the principal and the important secondary copies in chronological order. In addition he has made a study of the singers who sang for Handel, of the word-books of some performances (i.e. the libretti in which various portions of the text are described as 'Recit', 'Song', etc.) and of their pencilled annotations. This study is of great importance for, although much of this information has been known to Handel scholars, it is the first time that some of it has been presented and argued in print. It must, however, be remembered that little of the available evidence can be considered as conclusive. For example, the names of the artists pencilled in

---

[1] From article on 'The Church Music' by Basil Lam on page 170 of *Handel, a Symposium*, edited by Gerald Abraham.

the word-book of the first performance at Dublin in April, 1742, are unreliable as evidence, for, among other things, the unknown writer credited Mrs. Cibber with singing the 'rage' air for bass, 'Why do the nations', the soprano air 'If God be for us', and the chorus 'Behold the Lamb of God'. Then again the choice of the versions that different artists sang was possibly on occasion fortuitous. It could represent not even the most popular version but either the choice of the particular soloist or the version which happened to be in the particular set of orchestral parts that was available. As far as performance was concerned Handel was an opportunist, and the airs sung at the various performances would not necessarily represent his own preferences.

The Foundling material provides interesting evidence. This material consists of the score presented by Handel in the codicil to his will to the Foundling Hospital, the eighteenth-century chorus and solo part-books and the set of contemporary orchestral parts discovered among the Foundling papers. The various items of this material do not agree with each other. For example, in the score all the Passion airs are written as in the Autograph score for tenor, but the solo tenor part-book here contains only 'Thy rebuke hath broken His heart' and 'Behold and see' followed by the indication 'Accompg & Song Tacet'. Further, although in the tenor part-book the vocal stave of these two numbers is written in the soprano C clef, the second soprano soloist's part-book also has, immediately following 'He trusted in God', the indication 'Accompg & Song: Accompg & Song Tacet'. She therefore did not sing any of this music. One can only assume that the first soprano soloist sang 'He was cut off' and 'But Thou didst not leave His soul in hell', as unfortunately her part-book is missing.

Further, where whole settings or sections have been crossed out in pencil, who can say by whom they were deleted? Ink deletions are a serious matter; they have greater evidential value.

Even the order of the contents of a score which contains more than one version of a recitative, air, or chorus is not conclusive evidence. The scores have been rebound; the present contents are not necessarily the original contents. Some we know have been added to, but who can either prove or disprove Professor Larsen's suggestion that, although the Tenbury–Dublin copy contains only the $\frac{4}{4}$ setting of 'Rejoice greatly', the $\frac{12}{8}$ setting may have been included originally and removed later?

The Tenbury–Dublin copy presents a curious and this time not a hypothetical problem in the case of 'How beautiful' and 'Their sound'. In this copy the chorus setting of 'Their sound' is bound in *the middle* of the G minor air 'How beautiful'. At first sight it would appear to be an error on the part of the binder. It could, however, be something more, for curiously enough it is inserted immediately before the page that contains all but the first four bars of the middle section of the air that Handel had previously set to the same words: the first four bars are written at the end of the page before the insertion. It could indicate that at the first performance the first section of the G minor air was followed immediately by the chorus. But the word-book of that performance rules this out. When, therefore, was it bound in the copy, and is its position separating the two parts of the air accidental or not?

After presenting the evidence the most that one can say is, 'In the light of the evidence it is a reasonable assumption that . . .' or 'it is unlikely that Handel would. . . .'

Let us consider each case separately.

BUT WHO MAY ABIDE

1. Bass air;   D minor; Bass clef; $\frac{3}{8}$;   Autograph score
2. Recitative; D minor; Bass clef;   Marsh–Matthews copy
3. Alto air;   D minor; Alto C clef; $\frac{3}{8}$ and C; Autograph in the Tenbury–Dublin copy

No. 1 is the only setting Handel composed for the bass voice. It is in binary form, although a slightly extended form of the instrumental introduction is used as a final *ritornello*. The first section is set to the words 'But who may abide the day of His coming, and who shall stand when He appeareth?' It begins in D minor and modulates to the key of the relative major; it is founded upon the same *motif* as No. 3, but is essentially different, and consists of eighty-four bars (whereas No. 3 contains only fifty-nine bars). The second section is set to the words 'for He is like a refiner's fire'; it begins and ends in D minor, has two long *divisions* on the word 'fire', and with the closing *ritornello* consists of fifty-two bars.

No. 2 is not to be found in Handel's hand, but must be considered as there is some evidence that this was the setting that was sung at the first performance in Dublin on 13th April 1742. It is in the form of a recitative, is contained in the eighteenth-century manuscript copy in the Archbishop Marsh Library, Dublin, Ireland. Over the music the following statement is written: 'If the foregoing song [i.e. the $\frac{3}{8}$ air for bass 'But who may abide'] is to be left out as it was in the performance in Dublin, sing this recitative upon the very same words.' This statement, together with the fact that in the word-book of the first performance 'But who may abide' is described as 'Recit', gives the setting some authority.

No. 3, although based on the same *motif* as No. 1, is entirely different in its form, with the coloratura style of the second section and the time-change from $\frac{3}{8}$ to C. At the top of the page, in Handel's hand, is written 'For Guadagni.' The male alto Guadagni first came to England in 1748, so it would seem that this setting was composed some seven years after the first.

Handel seems to have cared little whether his music was sung by one voice or another. What mattered was that it be sung. Guadagni could easily have sung the original bass setting. Why did Handel compose another? It seems a not unreasonable assumption that, being dissatisfied with the original setting and having had in mind the idea of substituting a section of contrast in coloratura style for the relatively simple *division* previously quoted, he recognized in Guadagni's voice the suitable instrument and was moved to put his thoughts on paper. I find it difficult to agree with what would seem to be Professor Larsen's opinion—that Handel wrote this setting as the vehicle for a display of coloratura virtuosity. The coloratura arises naturally from the words, the music has strength, and the rondo-like structure is much more interesting for the listener than the original $\frac{3}{8}$ setting. The contents of the more important of the various manuscript scores copied after Guadagni arrived in England are of interest. Whilst the Fitzwilliam Barrett-Lennard contains both settings (in the body of the volume the original all-$\frac{3}{8}$ bass setting, and in the appendix the Guadagni setting in the alto C clef), the Foundling, Hamburg and RM 18.e.2 (the Smith presentation copy to George III) each contains only one setting, the Guadagni. True, in the Foundling it is transposed into A minor and is in the soprano C clef, yet in the Hamburg it occurs twice, once in its original key of D minor in the alto C clef and again transposed, this time into G minor in the soprano C clef, and in RM 18.e.2 it appears only in the Guadagni setting for alto. The original bass setting has disappeared from use. The alto setting has persisted, but is sung, generally, by a bass.

It is sometimes suggested that, having written the coloratura setting of 'But who may abide' for Guadagni, Handel would naturally have expected him to sing the preceding recitative (written in the bass clef in the Autograph score).

In the Foundling manuscripts 'But who may abide' is transposed into A minor for the soprano; in the solo part-book bearing Passerini's name, which contains this air, the words *accompago. tacet e poi l'aria subito* are written immediately after 'And the glory'.

The *basso principale* part-book contains the recitative 'Thus saith the Lord', after which are written the words *Aria tacet*. This is a clear indication that whichever voice sang the air, the recitative was to be sung by the bass.

Evidence of the air itself being sung by a bass is afforded by an item in the account of the Foundling expenses for the 1773 performance which reads:

> 'For writing the accompaniment for Mr. Reinhold   s   d
>   'But who may abide'   4   6

THOU ART GONE UP ON HIGH

1. Bass air;   D minor; bass clef; $\frac{3}{4}$; The Autograph score
2. Alto air;   D minor; alto C clef; $\frac{3}{4}$; Autograph in the Tenbury–Dublin copy
3. Soprano air; D minor; soprano C clef; $\frac{3}{4}$; Needler and Granville copies
4. Recitative;   Not extant, but so described in the 1743 word-book

No. 1. This is the only setting to be found in the Autograph score, and it is the first of three settings in the Tenbury–Dublin copy. It is also to be found in the Appendix, page 14, of the first printed score published by Randall and Abell.

No. 2 is what is known as the Guadagni setting. At the top of the page is written 'For Guadagni.' These words, even though written by Handel, are not by themselves sufficient evidence that this setting was *composed* for Guadagni, as in the same copy the original setting for bass (a copy of No. 1) composed some years before Guadagni came to England also has 'For Guadagni' written at the top of the page. Handel obviously thought highly of Guadagni's voice, and would have had him sing any air that was at all suitable. However, the coloratura style of this second autograph and the use of the alto C clef taken together suggest that it was, in fact, composed for Guadagni; it is a reasonable assumption that Handel inscribed the bass setting with Guadagni's name before he had composed the alto setting.

Again as in the case of 'But who may abide' the Barrett-Lennard copy contains two settings of which one is the Guadagni; and the Foundling, the Hamburg and RM 18.e.2 copies each contain only one—the Guadagni. The Dublin copy contains a third copy. It is not another setting but merely a transposition of the Guadagni setting into G minor and written in the soprano C clef.

No. 3 is not to be found in Autograph; but as it is contained in an early Smith copy and is the setting printed in the first published *Messiah* music, *Songs in Messiah* (circa 1749), it must be considered to be authentic. It is based upon the same theme as the other settings.

A word-book of *Messiah* 'as it is performed at the Theatre Royal in Drury Lane and Covent Garden', British Museum RM 5.e.7, describes 'Thou art gone up on high' as a recitative. But I have failed to find it in this form in any manuscript.

The following example of comparable passages, (a) and (b) of his treatment of the same text and (c) and (d) of *divisions*, show how completely dissimilar are the settings, despite their common origin.

(a) (From setting No. 1)

(b) (From setting No. 3)

ALTERNATE
SETTINGS

(c) (From setting No. 1)

might dwell

might dwell a - mong them

(d) (From setting No. 2)

Guadagni
Divisions

And re - ceiv - - - - -

- - - - - ed gifts____ for__ men.

AND LO! THE ANGEL OF THE LORD

1. Accompanied recitative; F major; soprano C clef; $\frac{4}{4}$; Autograph score
2. Arioso; F major; soprano C clef; $\frac{4}{4}$; Autograph score

No. 1 is short and expresses the general *Affekt* in a direct and simple manner. No. 2, 'But lo!' [*sic*], bearing Mrs. Clive's name written by Handel, is less direct. It stresses the *Affekt* of individual words, e.g. the word 'sore' first approached by a downward leap of a diminished seventh is repeated often with *affekt*-ive harmonic dissonance, and 'the Glory of the Lord' is extended by two *divisions* on the word 'glory'. The result is that the balance of the group is destroyed, the tension reduced and the choral climax delayed. Above all, this arioso setting is rather dull.

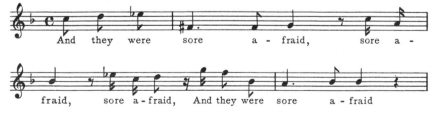

And they were sore a - fraid, sore a -

fraid, sore a - fraid, And they were sore a - fraid

In the Randall and Abell score, the arioso setting is printed in the body of the volume while the recitative setting is printed in the appendix. This would give the impression that the recitative was Handel's second thought. Particularly would this appear so as the index to the score contains a printed note declaring that the appendix contains airs that were 'set after the original performance a second time'. But a glance at the Autograph will suggest that Handel wrote the recitative setting immediately after he had finished writing the Pastoral Symphony, even before writing the recitative 'There were shepherds'. Then, realizing that he had forgotten to write that recitative and had not left adequate space, he squeezed it in by dividing the space left at the end of the Pastoral Symphony instrumental four-stave score horizontally into two two-stave scores for voice and continuo. The arioso 'But lo!', however, is on a separate sheet, the last two bars occupying a few inches of the reverse side, with the remaining staves quite empty. It appears to have been an insertion and this is supported by the fact that it throws Handel's numbering wrong: it was Handel's custom to number every four folios. The arioso page throws this out, for between Handel's 10 and 11 are not four but five folios. This arioso setting can hardly be described as a makeshift, but the recitative fits better into the general design. There is no evidence that Handel thought otherwise.

The evidence of the manuscripts is as before. The Fitzwilliam contains both the accompanied recitative and arioso settings whilst the Foundling, Hamburg, and RM 18.e.2 contain only the recitative.

Rejoice greatly

1. *Da capo* air; B♭ major; soprano C clef; $\frac{12}{8}$; Autograph score
2. *Da capo* air; B♭ major; soprano C clef; $\frac{4}{4}$; Autograph in Tenbury–
   Dublin copy

No. 1 at first consisted of an opening section of ninety-one bars (plus a cadence chord) ending in the tonic key, followed by a section of contrast of twenty-two bars beginning in G minor and ending in D minor, followed in turn by *da capo*. After a clear-cut opening statement of forty-three bars, the first section straggled on for a further forty-eight bars during which an attempt to obtain variety of key results only in a meaningless and ineffective modulation into C minor for seven bars ending with a sudden return to F major before continuing in the tonic key.   Handel then decided to shorten the first section by deleting bars 44–91 inclusive.   He showed the cut by running diagonal lines through bars 44–46 at the beginning of the cut and bar 91 at the end of the cut.   In order to make his intention quite clear he drew enclosing brackets, one at the beginning of bar 44 and another at the end of bar 91.

As bar 43 led to a perfect cadence in F major and bar 91 to a perfect cadence in B♭ major he first altered the first note in bar 92 from B♭ to F and then altered the harmony against the first note in the voice in the middle section from B♭ major to the first inversion of the dominant harmony of G minor, the key of the middle section.

The first section as it now stood ended with a perfect cadence in the dominant key of F major.   This made his original *da capo* instruction impracticable.   He therefore decided to use parts of the deleted section for the reprise; scribbled, in the totally inadequate space at the end of the middle section, an instrumental and vocal link which consisted of bars 1, 2, and the first half of bar 3 followed by the second half of bar 9, bar 10, and the first half of bar 11; he then indicated a return to beat 3 of bar 53, thus bringing the air to a conclusion in bar 92 with a perfect cadence in B♭ major.

In the Handelgesellschaft *Messiah* volume, Chrysander did not give either Handel's note alterations or his scribbled lead-in to the reprise; indeed, he failed to appreciate the purpose or to note correctly the extent of the cuts.

The second setting is contained in the Tenbury–Dublin copy.   The vocal stave is written in the soprano C clef, the key is B♭, and the time is $\frac{4}{4}$.   It is closely knit and well balanced: the opening statement consists of forty-three bars and the section of contrast of twenty-two.   It is based upon the same *motif* as the $\frac{12}{8}$ setting.   But the change from $\frac{12}{8}$ to $\frac{4}{4}$ is completely transforming.   Observe the difference between

re - joice . . .   greatly   and the same bar (27) in the $\frac{4}{4}$ setting:

re - joice . . .   greatly   And again between:

Violin

Voice

Shout_____   O daughter of Jerusalem

42

and the same bars (28 to 30) in the $\frac{4}{4}$ setting:

Shout‿‿‿‿ O daughter of Jerusalem

The triplet divisions of the $\frac{12}{8}$ setting have nothing like the virility of the quadruplets in the $\frac{4}{4}$ setting. It should be noted that in the $\frac{4}{4}$ manuscript only the voice and violin staves are in Handel's hand; the basso-continuo clefs and the signature were written by a copyist. In the Autograph Handel wrote the basso-continuo in $\frac{4}{4}$ and the voice and violin in $\frac{12}{8}$. This caused him some slight confusion in note values in the basso-continuo, in spite of the convention of writing simple-time groups against compound-time groups and vice versa.

The $\frac{4}{4}$ setting is obviously the later setting, but exactly how much later is not clear. The inscription 'Frasi' suggests that it was written for Frasi when she sang in the 1749 performance. But in addition to Frasi the Tenbury–Dublin copy bears the inscriptions 'Mr. Beard' and 'The Boy', so there is no conclusive proof that this setting was not sung much earlier than 1749. What is clear is that the $\frac{4}{4}$ is the only setting in the Tenbury–Dublin copy as it stands (there is no evidence either for or against an assumption that the $\frac{12}{8}$ was originally in this copy and later removed); and that in the Foundling, Hamburg, and R.M 18.e.2 copies also the $\frac{4}{4}$ is the only setting. It must be said, however, that it is not in the early copies—the Granville and Needler (dated by Larsen *circa* 1744–5), nor in *Songs in Messiah* (dated by W. C. Smith, 1749). But then neither is it in the post-Handel copy, R.M 18.b.10. It is difficult to imagine that Handel, having succeeded so well in his endeavour to compose a better setting, would use the other. The technical difficulties are much the same in both settings; therefore, the choice would not necessarily be affected by the availability or otherwise of a particular singer.

It is of interest to note the difference between the two settings in the word arrangement at the beginning of the middle section and the melodic shape in the cadence bars of the same section.

HE SHALL FEED HIS FLOCK

1. Soprano air;   B♭ major; $\frac{12}{8}$; Autograph score
2. 'Duet version' for   F major and B♭ major; $\frac{12}{8}$; Tenbury–Dublin copy
    alto and soprano;
3. Alto air;   F major; $\frac{12}{8}$; Marsh–Matthews copy

All three versions are identical except in the matter of key.
No. 1 was copied exactly into the Tenbury–Dublin copy.
No. 2 is formed by the insertion of additional manuscript sheets in the

Tenbury–Dublin copy between the copy of this all-soprano version and the previous number ('Rejoice greatly'). They contain a transposition down to F major of the first half of the air under discussion including the *ritornello* leading to and including the first note of the second half, and—of special interest—this note is written in the soprano C clef with a key signature of two flats and over the note is written 'Frasi'. The inserted manuscript contains also a similar transposition (downward, of a fourth) of the preceding recitative 'Then shall the eyes of the blind be opened'.

The purpose in making this alteration was obviously to break the monotony of key. The contrast in style between this air and the preceding air and subsequent chorus is made less effective by all three being in the same key.

There exists a third arrangement in which the whole air is transposed down into F, obviously for alto. This is to be found in two manuscript copies—one in the library of King's College, Cambridge, England (formerly Mn.17.25, now Rw.M.S.200) and the other the Marsh–Matthews copy. This all-alto transposition is not to be found in either of the primary or even the more important of the secondary scores. Further, the Tenbury–Dublin copy affords no evidence for the all-alto version but contains the actual alterations from the all-soprano version to the duet version—witness the name of the soprano, Frasi, written at the end of the first half of the manuscript containing the alto transposition. Also two of the more important secondary scores, the Hamburg and RM 18.e.2, contain only this duet version.

In the Hamburg copy above the violin stave to the left is written 'Signr. Tenducci', above the violin stave to the right is written 'Guadagni', and above the basso-continuo stave is written 'Signra. Moser'. Against the first note of the soprano section is written 'Frasi'.

As the name of Frasi on the additional manuscript in the Tenbury–Dublin copy is in the hand of the copyist it may well be that the alteration was not made before 1749. The two early manuscript copies, the Granville and the Needler, as well as *Songs in Messiah* (printed *circa* 1749), contain only the all-soprano version: it is, therefore, reasonable to assume that this version was sung before the duet version was introduced.

The Townley Hall manuscript contains this air only in the all-alto version. This is of special interest, for, previous to the discovery of the Townley Hall manuscript in 1960 the alto air, as the version to be sung and not merely as an alternative, was to be found only in the Mann 'Dublin' manuscript. True, the Marsh–Matthews manuscript also contains this version, but only as an alternative to the original all in B♭ major soprano air which occurs earlier in that manuscript. It has to be remembered that the Marsh–Matthews manuscript, with the probable exception of the recitative setting of 'But who may abide', was copied by Matthews while he was in England and therefore does not reflect any Irish tradition. Both the recitative and the statement written in the upper margin concerning (seemingly) the 1742 performance must have been given to Matthews after he moved to Ireland in the spring of

1776; certainly the manuscript of the recitative is a later addition to the volume, for it forms an upward extension of page 36, being pasted on to the top margin. The facts that in two 'Irish' manuscripts, the Townley Hall and Mann 'Dublin', the only form in which 'He shall feed His flock' appears is the transposition for alto solo, and that against this text in the 1742 word-book (British Museum K.8.d.4) is pencilled the name Cibber, could be regarded as support for the suggestion that Mrs. Cibber sang this version in Dublin at the first performance. Yet the alto solo version is not to be found either in the Tenbury–Dublin or the Hamburg–Schoelcher manuscripts. As for the word-book, if we are to believe the anonymous annotater, then Mrs. Cibber also sang 'Why do the nations'. However, the evidence provided by the Townley Hall, Mann 'Dublin', and Marsh–Matthews manuscripts is reasonable proof that the two stanzas 'He shall feed His flock' and 'Come unto Him' were sung in F major by an alto soloist and, because of the declared date of the Marsh–Matthews manuscript, 1761, quite possibly in Handel's lifetime. The order of contents here in the manuscripts is of some significance, see Appendix G. It will be seen that the Townley Hall and the Mann 'Dublin' manuscripts are identical, that one of the alternatives offered by the Marsh–Matthews manuscript, Alternative 3, agrees with the other two manuscripts and that, apart from the length (complete or shortened version) of the $\frac{12}{8}$ setting of 'Rejoice greatly', the only difference between the first two alternatives and the third rests purely in the key (original or transposed) of the following recitative and air.

From the Marsh–Matthews manuscript it will also be seen that the so-called 'duet' version of 'He shall feed His flock' is associated with the $\frac{4}{4}$ setting of 'Rejoice greatly' and not with the $\frac{12}{8}$ setting. This same grouping is found in the Tenbury–Dublin manuscript. This contains only the $\frac{4}{4}$ setting of 'Rejoice greatly' (this is in Handel's own hand although the volume as a whole is in the hand of his amanuensis, Smith) and the earliest source of the 'duet' version of 'He shall feed His flock'. The latter is not in Handel's hand, but the alto transposition of the first stanza, which is inserted before the original soprano air setting, may have had Handel's consent, for the last thing on this inserted page is a soprano C clef, the key signature of B♭ major, and the name of the soprano, Frasi, together with a direction to the second stanza of the soprano air.

Now let it be said that pages 117 to 132 in the Marsh-Matthews manuscript, i.e. the pages containing the $\frac{4}{4}$ setting of 'Rejoice greatly', the following recitative and the 'duet' version of 'He shall feed His flock', did not form part of the original binding but, like the alto transposition of the first stanza of 'He shall feed His flock' (from which the 'duet' version originated) in the Tenbury–Dublin manuscript, are a later insertion for they are gummed in.

The Townley Hall manuscript is of especial significance. It confirms opinions already formed as a result of collating the Marsh–Matthews and the Mann 'Dublin' manuscripts.

It will be seen, first, that in all three manuscripts the $\frac{12}{8}$ setting of 'Rejoice greatly' was followed by 'He shall feed His flock' as a solo; secondly, that, although in the Marsh–Matthews manuscript the solo following the $\frac{12}{8}$ 'Rejoice greatly' appears twice in the original setting for soprano, in both of the Irish manuscripts (the Townley Hall and the Mann 'Dublin') the solo is the transposed version for alto. This suggests that the earlier setting of 'Rejoice greatly' (in $\frac{12}{8}$) was followed in performance by a solo setting of 'He shall feed His flock', and that the later 'duet' version of 'He shall feed His flock' was intended to be sung after the later $\frac{4}{4}$ setting of 'Rejoice greatly'. This is supported by the manuscripts, for the Autograph and the early Needler and Egerton copies contain only the $\frac{12}{8}$ setting of 'Rejoice greatly' and the solo setting of 'He shall feed His flock', while the later Hamburg–Schoelcher (the copy containing the first 'clean' copy, i.e. by first intent and not by alteration, of the 'duet' version of 'He shall feed His flock') and the British Museum RM 18.e.2 contain only the $\frac{4}{4}$ setting of 'Rejoice greatly' and the 'duet' version of 'He shall feed His flock'.

The evidence of the printed editions issued between 1749 and 1813, however, is somewhat confusing.

PRINTED EDITIONS BETWEEN 1749 AND 1813

Edition		'Rejoice greatly'	'He shall feed His flock'
Walsh (*circa* 1749)		$\frac{12}{8}$	Soprano solo
Randall and Abell 1767	in body of score	$\frac{12}{8}$	Soprano solo
	in Appendix	$\frac{4}{4}$	—
Wright (*circa* 1785)	in body of score	$\frac{12}{8}$	Soprano solo
	in Appendix	$\frac{4}{4}$	—
J. Bland (*circa* 1782)		$\frac{12}{8}$	Soprano solo
Arnold (*circa* 1787)		$\frac{12}{8}$ followed immediately by $\frac{4}{4}$	Soprano solo followed immediately by 'duet'
Harrison (New Musical Magazine *circa* 1784)		$\frac{4}{4}$	Soprano solo
Harrison (corrected by Dr. Arnold *circa* 1786)		$\frac{4}{4}$	Soprano solo
Linley (*circa* 1785)		$\frac{12}{8}$	Soprano solo
Harrison and Cluse (The Pianoforte Magazine *circa* 1798)		$\frac{4}{4}$	Soprano solo
Preston (1807)	in body of score	$\frac{12}{8}$	Soprano solo
	in Appendix	$\frac{4}{4}$	—
Peck (1813)		$\frac{4}{4}$	'Duet'
Bland and Weller (1813)	in body of score	$\frac{12}{8}$	Soprano solo
	in Appendix	$\frac{4}{4}$	—

The above table shows:

1. That Peck declares clearly in favour of the $\frac{4}{4}$ 'Rejoice greatly' and the 'duet' version of 'He shall feed His flock'.
2. That Arnold, publishing a complete edition of the oratorio (his is the only eighteenth-century edition I know that includes the

recitative setting of 'But who may abide'), gives both the earlier and later settings in their correct order.

3. That the remaining editions, including those that contain the $\frac{4}{4}$ 'Rejoice greatly', either as the definite choice in the body of the score or as an alternative in an appendix, do not include the 'duet' version of 'He shall feed His flock'.

4. That of two editions (Peck and Bland & Weller) printed in the same year (1813) one includes 'He shall feed His flock' in the 'duet' version only, and the other includes the same air in the soprano setting only.

I consider that the weight of evidence lies with the manuscripts, that they, even the later 1760 copies, give the truer indication of what versions were sung during Handel's lifetime. Further to the opinion here expressed regarding the grouping of the different settings or versions it would appear that although in the Autograph score the $\frac{12}{8}$ 'Rejoice greatly' is followed by the soprano solo setting of 'He shall feed His flock', the contents of the two Irish manuscripts (the Townley Hall and the Mann 'Dublin') indicate that the alto solo version of 'He shall feed His flock' was in the nature of an Irish tradition. This supports the opinion held by some that it was this form that was sung in Dublin at the first performance of the oratorio in 1742.

It is not generally known that a duet form of this number in which the two voices sing together, in two vocal parts, is contained in the Schwencke edition of *Messiah* printed in Hamburg in 1809.

HOW BEAUTIFUL ARE THE FEET

1. *Da capo* air;   G minor;   soprano C clef; $\frac{12}{8}$;   Autograph score
2. Alto duet   D minor;   two alto C clefs $\frac{3}{4}$;   Autograph score (Appendix)
   and chorus;   for duettists;
3. Alto duet   D minor;   two alto C clefs $\frac{3}{4}$;   British Museum RM 20.g.6
   and chorus;   for duettists;   (Folio 25)
4. Soprano solo   D major;   soprano C clef; $\frac{3}{4}$;   British Museum RM 20.g.6
   and chorus;   (Folio 34)
5. Alto solo;   C minor;   alto C clef; $\frac{12}{8}$; The Barrett-Lennard copy

No. 1 is in the body of the Autograph score.   No. 2 is in the Appendix to
that score.   Nos. 3 and 4 are in a volume of miscellaneous autographs.   No. 5
is not to be found in autograph but as (a) it contains the same motif as the
G minor air and the D minor duet-chorus settings, (b) it is in the Barrett-
Lennard copy, and (c) it is printed in the appendix to the Randall and Abell
full score, it must be given consideration.

A sixth setting, for soprano and alto duet and chorus, is sometimes listed
but it does not merit being treated as an independent setting.   At some time
Handel pencilled in on the empty canto stave of No. 2 a rearrangement of the
second alto part for soprano.   Chrysander disregarded Handel's inked notes
for second alto and printed the soprano-alto duet as the authoritative setting.
Indeed but for Seiffert, who saw the *Messiah* volume through the press, the
original alto duet would not have appeared in the Handelgesellschaft edition
at all.   Even so it is printed very much as an afterthought for the sake of com-
pleteness.   Where a duet and chorus version is printed in modern performing
editions Chrysander's mistake is generally perpetuated.

It is continued also in the separate publication of 'How beautiful are the
feet', edited by Sir Ivor Atkins, published by Novello and Co. in their Octavo
Anthem Series, No. 1274.

The genesis of this publication is curious.   It is stated to have been edited
'From Chrysander's facsimile of the Autograph of *Messiah* in the King's
Library now in the British Museum'.   But why from a facsimile, when the
Autograph score itself was available in the same library?   Moreover the edition
is a hybrid.   The Chrysander facsimile is, as declared in its Preface, a facsimile
not just of the Autograph score, but also of all the additional settings and
fragments of *Messiah* music that then existed in Handel's autograph in other
volumes.   Atkins's edition may indeed be taken from the Chrysander facsimile,
but from two different parts of it, since it is a mixture of two quite different
settings.   The introduction in the Atkins edition begins at bar 24 of the
Chapel Royal setting in D minor (No. 3) and then jumps to the duet from
the Appendix to the Autograph score (but with the makeshift pencilled alterations for soprano and alto).   It then jumps to the Chapel Royal setting for
the choral section, but jumps back again to the Autograph in the final cadence
for the full close.

To recapitulate, Handel's soprano–alto duet rearrangement of No. 2 is not an independent setting; it is nothing more than an arrangement, a make-shift, pencilled on the empty canto stave, for some occasion when two altos were not available.   For no other reason would Handel have exchanged the relaxed effect of the falling third of the two opening alto notes for the relatively aggressive inversion to a rising sixth for the soprano entry shown at (*a*), with the resulting drop of an octave shown at (*b*), a drop which the crossed-out pencilled notes indicate he obviously had tried to avoid.   It is reasonably clear that he discarded this rearrangement for he smudged out the opening soprano notes with two characteristic thumb-like ink smudges.   As with a similar smudge in bars 59 and 60 in the basso-continuo in the same number, the ink has now faded to a light brown so that what was obscured in 1868 (cf. the Sacred Harmonic facsimile) is clearly to be seen today.

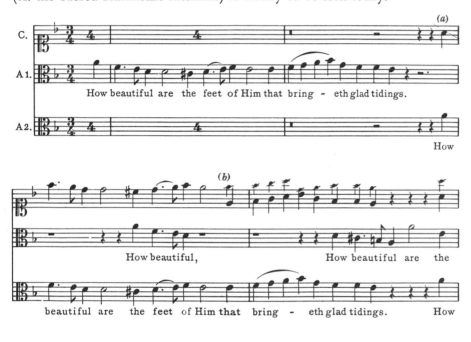

Although the titles of all five settings are the same there is a difference between the words of the air and the chorus settings; it is essential that this be understood when we consider the various changes made by Handel after he had composed the G minor *da capo* air.   The words of the G minor soprano and the C minor alto airs are from Romans X, which reads (verse 15), 'How beautiful are the feet of them that preach the gospel of peace, and bring glad tidings of good things', and in the G minor air only (verse 18), 'Yes, verily their sound is gone out into all the earth, and their words unto the ends of the world'.   Those of the settings with a choral section are all drawn from Isaiah LII, which reads (verse 7), 'How beautiful upon the mountains are the feet of him that bringeth good tidings, that publisheth peace; that bringeth good tidings of good, that publisheth salvation; that saith unto Zion, thy God reigneth!', and (verse 9), 'Break forth into joy. . . .'

In composing the G minor *da capo* air, Handel used the words 'Their sound is gone out into all lands and their words unto the ends of the world' for the middle section.   In the Autograph, the first bar of this middle section is crossed out, only in pencil but probably by Handel, for he later composed separate settings of the displaced words.

Nos. 2 and 3.   The two settings for alto duet and chorus, one in the appendix to the Autograph score and one in the British Museum (RM 20.g.6) said to have been written as an anthem for the Chapel Royal, are best considered together.   Both are in D minor and both begin with the *motif* of the G minor air.   After some twenty-one bars they begin to differ.   The duet in the Chapel Royal setting is six bars longer than the other.   In the choral section the Chapel Royal setting contains sixty-eight bars against the Autograph score's 111 bars, the key schemes of the two settings are quite different, and while the Chapel Royal setting ends with a half close, that in the Autograph score ends with a full close.   Further, there is considerable variation between the two settings in the orchestral introduction and accompaniment, both in matter and orchestration.   The introduction to the Autograph score setting consists of thirteen bars based upon the first seven bars of the duet theme extended by a sequential repetition of bars 5, 6, and 7, and is scored for strings and continuo.   The introduction to the Chapel Royal setting is taken from the first movement of the E minor sonata that Handel composed to precede 'As pants the hart!'

This sonata theme bears no resemblance to the theme of 'How beautiful are the feet'.   The sonata itself is scored for strings and continuo only, but when Handel used it for 'How beautiful' he added traverso and oboe to play an additional fourteen bars instrumental duet based upon the vocal duet (the flute and oboe are silent during the sonata theme itself with which the introduction begins).   In addition at the choral entry of this Chapel Royal setting he added two trumpets and timpani.

No. 4. The soprano solo and chorus version is essentially different from any of the other four settings. Here is the opening of the solo:

Note the strong resemblance of the first bars to the opening of the arioso 'Comfort ye'.

The main theme, beginning in bar 5 of the preceding music example, is almost identical with a setting in the same volume, folio 32, for 'the Boy' of the words 'The Lord hath given strength unto His people and hath given His people the blessing of peace'. The solo contains a number of *divisions*.

The chorus opens with a *motif* built on a rising arpeggio:

in complete contrast to the falling conjunct motion of the choral *motif* of the alto-duet and chorus setting in the Autograph score (No. 3). In spite of this difference, Handel contrives to use, in No. 4, the exact notes of the exciting quaver string accompaniment of No. 3, of course transposed from F to D major.

This setting, however, is incomplete; the last eighteen bars are unorchestrated and it finishes with a choral half close. It cannot be seriously considered as *Messiah* material.

51

No. 5.   The C minor air is not a *da capo* air. It is composed in one section and employs only the words of one verse (verse 15) of Romans X; there is no reference to 'Their sound is gone out'. It is more ornate than the G minor air, having written-out slides, various grace notes, and a moderately long *division* on the word 'glad'.

The significant point about this setting is its form.   Taken in conjunction with the suggested deletion of the middle section of the G minor setting, it indicates that although Handel was uncertain about this number as a *da capo* air he felt that the reference to the Messengers of the Gospel was incomplete without a further reference to the spread of the Gospel, for he composed a separate setting of 'Their sound is gone out into all lands'. In the end he composed not one but two other settings.

The first of these is in the Appendix to the Autograph score. It is for chorus, is in the key of E♭ major and the time is $\frac{4}{4}$.

The second is also in the Appendix to the Autograph score, but it is not in Handel's writing.   It is an arioso, the vocal stave is written in the tenor C clef, the key is F major and the time is $\frac{4}{4}$.

Although the manuscript is not in Handel's hand, the pencilled 'Sra Avolio' in the top margin most certainly is.   Further, it is written on the reverse of a page that is written in Handel's own hand.   Moreover it is based upon the opening motif of the E♭ major chorus setting.   Therefore it may reasonably be accepted as authentic.

The question remains, how are the various settings of 'How beautiful' and 'Their sound' to be paired?   At first sight it would seem that:

(1) the E♭ major chorus ('Their sound') is the natural complement of the G minor air ('How beautiful');

(2) the E♭ major chorus ('Their sound') is equally well the natural complement of the C minor alto air;

(3) the F major arioso ('Their sound') is the complement of the C minor air ('How beautiful'), although less naturally so;

(4) the settings for alto duet and chorus in D minor are complete in themselves; the words sung in this setting by the chorus, 'Break forth into joy' being the equivalent of the triumphant 'Their sound is gone out'.

The first assumption is musically acceptable, The second is equally acceptable; the key relationship C minor to E♭ major is most natural. It must be remembered that the late Baroque composer, in spite of the lingering modal influence, had completely accepted key (as distinct from tonality) and the consequent aural relationships.   Moreover, it is worthy of note that in the Appendix of the Barrett-Lennard copy the E♭ major chorus is immediately preceded by the C minor air.   Let me repeat: this C minor air is not merely a transposition of the G minor air but an independent setting.

The third and fourth assumptions, however, require examination. Let us take (4) first.   It is supported in the 1742 word-book, for in this the words of the alto duet and chorus 'How beautiful . . . break forth into joy' are followed directly by 'Why do the nations'. What, then, is the meaning of the words *da capo* printed in both the 1742 and 1745 Dublin word-books immediately following the words of the choral section of 'How beautiful'? This could, of course, be dismissed as a printer's error, for there is no *da capo* in the autographs (the copyist of the Hamburg and Foundling scores and copies was guilty of a more obvious error when, having copied the G minor air *without a middle section*, he wrote in a meaningless *dal segno* sign). Still, it has to be remembered that the Chapel Royal setting ends definitely with a half-close. Did Handel intend a *da capo?*

It might be argued, and this could apply equally to the setting ending with the choral full-close, that the *da capo* could consist solely of the instrumental introduction which ends in the tonic key. On the other hand, it might be argued that Handel felt that 'How beautiful', with or without the choral ending, was not complete unless followed by some form of 'Their sound'. There is some pertinent evidence regarding this. Firstly, the F major arioso of 'Their sound' is written on the back of the final page of the Autograph setting of the D minor alto duet and chorus 'How beautiful'; this is not without significance; the D minor–F major key relationship of the duet–chorus and the arioso is much more reasonable than the C minor–F major relationship of the alto air and the arioso. Secondly, the Granville and the Needler copies contain only the D minor alto duet and chorus 'How beautiful' followed by the F major tenor arioso 'Their sound'. Thirdly, there is evidence that they were actually coupled in performance as early as 1745, for in the word-book of the performance at Dublin in that year the words of the Isaiah text of 'How beautiful' (used only for the settings with chorus) are followed by 'Their sound is gone out', described as a 'Song'. This song could, of course, only be the tenor arioso.

The Marsh–Matthews manuscript confirms this sequence and offers a solution of the *da capo* question. This copy contains 'How beautiful are the feet' in the original *da capo* air setting for soprano in G minor with the middle section set to the text 'Their sound is gone out'. This is directly followed by 'Why do the nations'. Then comes 'How beautiful are the feet', 'Break forth into joy' in the alto duet and chorus setting, followed in turn by 'Their sound is gone out' in the tenor arioso setting and, it is to be noted, at the end of the arioso is written the instruction '*da capo* page 113'; on page 113 is the beginning of the chorus section 'Break forth into joy' of the alto duet and chorus 'How beautiful'.

As manuscript copies either were made for performance or reflected a performing tradition we may safely assume from the evidence of the Marsh–Matthews copy that when the D minor alto duet and chorus 'How beautiful' was sung it was followed by the tenor arioso 'Their sound is gone out' and completed by a reprise of the chorus 'Break forth into joy'.

In order to arrive at a decision as to the relative importance of the different settings it is necessary to consider the following evidence:

C

(1) that in the Tenbury–Dublin copy not only is the middle section of the G minor *da capo* air crossed out but also the first section, i.e. the whole air;

(2) that Handel made no less than three attempts at a setting containing a choral section to the words 'Break forth into joy . . .';

(3) that the word-book of the first performance at Dublin on 13th April 1742 contained under 'How beautiful' the words of this choral section;

(4) that of the settings with a choral section only one ends with a full-close—the D minor from the appendix to the Autograph score; and finally,

(5) that this latter is the only choral setting to appear in any of the principal eighteenth-century copies. It was the setting sung at the first performance—the setting over which Handel took considerable trouble.

Thus saith the Lord
The Pastoral Symphony

Whilst 'Thus saith the Lord' and the Pastoral Symphony have not alternative settings in the true sense, they deserve mention here because of the alterations made by Handel in the Autograph score to their original form.

Handel originally conceived the opening bars of 'Thus saith the Lord' in the style of an arioso. It was first copied in this form in the Tenbury–Dublin copy.

He later altered it in the Autograph so:

A comparison of the two examples shows that the voice first began at bar 4 with the measured theme stated in the instrumental introduction; that Handel decided to change the style at bar 6 where he wrote the word 'recit'; that he later decided to discard the arioso-like introduction, rewrote the first bars as we now know them, crossed out the word 'recit' at bar 6 and wrote it in the margin at the beginning of the stave and, in order to make the change to *recitativo accompagnato* clear beyond all doubt, crossed out the tempo indications for the arioso (*a tempo ordinario* and *grave*) and over the first violin stave wrote 'accomp'.

The manuscript after Handel had made the alterations was far from clear, but Smith deciphered it, copied it on a piece of manuscript only half the depth of the page and inserted it in the Tenbury–Dublin copy as a loose leaf over the top of the arioso-style bars. Both forms, therefore, are clearly to be seen in the Tenbury–Dublin copy.

A close examination of the Autograph, bar 5, discloses that, in the first form of this number, in writing all the groups so 𝄾 ♪ ♩. ♩ Handel was following a convention of the period, that he expected the rest to be lengthened and the following note to be shortened, that he expected the group in each case to be played as 𝄾 𝄿 ♪♪. ♩ . Later, when making the alteration in bar 5 he wrote, not according to the convention, but, as he often did, the exact sound effect that he desired. Observe the quaver rest followed by a semiquaver rest which Handel substituted for what previously was a dotted quaver. The alteration obscures this note but it is clearly to be seen in the second violin. Handel altered all the parts but the alteration in the basso-continuo stave is difficult to see. Smith failed to see it and so altered only the two violins and the viola staves, leaving the dotted quaver note in the basso-continuo with its implication of a cembalo chord instead of a rest (cf. facsimiles, pp. 54, 55). All the copies except the Tenbury–Dublin contain only the altered version. But it is worth noting that in the two early copies one, the Needler, has the correct basso-continuo at bar 5: 𝄾 𝄿 ♪♪. ♩ , while the other, the Granville, repeats the error from the Tenbury–Dublin copy ♩. ♪♪. ♩ . This supports Professor Larsen's finding that the Granville is a Smith copy. Needler was evidently the more observant.

THE PASTORAL SYMPHONY

In its first form Handel's 'Pifa' (the only title in the Autograph, really an indication of style) was but eleven bars in length. Originally he had no thought of a possible extension for, immediately following the final eleventh bar, on the same page, he wrote the *secco* recitative 'There were shepherds' and the *accompagnato* 'And lo!'. His later decision to extend the Symphony was possibly because he felt that eleven bars did not give sufficient time for the climax built up by the group beginning with the recit. 'Behold a Virgin shall conceive' and culminating in the chorus 'For unto us a Child is born' to subside into the serenity of the recitative 'There were shepherds'.

Handel wrote the middle section on a piece of manuscript paper just four staves deep; it is inserted in the binding at the foot between the page containing the final bars of the original Pastoral plus the *secco* and *accompagnato* recitatives, and the page containing the arioso setting of 'And lo!' Having written the middle section he then proceeded to make the link between the two sections in the basso-continuo. He filled in the open head of the dotted minim C in bar 11 (all Handel's very large crotchets invariably had first been minims) and in the remaining and inadequate space wrote the notes D, E and F♮. Realizing that they were almost indecipherable, he wrote their names over the respective notes and marked the connecting bars with his usual N.B. sign.

Chrysander, the editor of the Handelgesellschaft, declared that this middle section was cut by Handel, and that in the Tenbury–Dublin copy it was

pasted over with paper (Chrysander worked on this score in the latter part of
the last century). It is not so now, but there are marks in the score consistent
with the use of paste. But pastings over and, still more, crossings out rarely
provide satisfactory evidence either as to by whom or when the deletion was
made. The facts are that in the Tenbury–Dublin copy, which contains the
first complete copy of the Pastoral, the notes in the basso-continuo which lead
to the middle section are crossed out rather in the manner of Handel. There
is also a faint double bar at this point as well as faint pencil lines which indicate
a cut. In the Foundling and Hamburg copies this Symphony consists of only
the eleven bars which Handel first wrote. All the remaining manuscripts
from the early Needler and Granville copies to the late RM 18.e.2, contain
the Symphony complete with middle section and consequent *da capo*.

It is not generally known that Handel made a second attempt at composing
a middle section.. This he wrote on the back of this same four-stave insertion.

A musician can have little difficulty in believing that Handel discarded this attempt; but there seems little reason, in this case certainly not length of performance, for his discarding the accepted middle section.

WHY DO THE NATIONS

There are two Autograph manuscripts concerning this air. One is a complete setting, the other is an alternative ending to that setting.

The complete setting is contained in the Autograph score. It is written in the bass clef, the key is C major and the time signature $\frac{4}{4}$. From its structure it looks like a *da capo* air. There is a first section of seventy-four bars ending in the key of the tonic. This is followed by a section consisting of twenty-two bars beginning in the relative minor and ending in the mediant minor; further, the first section closes with a *ritornello* which ends in a typical *fine* bar. In the Autograph, however (also the early copies, the Needler and Granville), there is neither a pause nor other indication of a *fine* bar at this point, nor is there the indication *da capo* at the end of the second section. But in *Songs in Messiah* (*circa* 1749) a *fine* pause was printed in bar 74, as was also *da capo* after the final bar. This would seem to indicate that Handel intended this to be a *da capo* air. There are, however, two pieces of evidence to the contrary: one, the not merely satisfactory but the brilliant completion of the expected ternary structure by the following chorus 'Let us break their bonds asunder' which is in C major, the tonic key of the air; the other, the instruction written by Handel, immediately following the cadence bar on the manuscript of the alternative ending: '*Segue il coro* Let us break'.

The alternative ending is to be found in the Tenbury–Dublin copy, not in the body of that copy but in the Appendix (the body of the copy contains a copy of the original complete air from the Autograph score). The 'Amen' chorus finishes verso folio 138; folio 139 is empty. On folio 140, recto, in autograph, is a recitative seven bars in length. This is the alternative ending. It takes the place of some fifty-eight bars of the original air, beginning at bar 39. In that bar on the first beat a $\frac{6}{3}$ on the note G♯ is substituted for a chord of G major, so preparing for an immediate transition through A minor, ending, as does the original air, in E minor. The connecting points for the beginning of the cut have not Handel's usual N.B. sign. On the manuscript of the recitative there is not any mark but in the same score (the Tenbury–Dublin copy) in the copy of the original complete setting is a small 'x' in ink exactly over the bar line between bars 38 and 39.

The Foundling and Hamburg scores contain only this shortened version of the air ending with the recitative. Chrysander regarded the Hamburg copy as the final authentic form of the oratorio. But, while one can easily believe that Handel accepted this version for some occasion when the bass soloist was inadequate, it is very difficult to believe that, given the adequate soloist, he would prefer it. From the instrumental introduction itself it is obvious that Handel intended this to be a full length typical 'rage' aria. This sudden truncation of it after a mere twenty-three bars of the voice can only be regarded as a makeshift. It may be reasonably assumed that Handel would prefer the original complete air, and that it should run straight into the following chorus without *da capo*. The collation of the recently discovered Townley Hall manuscript with the Marsh–Matthews and Mann 'Dublin' manuscripts, however, throws further light upon this question. For the order of contents in the three manuscripts of this part of the oratorio, see Appendix H.

It will be seen that all three manuscripts contain 'How beautiful' in the alto duet and chorus setting followed by 'Their sound is gone out' in the tenor arioso setting, and that in each manuscript the air that follows, 'Why do the nations', is in the shortened version with the recitative ending. Therefore, it may well be (a) that this shortened version was written expressly to follow the more elaborate duet and chorus setting of 'How beautiful' with its complementary tenor arioso; and (b) that the original complete setting of ninety-six bars was sung only if preceded by the more simple setting of 'How beautiful' as a *da capo* air. The following note written after the final cadence of the complete setting of 'Why do the nations' on page 108 of the Marsh–Matthews manuscript supports these conclusions.

> The next duet on the opposite side with the chorus of the same[1] together with the tenor song[2] after the chorus, is taken from Mr. Harris's score, but the words are the very same as in the fore-going treble song (How beautiful &c), and after that this bass song with alterations and cut shorter, which is likewise taken from Mr. Harris's score, but the words are the same as the bass song that ends on the top of this page.

This grouping was clearly an established practice, for when the alto-duet and chorus setting of 'How beautiful' came to be omitted in performance (at some later period, for in the Rowe score—dated by the copyist 1761—in the top margin of the G minor air is written 'A song omitted in the performance'; and over the duet and chorus which follows 'Duet which is played instead of the last song'), the conductor, for more convenient use of the score, doubled over the pages containing all three settings (the alto-duet and chorus, the tenor arioso, and the shortened bass air); the crease down the centre of these pages is still clearly to be seen.

It is not unreasonable to assume that this truncated version of 'Why do the nations' with the recitative ending was made as a compromise for some less accomplished singer. For who could imagine that Handel, a sensitive artist and craftsman, would as a regular practice and not merely in a moment of necessity, allow the completely satisfying and expressive tripartite structure (the bipartite air with the following chorus taking the place of a *da capo*— the air itself was never intended as a *da capo* air) to be wrecked by such a stop-gap as this truncated, mis-shapen alternative in which at bar 39, when we have

[1] 'How beautiful'; 'Break forth into joy'.
[2] 'Their sound is gone out'.

only begun to savour the air, we are suddenly switched to a closing recitative of seven bars, in itself a dramatic recitative but a poor substitute for the final fifty-eight bars of one of the finest of Handel's 'rage' arias. However, with or without Handel's consent, the singing of this alternative was reasonably established, for the evidence of these manuscripts cannot be ignored.

Thou shalt break them

1. Air; tenor C clef; A minor; ¾; Autograph score
2. Recitative; Tenbury–Dublin copy

The recitative is to be found in the Tenbury–Dublin copy, immediately following the end of the air, on the remaining four staves of folio 87 verso. Surely this was only written for some occasion when the tenor soloist was not equal to singing the air. It is not to be found in autograph but, in its situation in the Tenbury–Dublin copy, may well be authentic. It seems hardly likely that, given an adequate soloist, Handel would forego the air.

Chrysander omitted the air in his performing edition, substituted the recitative, transposed it down a major third into D minor for the bass voice, ornamented it, and omitted the final cadence chord in order to go directly, without any break, into the 'Hallelujah' chorus:

O DEATH WHERE IS THY STING

In the *Musical Times* of October 1948, Julian Herbage called attention to a previously unknown setting of 'O death where is thy sting'. It is contained in the Marsh–Matthews copy in Dublin. The setting is in the form of a recitative; it is six bars in length, is written in the alto clef, ostensibly in B♭ major and, written with the conventional signature of one flat less, it really begins in E♭ major and moves through B♭ major and C minor to a final cadence in G minor. There is not any evidence in support of its acceptance as authentic *Messiah* material.

4 *The Orchestra*

ORCHESTRATION

ALTHOUGH Handel took only twenty-four days to compose *Messiah*, the orchestration in the Autograph score is complete in all essential features. Quite naturally he took advantage of any reasonable device to avoid wasting time in writing unnecessary notes; in the middle section of 'He was despised', having established the repeated note figure in the time group ♩. ♪♪. ♪, he troubled only to write, for each crotchet beat, one filled-in note-head just to indicate the pitch of the notes; in 'Why do the nations', having established a semiquaver bowed tremolo, once again he troubled only to write four filled-in note-heads in each bar to indicate pitch (indeed, the copyist of the Foundling copy took advantage of the same abbreviation in 'But who may abide'); in a choral fugue where the strings double the voices he saved himself the trouble of writing the notes on the orchestral staves by writing the indication to the copyist 'Ut . . .' on the appropriate stave filling in the dotted space with the appropriate voice.

These were clear instructions to the copyist; in effect every note was written by Handel. The only notes to be heard in performance that were not written by him were the notes to be played by the keyboard continuo players, but then the realization of the basso-continuo was by convention a matter of improvisation.

Handel scored *Messiah* in the accepted manner of the period; for continuo accompaniment alone, for continuo with obbligato instruments, for continuo with full strings (it being understood that in choral numbers the oboes would double either the choral soprano or violin and that the bassoons would double either the choral bass or the basso-continuo) with, in certain numbers, the addition of trumpets and of timpani.

All the choruses are scored for continuo and full strings with the following additions:

'Glory to God': 2 trumpets.
'Their sound is gone out': 2 oboes.
'Hallelujah': trumpets and timpani.
'Worthy is the Lamb'; 'Blessing and honour'; 'Amen': trumpets and timpani.

With the one exception of the trumpet in the air 'The trumpet shall sound' Handel did not score for trumpets or timpani elsewhere in *Messiah*. The statement on page 24 in *Handel's Oratorio 'The Messiah'* by Edward C. Bairstow[1] that, in 'For unto us a Child is born', 'The trumpet and timpani parts are

---

[1] Oxford University Press, 1928.

62

Handel's', is completely incorrect. The statement in the same book that in 'Glory to God' 'Handel scored for trumpets, drums and strings' is also incorrect: Handel did not introduce timpani until the 'Hallelujah' chorus. His reserve in the use of brass and percussion, not only in relation to the complete work but also within those numbers in which he scored for these instruments, makes their use the more effective; note, for example, in 'Worthy is the Lamb' their effective re-entry in bar 19 after their silence in the preceding *largo;* and similarly their re-entry in bar 53 of the same chorus and not, as a lesser composer might well have made it, in bar 24 (the first statement of the same 'Blessing and honour' theme). The score contains many eloquent orchestral silences.

It is apt here to refer to the choral sequence 'Since by man'. The late Professor Tovey once declared that neither Bach nor Handel wrote a line of vocal music with the intention that it was to be unaccompanied.[1] Here again we see the perpetuation of the false idea of an *a cappella* Renaissance and a *sempre-continuo* Baroque. Handel wrote an accompaniment of full strings and continuo for 'By man came also the resurrection of the dead' and 'Even so in Christ shall all be made alive'. Not only did he not score the other two parts of the sequence ('Since by man came death' and 'For as in Adam all die') in similar fashion but, after writing the first crotchet for the key-chord, he took the positive action of writing rests in the remaining bars of the basso-continuo. Further evidence is that in the orchestral continuo parts in the Foundling orchestral material these sections are marked *senza stromenti*. Therefore, we may justifiably assume that in this sequence Handel intended an alternation of true *a cappella* and *con stromenti*.

Of the thirty-three numbers for solo voice, seven are *secco* recitatives and one other number, the duet 'O death where is thy sting', is scored for continuo alone, making eight numbers scored for continuo accompaniment alone. Of the remaining twenty-five solo numbers (airs, ariosos, and accompanied recitatives) eight are scored for continuo with *obbligato* violins, one for continuo and strings with *obbligato* trumpet, and sixteen are scored for continuo with full strings.

Where Handel scored for continuo only it may generally be assumed that he did so because he considered it to be the correct scoring, both for the number itself and in its context in relation to the scoring of the work as a whole, and not because he was pressed for time. For example, some recitatives he wrote as *secco* but others, impelled by the *Affekt*, he wrote as *accompagnato*. In some works he used both forms in one recitative because the text demanded it.[2] In *Messiah* itself observe the alternation of the two styles in the Christmas recitatives and the use of *accompagnato* for the more exciting 'And lo! the Angel of the Lord' and 'And suddenly there was with the Angel'.

[1] *Essays in Musical Analysis* (Vol. V, p. 73), Tovey, Oxford University Press.
[2] *Cf.* the recitative before Cleopatra's final aria in *Alexander Balus* as but one example.

The Foundling manuscripts include a set of orchestral parts. The authenticity of these parts has been questioned, and in this regard it is of interest that the Foundling minute of 13th June 1759 refers to the delivery of a score only, no reference being made to any parts. The watermark in the parts, however, is the same as that in the Autograph score. It consists of the design known as the Strasburg Bend and Lily together with the initials L.V.G. and J.W.; the last two letters are the initials of James Whatman, who made paper in England and Holland; L.V.G. are the initials of L. Van Gerrevink of Egmond an der Hoef, North Holland (from whom Whatman learned the art) and indicate that the paper was made at Whatman's Mill in Holland. The Whatman–Van Gerrevink mark is to be found on various folios in the Foundling parts: e.g., in the viola part, (a) the folio containing 'thy rebuke hath broken His Heart is marked with the Strasburg Bend and L.V.G.; (b) the next folio, 'Lift up your heads', is marked with the Lilies design; and (c) the following folio is marked with the initials J.W. Paper made abroad for the British market also had the British Royal Cipher as countermark; the initials G.R. are also to be found in the paper used by Smith.

The oboe and bassoon manuscript parts afford an insight into the conventional use of these instruments.

In the *Grave* of the Overture the oboes play in unison and double the first violin; in the *Allegro* they are *divisi* and double first and second violins respectively. In fourteen choruses the oboes play in unison and double the choral soprano. In Handel's own performances the sopranos were boys; moreover, the *tessitura* of the choral soprano part is low and the boys doubtless needed the support of the oboes. At each of the Foundling performances of *Messiah* Handel used four oboes.

Of these fourteen choruses the oboe parts in the following are of interest:

'Glory to God'

Bars 30 to 31. The first telescopes the two bars into one, in error, while the second oboe plays the correct time values:

'Behold the Lamb of God'

Bar 18, beat 2 repeats the often made mistake of turning Handel's even quavers into a dotted group.

'Amen'

The oboes are in unison throughout and, with one exception, double the sopranos throughout. The exception is the first entry of the soprano in bars 87 to 91; and the reason is that Handel scored the *exposition* of this chorus for continuo only, therefore there is no orchestral ensemble in which the oboe may join.

In the following choruses the oboes do something more than double the sopranos in unison:

'And the glory'

The first and second oboes play in the instrumental introduction. They are *divisi* and double the first and second violins respectively. But from bar 14 to the end they revert to the usual practice of doubling the soprano in unison. There is one exception to this, bar 14 beat 2, when the second oboe plays a¹ against the soprano and the first oboe note e''.

'For unto us a Child is born'

The first and second oboes play in the instrumental introduction, *divisi* and doubling the first and second violins respectively for six bars and one beat, after which they revert to the usual practice.

The part contains two copyist's mistakes. The one that is of interest occurs in bar 29 beat 3 where, while the second oboe has the correct time group: ♪♫ , the first oboe has the here incorrect: ♫♪ ; in bar 64, however, both oboes are correct.

'His yoke is easy'

Although first and second oboes play in unison and double the choral soprano from bar 11 to the end, yet, during the opening statement of the theme by the sopranos, the second oboe is silent.[1] The four oboes were possibly too heavy for the boy sopranos in a theme so light in character.

'Lift up your heads'

The first and second oboes play in the instrumental introduction, *divisi* and doubling the first and second violins respectively. At the choral entry, still *divisi*, they double the first and second sopranos respectively. From the last quaver of bar 33 to the end they revert to the usual practice.

'The Lord gave the Word'

The first oboe doubles the choral soprano throughout; but the second oboe for the first thirteen bars plays a mixture of choral alto, second violin and choral tenor. Further, in bars 9 and 10 the choral soprano and alto motive is included in the oboe parts; in the Bourne 'Original' printed parts (Novello), the oboes are *tacet* in these bars.

In the body of the Autograph score, Handel did not write oboe parts for any chorus. But bound in the Autograph volume at the end, after the alternative alto-duet and chorus setting of 'How beautiful are the feet' and the tenor arioso setting of 'Their sound is gone out into all lands', is the Autograph of the chorus setting of 'Their sound is gone out' which Handel scored for first and second oboes in addition to continuo and full strings. In a number of bars the first oboe doubles the choral soprano and the second oboe the choral alto; but in some bars, e.g. bars 8, 19, and 30, they reverse the procedure. In other bars an independent part is made out of odd beats from several voice parts: e.g. in bar 28 the first oboe doubles the tenor for the first

[1] Handel's orchestra included two first and two second oboes.

two beats and the soprano for the last two beats in the bar; or, as in bar 20, the second oboe and second violin in unison play an independent part in thirds with the alto; or again, the oboes play a sustained note against choral passing-notes or, as in bars 22 and 23, a decoration of a vocal cadence:

This is the only autograph *Messiah* manuscript to have oboe parts.

In the Foundling parts in the Overture and the Pastoral Symphony the bassoons double the basso-continuo. They are silent in all accompanied recitatives with the exception of 'Behold, darkness shall cover the earth', in the arioso 'Comfort ye', and in the first and third choruses of the choral sequence 'Since by man came death'. In the airs they play in the *ritornelli* and *con ripieno* passages but generally not actually against the voice; an obvious exception is the air 'The people that walked in darkness', in which they play throughout. But, for example, in 'Every valley' they have thirty bars rest after bar 11 and then play only the *con ripieno* orchestral points of imitation. In the choruses they double not the choral bass but the basso-continuo. Only where the basso-continuo is *seguente* do they play with the choral bass (sometimes the choral tenor).

ADDITIONAL ACCOMPANIMENTS

Although the additional accompaniments in *Messiah* are usually attributed to Mozart it is doubtful whether he was completely responsible for the whole of them. It is fairly safe to assume that Johann Adam Hiller, sometimes known as 'The Father of the Singspiel', must take the blame for the less worthy additions; the least worthy being unquestionably the alterations to the content and structure of the air 'If God be for us' and the turning of Handel's *obbligato* for violins in the same air into a vulgar bassoon *obbligato*. It is true that Mozart considered this air unsatisfactory, for in a letter to Mozart dated 22nd March 1789, Baron Van Swieten writes that he considers Mozart's idea of turning 'the cold aria' into a recitative to be excellent; but a recitative is one thing and the maltreated air, in what in the absence of definite proof we may call the Mozart–Hiller arrangement, is quite another.

It is said that Hiller prepared a special score for his Leipzig performance, *circa* 1787. The question of the authorship of the 'Mozart' additional accompaniments was raised in 1862 by C. F. Baumgart (Headmaster of the Mathias Gymnasium, Breslau) by an article in the *Niederrheinische Musik Zeitung*, 'Ein' Falsum in Mozarts *Messias* Partitur'; again in 1881 by Julius Schäffer (successor to Reinecke as conductor of the Breslau Singakademie) by an article in the *Musikalisches Wochenblatt*, 'Fälschungen in den Bearbeitungen des Händel'schen *Messias* durch Johann Adam Hiller'; and again in 1903 by Hermann Schönfeld, Cantor of the Church of Maria Magdalena, Breslau.

Schäffer asked Breitkopf to clarify the matter by publishing a new edition together with any papers or music manuscripts left by Mozart referring to his work on *Messiah*, but Breitkopf did not reply.

Putting aside the maltreated 'If God be for us' and the badly truncated 'The trumpet shall sound' and the orchestration stylistically at fault, it is understandable that Mozart should consider it necessary to rewrite Handel's trumpet parts, for somewhere about the time Mozart was born the function of the trumpet in the orchestra had changed; it was no longer used as a melodic instrument, but as harmonic support for the middle of the harmony. As a result the players' *embouchure* loosened and the art of *clarino* playing died out; only the *principale* remained.

For the alterations to the timpani parts, however, there is no such excuse. It is hardly credible that Mozart could be responsible for the meretriciously effective variations upon Handel's dignified and completely *affekt*-ive rhythms, indeed in some cases upon Handel's wisely judged silences. For example, in the 'Amen' chorus against the majestically flowing even quavers in the

bass in bar 121  for Handel's

rests in the timpani part was substituted

Again in bars 146–147 in the same chorus

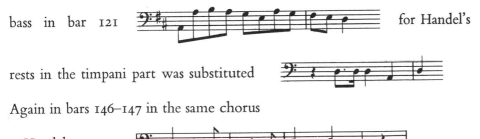

Handel

Mozart-Hiller

And against the final two *sostenuto* 'Amens'

Handel

Mozart-Hiller

Handel's notes were, of course, rolled.

Rochlitz summed up the case justly in a review of the Breitkopf 1803 edition when, in referring to the additional accompaniments, he wrote, 'Every period has its own essential characteristics and should be allowed to keep them.'

Handel may not have added greatly to eighteenth-century orchestral practice (in passing, his anticipation in *Giulio Cesare* of the use of four horns must not be forgotten) but he took every possible advantage of accepted practice. He was a practical wind, string, and keyboard performer and this shows in his use of the orchestra, not merely in such technical details as the *louré* string accompaniment to 'Comfort ye', the use of the bowed tremolo in the contrast sections of 'But who may abide' or the couplet bowing in 'All we like sheep', but in more vital things. Note the style of the second oboe in the first twelve bars of the chorus 'Their sound is gone out'; the excellent string writing in the introduction to 'Thou art gone up on high', and the exciting octave-leap in reverse string accompaniment to the choral voices in bars 52 *et seq.* of the alto duet and chorus 'How beautiful are the feet'; the *concertato* style dialogue between choir and orchestra and between the upper and lower choral groups in 'Lift up your heads'; the lightness of texture in 'His yoke is easy' varied by the sudden superimposition of *con ripieno* upon the general *senza ripieno* background; the effective alternation of continuo with a full string accompaniment in 'And He shall purify'; the choral shouts in 'For unto us a Child is born' of 'Wonderful, Counsellor' against the brilliant semiquaver passage in thirds in the violins, suspended, as it were, in the heavens almost without any terrestrial support; the characteristic figure of the introduction to 'O Thou that tellest' given to the first violin in bars 127 and 128 while the chorus merely supplies accompanying harmony; and the cadential melody of the theme of 'His yoke is easy' given in bars 36–7 and 45–6 to the second violin against independent choral writing.

Unfortunately in many performances today these marvellous touches are lost in an insoluble mass of sound.

In other works Handel scored for theorbo, harp, lute, flute, clarinet, mandoline, carillon, trombone, strings muted, strings pizzicato, and string basses playing three-part harmony. None of this is experimental in effect for within the style of the period he did it all with a sureness of touch to be envied by the most virtuoso of orchestrators. But in *Messiah* he used none of these things. In *Messiah* he gave proof of the wealth of his genius by his economical use of the orchestra.

THE FIRST PERFORMANCE

Handel received an invitation from the Lord Lieutenant of Ireland, William Cavendish, fourth Duke of Devonshire, to visit Ireland and to perform his music for the benefit of charity.

It has often been stated that *Messiah* was composed for this visit, and an advertisement in *Faulkner's Dublin Journal* '. . . well-wishers to this Noble and Grand Charity for which this oratorio was composed . . .' lends support to this view. But although Handel travelled to Ireland in November 1741, a few weeks after completing the oratorio, he did not announce *Messiah* until the April of 1742. It was first heard at a public rehearsal on 9th April and given its first public performance on 13th April in Neale's Music Hall,

Fishamble Street, Dublin. The leader of the orchestra was Dubourg (a pupil of Geminiani); the sopranos were Signora Avoglio and Mrs. Maclean; the mezzo-soprano was Mrs. Cibber (a former actress and the daughter of Arne); the male altos were Joseph Lamb and Michael Ward, the tenor, James Bailey, and the bass, John Mason. The word-book of the first performance bears the imprint 'George Faulkner—Dublin 1742'—the price is given as a 'British sixpence'. It is in the British Museum: shelf-mark Mk 8.d.4.

For chorus Handel had the choirs of the two cathedrals. The singers were:

St. Patrick's Cathedral		Christ Church Cathedral	
Gentlemen of the Choir		Gentlemen of the Choir	
Mr. Worrall	Mr. Jones	Mr. Worrall	Mr. Smith
Mr. Church	Mr. Phipps	Mr. Taylor	Mr. Mason
Mr. Bailey	Mr. Tavenor	Mr. Jones	Mr. Church
Mr. Hall	Mr. Woffington	Mr. Phipps	Mr. Ward
Mr. Lambe	Mr. Smith	Mr. Bailey	Mr. Carter
Mr. Colgan	Mr. Hill	Mr. Lambe	Mr. Hill
Mr. Ward			
and 8 choristers		and 8 choristers	

The choristers were boy trebles.

Roseingrave was organist of both cathedrals. It will be seen also that several of the singers sang in both choirs. Therefore, in the first performance the choir consisted of sixteen men and sixteen boys.

Professor Larsen, writing about the shortened version with the recitative ending of 'Why do the nations', suggests that it was written for the Dublin performance because the air was sung by an inferior singer, Hill, declaring that Hill's name is written against the air in the 1742 word-book and in the margin of the air in the Tenbury–Dublin copy. This is not so. The name in the word-book is Cibber, but the first and last two letters are extremely faint—hence Professor Larsen's error. The only name now to be seen in the margin of the air in the Tenbury–Dublin copy, however, is Reinhold.

OTHER PERFORMANCES

After Handel's return from Ireland, during his lifetime, i.e. in the course of seventeen years, England provided some fifty-six performances, all but twelve in secular places of entertainment, variously announced as 'A New Sacred Oratorio' (1743), 'A Sacred Oratorio' (1745), 'An Oratorio called *Messiah*' (1749), '*Messiah*, or the Sacred Oratorio' (1757). Bath, Bristol, Durham, Gloucester, Hereford, London, Oxford, Salisbury, and Worcester provided forty-five (on two occasions Oxford spread the oratorio over two perform-ances; the advertisement for the second announced 'will be performed so much of the *Messiah* as was omitted in a former performance'). The Foundling Hospital provided eleven performances. There were nine other occasions when either a single part or a selection from the oratorio was given, when the 'Hallelujah' ('The Grand Chorus from the *Messiah*') was sung, or when Galli or Frasi sang an air 'in the *Messiah* by Mr. Handel'.

Messiah was first performed in Germany at Hamburg, in English, conducted by an Englishman, Michael Arne, in 1772. Afterwards it was sung in German in Hamburg, with the Klopstock-Ebeling translation, conducted by C. P. E. Bach in 1775, at Mannheim under Vogler in 1777, in Weimar, with a musically sensitive translation by Herder, under Kapellmeister Wilhelm Wolf in 1780 and 1781, and in Berlin (the Cathedral), in Italian, under Hiller in 1786.

HANDEL'S OWN PERFORMANCES

It will be seen from the extracts from the Minute Books of the Foundling Hospital[1], that the balance of orchestra and choir remained constant during Handel's lifetime; twelve to fourteen violins, three violas, three violoncellos, two contrabassi, four oboes, four bassoons, two trumpets, two horns, and timpani, 'The Children of the Kings Chapel', and about a dozen male singers. But in 1771 the oboes were reduced to two, likewise the bassoons; the male singers (these, of course, include altos) increased to eighteen, and in addition to twelve boys (eight supplied by Dr. Nares and four by Mr. Cooke) there were '26 Chorus Singers Volunteers not paid'.

In all the lists of players two horns are included, although no horn parts are to be found among the Foundling manuscripts. Handel scored for the horns in other works and it was his custom to have the horns double the trumpets at the lower octave. In general, however, he associated the horns with un-believers and the only such chorus in *Messiah*, 'He trusted in God', is without opportunity for the use of any kind of brass except in the final cadence. That horns were used in *Messiah* would seem fairly certain, and, therefore, in the absence of parts one can only assume that they doubled the trumpets at the lower pitch.

The Minute of 25th June 1754 makes it very clear that the 1754 performance was to be the last Foundling Chapel performance to be conducted by Handel; in the Minute he hands over to Smith both the conducting and the administration. Yet a Minute dated 18th May 1757 refers to the performance 'under the direction of Mr. Handel'. It is amusing to note that the 'very numerous audience' of 1750 became in a Minute of 15th April 1752 'a most noble and grand audience' but receded in a Minute of 18th May 1757 to a 'numerous and polite' audience.

THE FUNCTION OF THE HARPSICHORD

The core of the orchestral sound is the keyboard continuo; in the solo sections the harpsichord, in the choruses the organ and harpsichord. With the exception of those bars where a melody in the upper parts stands entirely alone there is no place where the keyboard continuo can be omitted without detri-ment to the balance, timbre, and style. In some cases the omission would result in the misrepresentation of Handel's harmonic intentions and in others

[1] See Appendix D.

the loss of a particular and essential colour.

Handel knew well how to write for strings, but often he scored somewhat thinly, as in the following examples, leaving the filling out of the harmony to the keyboard continuo.

On occasion he would rest the upper strings with the voice, intending the harpsichord to make itself heard in a spread chord during the momentary cessation of string tone. Such a case is to be found in bar 43 of 'He shall feed His flock'. Here in the vocal rest the four-part string accompaniment is suddenly reduced to two parts, the bass instruments and the viola, playing respectively the third and the root at the interval of a thirteenth.

Again he would write only the root and fifth in the strings, as in the final chord of 'Thy rebuke hath broken His heart', indicating by the figuring ♯ that the harpsichord was to supply the missing third.

Or again he wanted the harpsichord not merely to supply the harmony but with its quilled tone to intensify the dramatic effect. In the accompanied recitative 'All they that see him laugh him to scorn' the strings are in complete four-part harmony during the introduction. At the entry of the voice in bar 4 they are abruptly reduced to the bass instruments and the first violin and, as was customary against the voice, marked *piano*. But the character of the violin figure in bar 5 with its final octave leap, the contrary movement between the two widely separated parts and the chord on the full strings on the third crotchet indicate the usual after-voice *forte*. It surely is obvious that Handel here in accord with the *Affekt* would play not a solitary minim chord but, at the very least, repeated quaver chords, forte and with four notes in each hand.

Or yet again in a movement scored for continuo trio, having at some point given a moving figure to the violins against a sustained note in the voice he would in a comparable place elsewhere silence the violins, intending himself to improvise a moving figure on the harpsichord. An outstanding example of an *obbligato* figure being halted in order to obtain contrast by means of imitation in another instrumental timbre (the harpsichord) is the accompanied recitative 'Wiewohl mein Herz in Tränen schwimmt' from Bach's *St. Matthew Passion*. No keyboard continuo player with understanding of and love for his art could allow the flowing semiquaver triplets of the two oboe d'amore to disappear in bar 4 into dull repetitive quaver chords on the harpsichord. Certainly not Bach nor Handel. They, we may be sure, would improvise a flowing figure on the harpsichord.

Indeed, in bar 8 of this same recitative Bach himself indicated the need in such cases for maintaining movement of some sort when against the sustained first oboe d'amore he wrote semiquaver couplets for the second oboe d'amore. Much has been written about the keyboard mastery of Bach and Handel, but there is nothing in the nature of irrefutable evidence concerning their practice when improvising basso-continuo realizations. In the absence of such evidence, one's own musicianship must be the arbiter.

In 'O Thou that tellest glad tidings to Zion' bars 25 to 28 Handel wrote:

It is a reasonable assumption that in bar 10 the figure

might flow from his fingers. In the same air in bars 89–93 against the sustained note following the scale-wise descending passage he wrote a broken arpeggio figure in the violins, again repeating the figure in bars 102 and 103.

Again it is a reasonable assumption that in bars 54–57, and 64–66 a similar broken arpeggio figure would arise from either hand on the harpsichord.

The timidity evinced by the generality of musicologists in relation to basso-continuo realization has much delayed the resurgence of the art and the development of a suitable style. In his invaluable book *The Art of Accompaniment from a Thorough-bass*,[1] F. T. Arnold, writing of an informal congress of members of the Neue Bach-Gesellschaft held at Duisburg in 1910 writes, 'A desire was expressed for a fully set-out accompaniment in place of or in addition to Bach's figured basses. Various reasons against this were advanced; buildings differed in their acoustical properties, and so forth, and the accompaniment required to be modified accordingly. But the writer had little doubt that the real (if subconscious) reason in the minds of those concerned was the wise reflection that, in playing from a figured bass, it is often convenient to do things *which do not look well on paper*'. And as late as September, 1957, in the *Musical Times*, Julian Herbage, in reviewing the Purcell Society's Vol. XXVII, described a particular harpsichord realization as one 'that (unlike little children) should be heard and not seen'. Obviously there is need for greater honesty in this regard. Saint-Lambert at the beginning of the eighteenth century wrote, '*Comme la Musique n'est faite que pour l'oreille, une faute qui ne l'offense point n'est une faute.*' If a realization is fit to be heard then not only is it fit to be seen—it ought to be seen. Certain is it that the unimaginative chordal style of the school castigated by G. M. Telemann as 'Thorough-bass threshers' is far removed from all that we know of Handel. It is impossible to imagine such a style falling from the fingers of one who in addition to the power of creating massive harmonic structures was possessed of such endless melodic invention and contrapuntal skill.[2]

[1] Oxford University Press, 1931.
[2] See the music examples of harpsichord style in Chapter 5, under Ornamentation.

5 Style in Performance

DYNAMICS

In the Autograph score, Handel gave general indications of dynamics. In the Tenbury–Dublin copy he added detailed *senza* and *con ripieno* instructions. These instructions must be given much consideration when preparing for performance. If carefully followed they provide a considerable amount of tonal contrast and colour. Indeed, they are essential to his scheme of dynamics. Note the detailed contrasts in 'Every valley'; the burst of tone in 'And the glory' at bar 14 where after a *senza ripieno* orchestral introduction followed by the choral alto entry, the full choir enters with the orchestra *con ripieno;* the *forte* cadences, reinforced by the orchestra *con ripieno*, that are periodically superimposed upon an otherwise light texture in 'His yoke is easy'; and the build up of the first bars of the 'Hallelujah' chorus where first the orchestra enters alone *senza ripieno*, then the voices are added and six beats later the orchestral *ripieno* is added for the vigorous antiphonal orchestral and vocal hallelujahs. There are places, however, where one suspects that Handel's *ripieno* instructions were sometimes governed by the less-than-facile technique of his *ripieno* players: e.g. 'The trumpet shall sound' is *con ripieno* but 'Why do the nations' is *senza ripieno*. Therefore, in these days of greater technical proficiency the conductor should use his discretion in such cases.

The *ripieno* instructions and the normal contrast between *piano* and *forte* playing produce a terraced expression which is a feature of the period. Rosamond Harding in her *Origins of Musical Time and Expression*[1] writes, 'Even Handel, impregnated as he was with Italian music, only uses the term *forte*, *piano*, and *pianissimo* in the *Messiah*'. But in the Autograph he also wrote *mezzo piano* at the beginning of the Pastoral Symphony and *un poco piano* both at the beginning of the middle section of 'He was despised' and under the basso-continuo bar 77 of 'But who may abide' in the Autograph Guadagni setting in the Tenbury–Dublin copy, so narrowing the terraces. Elsewhere he narrowed them still further by '*piano, piu forte, fortissimo*' (RM 20.d.7, folio 44 recto).

But the absence of *crescendo* and *diminuendo* marks from the score does not mean that there should not be any nuance within each terrace. It should be remembered that the early vocal device *messa di voce* had been adopted instrumentally for some time, that Matthew Locke in *The Tempest* wrote 'louder by degrees' and that Handel's 'terraced' markings in the final *ritornello* of 'Glory to God' in effect constitute a *diminuendo*. Further, even where a general level of *forte* is to be maintained for a relatively lengthy period, as in the 'allegro' of the *Messiah* overture, there is little doubt that Handel meant it to

[1] Oxford University Press, 1938.

75

be what Schweitzer in his life of Bach describes as a 'flexible *forte*'.

I have said that in the Autograph score Handel gave general indications of dynamics; but they are general only in comparison with later practice.

Handel's music was conceived on broad lines and it sounds best when its interpretation is realized on broad lines. This is not to advocate a dull colour-less performance. Handel may have worked on a large canvas, but his wrist was exceedingly flexible and his brush-work often extremely delicate; but it was a flexibility and a delicacy born of strength. The interpretation must not be finicky or fussy but it must not lack variety.

Handel's music calls for all degrees of dynamics from *pianissimo* to *fortissimo*. It contains inherent *crescendi* and *diminuendi*, *accelerandi* and *rallentandi*, it even calls for an appreciation of the difference between dynamic and agogic accent—but it does not call for rapidly changing subtle nuance or the restless rubato of Romantic music. Flexibility there must be, but it must be within clearly defined terraces, for clearly marked contrast (the root of the *concertato* style) is the very heart of the Baroque. The search for the historically correct per-formance if wrongly directed becomes a sterile inquiry. Wisely directed it will give life to music which otherwise sounds dull; it will enable us to hear the works of composers of past ages—no less living, sentient beings than we—as they themselves conceived them. The basic materials of musical expression have been essentially the same for at least three centuries; the stylistic differences lie in their application.

Examination proves Handel's marking to be adequate. It is true that there appear to be many omissions, e.g. the opening of a movement is more often than not without any indication of dynamic, but this was not an omission, for it was a performing convention of the period that a movement began *forte* unless otherwise marked.

An analysis of Handel's own markings in *Messiah* yield the following results.

Out of the total number of sixty movements there are thirty-three without a single indication of dynamic.

The Beginning of the Movement

Out of the remaining twenty-seven there are only five with an indication of dynamic at the beginning of the movement and three of these contain the word *piano*. (Handel did not write *forte* at the beginning of any movement of *Messiah*.) Of those three there are two with a combined tempo and dynamic indication (*larghetto e piano*, *larghetto e mezzo piano*), and one with *piano* over the stave and *andante* in the margin.

Out of the remaining twenty-two, there are seventeen in which the first indication, a number of bars distant from the beginning, is *piano*. This is not only an indication for the particular bar, it has significance as a cancellation of a previously understood *forte* and suggests that all movements are to begin *forte* unless otherwise marked. This holds good even for such movements as the accompanied recitative 'For behold, darkness shall cover the earth' and the

chorus 'Glory to God', both of which more often than not are begun *pianissimo*.
It will be found that a flexible *forte* introduction best suits the prophetic utterance
of the recitative, and that a brilliant *forte* attack of the chorus provides the true
climax for the *crescendo* of excitement created by the preceding Christmas
recitatives.

Ritornelli and Codas and other Purely Orchestral Passages

Out of the twenty-seven that contain indications there are twenty in which
ritornelli, *codas*, thematic imitations of the voice, quotations from introductions,
or detached chords in accompanied recitatives are marked *forte*. In five
movements there are sixteen instances in which such passages are marked *piano*,
and in one coda ('Glory to God') there is *pian* and three bars later *pian pian*.
This suggests that all after-voice orchestral passages should be *forte* unless otherwise marked.

With the Voice

Handel marked *forte* in the orchestral accompaniment to the voice in one
movement only, the Guadagni setting of the air 'But who may abide' (in
autograph in the Tenbury–Dublin copy). He wrote it eleven times in this movement in two different styles of accompaniment: one, short detached chords
(in bars 77 to 83) and the other a bowed-tremolo passage (bar 85 and continuing for three bars till bar 87; in bar 88 on the first beat he wrote '*p*'). By
implication the bowed-tremolo passage in bars 59–77 and bars 115–140 should
also be *forte* (against the first beat of bar 141 Handel again wrote '*p*'). For
the rest, at every vocal entry the accompaniment is intended to be *piano*. It
is marked so in certain cases; in one case, bar 14 of the air 'He was despised',
it is marked '*pianiss*' because the orchestral point-of-imitation in the previous
bar is already *piano* and whatever the dynamic before the voice it must reduce
further at the vocal entry.

The Obbligato

The reduction of the dynamic at the vocal entry applies equally where the
voice enters before the *ritornello* theme is completed. In the air 'Thou art
gone up on high' (Autograph score setting) the *ritornello* beginning in bar 74
is marked *forte*, but although at the vocal entry in bar 79 the *ritornello* still has
five beats to its completion Handel marked it '*piano*'.

Even when the *obbligato* instruments have a definite counter-theme against the voice they still must play *piano*. In the same air ('Thou art gone up on high' in the Autograph score) where the violins have a passage of marked character to play in bars 67–72, a quotation from the introduction, Handel expressly marked it *pian*.

In the air 'I know that my Redeemer liveth' the dotted *motif* in bar 84 is marked *piano* even though the preceding figure in bar 78 was marked *piano*. Note also the *pianissimo* in bar 58 of the air 'Rejoice greatly'.

In those days the reign of the soloist was undisputed. The function of the accompanist was to accompany. It was expressed somewhat later in the century by Burney in the preface to his 'Four Sonatas or Duets for two performers on one Pianoforte or Harpsichord' (dated St. Martin's Street, 1777): 'And with respect to the Pianos and Fortes, each performer should try to discover when he has the *Principal Melody* given to him or when he is only to accompany that melody; . . . There is no fault in accompanying so destructive of good melody, taste, and expression, as the vanity with which young and ignorant Performers are too frequently possessed of becoming *Principals*, when they are only *Subalterns;* and of being heard when they have nothing to say that merits particular attention. If the part which would afford the greatest pleasure to the hearer be suffocated, and rendered inaudible, by too full and too loud an accompaniment, it is like throwing the capital figure of a piece into the background, or degrading the Master into a Servant.'

The matter is well summed up by another quotation from the air 'I know that my Redeemer liveth', bars 104–108:

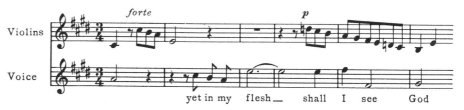

Points of Imitation in a Higher Register

Orchestral points of imitation or quotations, no matter how short in length, are *forte* if pitched in a high register. Take, for example, the point of imitation that begins on the last quaver of bar 42 in the air 'O Thou that tellest'. This is not marked *forte* but is clearly so by implication as the quotation in bar 44 is marked *piano*.

Again, in 'Thou shalt break them' the quotation in bar 43 is *forte* by implication as the following bar is marked *p*. The air 'I know that my Redeemer liveth' makes this point very clear. The point of imitation that begins in bar 22 is marked *piano* but the similar point of imitation that begins in bar 35 is marked *forte*—it is a fifth higher than that of bar 22. This is emphasized by the exception in bars 137–141 where Handel marked the quotation of the dotted figure pitched above the stave *piano*.

Dynamics by Implication

Many passages though not marked are nevertheless marked by implication. For example, in 'The trumpet shall sound' Handel has not marked a single *piano;* but a *piano* against the voice is made clear by his *forte* at the beginning of the following *ritornello.*

Immediate Repetitions

An immediate repetition should generally be treated as an echo. The echo was not merely a part of the technique of performance by means of which repetition was made bearable, it was part of the very stuff of the Baroque.

The Da Capo

In the *da capo*, as distinct from the immediate repetition of a passage, the dynamics are unchanged except for the intensification caused by added ornamentation. But the middle section of a *da capo* air is almost invariably contrasted in tone with the first section; note the *un poco piano* at the middle section of 'He was despised'.

Sudden Dynamic Contrasts

Dynamic contrasts, such as the introduction to 'Rejoice greatly', where the trilled couplets marked *p* are followed by a sudden *f* on beat 3 of bar 8, and the introduction to 'Every valley', where the slurred quavers in the violins in bar 6 marked *p* are followed by a sudden *forte* of the whole strings on the last quaver of the same bar, must be most clearly marked. (See also the chorus 'His yoke is easy' and the air 'He was despised'.) The 'Every valley' example is frequently completely spoiled by a *crescendo* through the couplets. This is unquestionably contrary to the composer's intentions. Interpretation must not be superimposed upon the music, it must arise from the music.

Detailed Analysis

'Glory to God'; 'If God be for us'.

The application of these general rules is shown by way of example in the following detailed analysis of just two numbers from *Messiah*, the chorus 'Glory to God' and the air 'If God be for us'. The only indication at the head of the chorus 'Glory to God' is one of tempo, *allegro*. The indication of dynamic, *da lontano e un poco piano*, is clearly written between the two trumpet staves and refers to these instruments only; the first indication was *in disparte* (aside), also written between the two trumpet staves.

These words have been responsible for an interpretation voiced by Cusins in 1874: 'Handel first writes "In disparte" (aside)—then crossed it out and substituted *Da lontano e un poco piano* evidently to indicate the gradual approach of the Heavenly Host as the *piano pianissimo* at the end may correspondingly depict the departure of them from the Shepherds into Heaven.'

The facts are: in bar 7 Handel wrote *pian* over the repeated quaver chords. This cancelled an implied *forte* beginning. This is supported by the *forte* he wrote in bar 10. In bar 16 once again over the repeated quaver chords is *pian*. He omitted to write a *forte* at the following choral entry ('Goodwill toward men') but it is *forte* by implication for once again in bar 31 over the repeated quaver chords is *p* followed this time by *forte* at the choral entry in bar 33.

The phrase 'And peace on earth' is generally sung softly. This is quite mistaken—it should be sung *forte*. Handel wrote *pian* not over this choral unison but each time over the instrumental quaver chords two bars later. Further, in bars 5 and 14 against the basso-continuo of the choral unison he wrote '*Tasto solo*'; this is an indication of strength. He wrote it in the 'Hallelujah' chorus against the bass statement of the *subject* 'And He shall reign for ever and ever' beginning in bar 41, in the alto and tenor and bass 'Blessing and honour' phrase beginning bar 53 of 'Worthy is the Lamb', and in the opening bass statement of the 'Amen' *subject*.

In 'Glory to God' the choir should never be less than *forte* from the first chord (the climax of the *crescendo* of excitement created by the preceding Christmas recitatives) till the final chorus cadence in bar 42.

With reference to the indication in the coda of this chorus, Handel wrote *pian p* over the viola stave the fourth bar from the end and *pian pian* over the basso-continuo stave overlapping the third and fourth bars from the end. As elsewhere he wrote: *pianiss* ('His yoke is easy'), his *pian pian* and *pian p* here possibly indicate a shade between *piano* and *pianissimo*, for in the book *A short explication of such Foreign Words As are made use of in Music Books*, printed for J. Brotherton at the Bible in Cornhill, near the Royal Exchange (1724), *pp* is defined as an abbreviation of *piu piano* and *ppp* as an abbreviation of *pianissimo*.

The indication at the head of the air 'If God be for us' once again is purely of tempo. The first indication of dynamic is *piano* against the voice in bar 26 implying the usual *forte* beginning. The six-beat thematic imitations in the violins beginning in bars 29 and 35 have no markings, but, in view of the *forte* written against the *ritornello* beginning in bar 41, should be exceptions to the general treatment of such imitative comments and played *piano*. After the *forte* in bar 41 Handel wrote nothing until the warning *p* in bar 62 where the violins have a quotation from the introduction against a long sustained note in the voice. But although there is no mark the accompanist must be *piano* against the voice at bars 48 and 59. The after-voice passages, bars 52–54 and 56–58, will be *forte* as contrasts to the surrounding *pianos*. After the *p* in bar 62 Handel wrote nothing till the *forte* in bar 91, but there is little doubt but that the *ritornello* beginning in bar 68 should be *forte* with a return to *piano* against the voice in bar 74. Handel omitted the *piano* against the voice in bar 100 but implied it by the *forte* against the *ritornello* in bar 107. He again omitted the *piano* at the re-entry of the voice and, in fact, marked nothing more for 55 bars till the coda, where in bar 162 he wrote *forte*. In the light of his usage I suggest that the thematic imitation beginning at bar 118 should be *forte* by reason of its high register; that the long sustained notes in bars 124–129 and 150–155 be played as *messa di voce;* and that the repeated trill figures in bars 142 and 143 should be played as 'after-voice' *forte* (cf. bars 52–53 and 56–57), the remainder of these fifty-five bars being *piano*.

TEMPI IN *MESSIAH*

There is no definite record of Handel's tempi in *Messiah*, for although many efforts had been made to measure time it was not until fifty years after Handel's death that it became possible for composers to indicate the exact tempo at which they wished their music to be performed. Therefore, the only guide is Handel's general indication, by means of a musical term, at the head of the movement.

Composers have been reputed to be careless and inconsistent, and it is true that Handel has given different tempo indications in different manuscripts to what is essentially the same music. Yet in general in the oratorios, and certainly in *Messiah*, he was meticulous in selecting the indication for the movement. Indeed, the following alterations of tempo indications in the Autograph are proof of this.

At the beginning of the fugal section of the Overture he first wrote *allegro giusto*. He then altered it to *allegro moderato*. Now according to Crotch, *giusto* was the least precise of all indications, for it varied 'with the fancy or judgement of the performers'. But Ralph Dunstan in the *Cyclopaedic Dictionary of Music* (for which he drew upon, among others, such authorities as Albrechtsberger, Burney, Grassineau, Gevaert, Helmholtz, Hawkins, Rousseau, Riemann, and Rockstro) gives: 'Tempo giusto. In just, steady time. With Handel $\frac{4}{4}$ at a moderate speed.'

And Scholes in the *Oxford Companion to Music* gives: 'Tempo giusto (1) just or exact rhythm; or (2) the speed that the style of the music demands (really *moderato*).'

Both Dunstan and Scholes, in the final analysis, define *giusto* as *moderato*. Dunstan explicitly associates this interpretation with Handel's music. But, quite obviously, for Handel *giusto* was not synonymous with *moderato*, for he ran his pen through the former and substituted the latter.

When he first began to set the text 'Thus saith the Lord' (*i.e.* as an arioso) he wrote the indication *grave*, later altering it to *a tempo ordinario*. Then, deciding to change the form to an accompanied recitative, he crossed out *a tempo ordinario* and wrote simply *accomp*.

His first indication for the opening of 'Worthy is the Lamb that was slain' was *a tempo ordinario*. Then running his pen through the *a tempo ordinario* he wrote the slower *larghetto*.   Then again he ran his pen through the last three letters of that indication and altered the 'e' to 'o', so ending up with the still slower *largo*.

He marked 'Why do the nations' as *allegro* but almost immediately added some other indication, which he then blotted out with much ink so thickly that the underlying characters will not yield to any form of examination.   To make his intention clear beyond all doubt he wrote *allegro* again, but over the basso–continuo stave.

Over the first violin stave of 'The trumpet shall sound' towards the left margin is *pomposo*.   This is followed by *andante*, later crossed out with long ink strokes, and this, in turn, is followed by *ma non allegro*.   The word *pomposo* stands somewhat apart from *andante*, but the *ma non allegro* follows so closely upon (and on the same level as) *andante* that it would appear that Handel first wrote *andante ma non allegro*.   However that may be, it is clear that he altered *andante* to *pomposo* and either left or added the last three words in order to qualify *pomposo*.

Crotch, writing in 1800, divided musical terms into two classes, one dealing purely with tempo, the other with expression.   In *Messiah* Handel made no such distinction.   He qualified tempo in some numbers:

Allegro moderato: The Overture, 'All we like sheep', the 'Amen'.
Alla breve moderato: 'And with His stripes'.
Andante allegro: 'For unto us', 'The Lord gave the Word'.
Andante larghetto: 'But who may abide' in the all-$\frac{3}{8}$ setting, 'For behold, darkness', 'But Thou dids't not leave His soul in hell'.
Pomposo, ma non allegro: 'The trumpet shall sound'.

In others he added nuance:

Allegro e staccato: 'Let us break their bonds asunder'.
Larghetto e mezzo piano: the Pastoral Symphony.
Larghetto e piano: 'He shall feed His flock'.
Largo e staccato: 'Surely He hath borne our griefs'.
Largo e piano: 'Behold and see'.

All his other indications would seem to be concerned strictly with tempo, but his tempo indication reflects much more than the effective tempo in relation to the characteristic time-group, the value of the average shortest note, and the character or size of the forces used in performance.   For example, the verbal text and the separate groups of semiquavers in 'Thou shalt break them' taken together suggest *allegro* as the suitable tempo.   But for the expression of the *Affekt* it is essential that not only the staccato quavers but each of the four semiquavers shall, as it were, exist in its own right.   If taken *allegro* the leaping quavers sound merely hurried and the semiquavers sound as an ornamental extension of a single note—a double mordent.   Handel's choice of term, *andante*, sounds completely unsuited to the mood of the air, but it enables not only the quavers but each separate semiquaver to have the vigour essential to the *Affekt*.   His *andante* implies much more than mere tempo.

Still, the need for a definite expression of speed by mechanical means had been recognized for some time. Loulie, in 1696, devised a chronometer for the purpose, but neither this nor the further attempts made during the eighteenth century were practical solutions. It was not until 1815 that Maelzel patented the metronome known by his name. (For the name of the true inventor and the story of the metronome, see Rosamond Harding's *Origins of Musical Time and Expression*.[1]) But before this, Crotch, in the *Monthly Magazine* for January 1800 (page 940 of the 1799 volume), gave a set of figures based upon the use of a weight on the end of a swinging string. The figures represent the length of string in inches from the point where it is held between the fingers to the middle of the weight. This idea was not new, for some years before, *circa* 1795, one Thomas Wright had composed a harpsichord concerto, to each movement of which he gave a rate in figures. Wright's figures, however, represented not inches, but the breadth of the harpsichord's keys; e.g. ♩=28 indicated that a minim was equal to the swing of a pendulum the length of which equalled the breadth of 28 keys of the harpsichord.

While we have no record of Handel's own tempi, the tempi given by Crotch, whether we agree with them or not, may be assumed to be reasonably near the tempi that were generally observed during the eighteenth century; for Crotch (1775–1847, Professor of Music in the University of Oxford in 1797) was a pupil of Randall (1715–1799, Professor of Music in the University of Cambridge in 1755) who, as a boy, sang the name-part in *Esther* and, it is reported, turned over the music pages for Handel at the funeral of Queen Caroline in 1737, and who, later, in the course of his duties at Oxford, conducted performances of Handel's works, including *Messiah*. Crotch's list in the *Monthly Magazine* included only some dozen numbers from *Messiah*, but in 1813 Birchall published *Chorus & Symphonies from* Messiah *arranged for Pianoforte by Dr. Crotch*. In this Crotch gave a rate of inches for each number in the volume. His figures, expressed here in metronome rates, show a considerable pace-range for any one tempo-word. Indeed, as may be seen by comparing the list in the *Monthly Magazine* letter (see pp. 85-7) and the figures from the *Chorus & Symphonies* publication (to be found in the Table of Tempi in Appendix F), Crotch's own tempi varied between 1800 and 1813 for the same music.

	In *Monthly Magazine*	In piano arrangement
Overture, *grave*	♪ = 116	♪ = 100
And the glory	♩ = 108	♩ = 96
And with His stripes	𝅗𝅥 = 100	𝅗𝅥 = 84
He trusted in God	♩ = 92	♩ = 80
Let us break	♪ = 152	♪ = 138
Since by man	♪ = 69	♪ = 72
O Death, where is thy sting	♪ = 152	♪ = 108
Worthy is the Lamb, *largo*	♪ = 69	♪ = 60
Worthy is the Lamb, *larghetto*	♪ = 138	♪ = 120

[1] Oxford University Press.

Although it is essentially true that any *musician*, without any tempo indication either by word (pace or style) or metronome rate, could find (within a hair's-breadth) the tempo at which the composer conceived the music, the 'hair's-breadth' is, of course, sensitive to interpretation! There is much more than Crotch's theory of modification by reason of context. Tempo, the basic element in interpretation, is a very personal matter. It varies not only between different persons but between different moments and moods in the life of one person.

The tempo tables may not disclose any pattern for logical conclusions. But they may at least cause us to consider the music more carefully in relation to the period and style in which it was composed rather than that of our own. For the Table of Tempi I have selected seven editions, four of which—Crotch (almost in direct succession from Handel); Clarke; Rimbault, for the English Handel Society; and Elvey for the Sacred Harmonic Society—cover roughly the century following Handel's death; the remaining three—Chrysander, Prout, and Coopersmith—cover say the last quarter of the nineteenth century and first half of the twentieth century. Crotch in his letter suggests that tempo was much faster at the end than in the early years of the eighteenth century. This trend, if it was so, has been repeated. A comparison of Crotch with Prout and Chrysander shows that, of the twenty-two movements that it is possible to compare:

Nineteen have increased in speed.

Two are border-line cases, either because Crotch gave one tempo in the *Monthly Magazine* and another in the *Chorus & Symphonies*, or because Prout and Chrysander differed.

Only in one case has the speed decreased, in the chorus 'And with His stripes': Crotch in 1800 (the *Monthly Magazine*) gave $\half = 100$. Thirteen years later he reduced it to $\half = 84$, Prout in 1901 gave the still slower $\half = 80$, and Chrysander (Seiffert) in 1901–2 gave the even slower $\half = 69$.

It is of interest, however, that wherever Crotch gave two different tempi his 1813 tempo was generally the slower tempo. In 'O Death' it is as much as forty-four degrees ($\eighth = 152$ becoming $\eighth = 108$). A comparison between Prout and Chrysander shows that Chrysander's tempo was generally the faster. It was the slower only in four cases—the *grave* of the Overture (Prout $\eighth = 120$, Chrysander $\eighth = 116$); 'O Thou that tellest' (Prout $\eighth = 138$, Chrysander $\eighth = 120$); 'For unto us a Child is born' (Prout $\half = 76$, Chrysander $\half = 72$); 'And with His stripes' (Prout $\half = 80$, Chrysander $\half = 69$). They were identical in only one case—'All we like sheep'; here they agreed on $\half = 92$, against Crotch's $\half = 76$. For the remainder Chrysander was faster but only a few degrees, except for the Pastoral Symphony (Prout $\eighth = 132$, Chrysander $\eighth = 160$); the *andante* of 'Worthy is the Lamb' (Prout $\eighth = 120$, Chrysander $\eighth = 152$); the 'Amen' chorus (Prout $\half = 84$, Chrysander $\half = 112$); and—a very considerable difference—'He was despised' (Prout $\eighth = 72$, Chrysander $\eighth = 120$).

It must be obvious that there is no one tempo at which, under varying conditions of performance, the music of any movement will come to life. Tempo stems from rhythm, and rhythm must be felt within. There is a subtle difference between a performance of, say 'O Thou that tellest' when *felt* by the performer as six quavers in the bar, and when felt as two dotted crotchets in the bar, even though, measured in time, the tempo in each performance is identical. The metronome rate is by no means the complete answer, but it is essential to study it, as a necessary part of the answer, in relation to the various constituents of performance, above all in relation to style.

In order to assist such a study I have provided a table of representative tempi for comparison, together with a summary in terms of speed (see Appendix F).

Here is the letter[1] from Dr. William Crotch to the *Monthly Magazine*, January, 1800.

Remarks on the terms at present used in Music for regulating the time.
Sir,

My endeavour is to prove that those terms are indefinite or at least misapplied; and that it would be easy to substitute definite characters; and that much trouble and difficulty would be removed by the proposed alteration. Dr. Nares in the Preface to his Anthems remarks that Music performed in just time is like a painting set in a good light, and is therefore anxious that the terms of Time should be particularly regarded.

In Rousseau's Dictionary of Music, time is divided into five principal terms, *largo, adagio, andante, allegro* and *presto*. There are also other collateral terms. In ancient music, *grave alla breve, tempo ordinario,* and *tempo giusto.* In modern music, *lento, andantino,* and *allegretto.* And in both ancient and modern, *larghetto, vivace, prestissimo.* There are also various modifications of these, by the addition of the words *molto, poco, con moto, moderato, non troppo,* etc.; and by combinations, as *andante allegro, andante larghetto,* etc. These terms are, perhaps, only intelligible when considered in succession. Slow and quick, like great and small, exist only by comparison. It is, I believe, generally understood, that the order of succession is as follows:

Grave, Largo, Larghetto, adagio, lento, andante, andantino, allegretto, allegro, vivace, alla breve, presto, prestissimo. I am perfectly aware, however, that this order will be disputed. By some, *adagio, lento, andante, andantino, alla breve,* and *vivace,* are regarded, rather as terms of expression and taste, than of time. *Adagio* is by others considered as denoting a slower time than *largo,* also *Andantino* than *Andante.* And it is not surprising, that Composers should be misunderstood, since we find they are themselves inconsistent. Handel has marked the Bass Air in the Messiah, 'But who may abide', with the word *larghetto;* but he has marked the same song *Andante Larghetto* in the appendix. The recitative 'For behold, darkness shall cover the earth', is marked *Andante Larghetto,* and the succeeding Air *Larghetto.* Now *Larghetto* is certainly slower than *Andante Larghetto,* yet the quavers in the air are always performed full as quick as the semiquavers in the recitative. The Air, 'Thou art gone up on high' for a Soprano voice is marked *Andante;* the same song with the slightest variation for a Bass voice is marked *Allegro.* In old, and especially Church Music, where the notes of the shortest value were quavers, and those but seldom used, the minims were no longer than our crotchets. Pleyel, and some others of the later composers, seem to have revived this long neglected species of notation, in the *prestos* and other quick movements of their *sinfonias.* Indeed, time frequently seems to depend on the number of notes contained in a bar.

I am convinced both from my own observations on the admirable and accurate performance

[1] I am indebted to Mr. Vere Pilkington for calling my attention to this letter.

D

of Handel's works at Westminster Abbey, and those of other great Composers of the same period at the Concerts of Ancient Music, and also from the assurances of many elderly musical gentlemen that the time at the beginning of this Century was performed much slower than in modern music.   I am confirmed in my opinion that the terms of time, now used, are indefinite, and of very little service, from a series of experiments which I have made with a pendulum; and of which the following Table is a selection and will, I trust, be found tolerably accurate.

Table of the Times of various Pieces, measured by a pendulum.

Terms of time	Names of Pieces	Time	Notes which one swing of the pendulum expresses	Length of the pendulum	
				Feet	Inches
Grave	Chorus, 'Since by Man came death'	C	Quaver	2	6
	Final movement of the overture to the Messiah	C	ditto	0	10½
Largo	Song, 'Sommi Dei' in Radamisto, Handel	¾	ditto	1	0
	Fourth movement in the Passione Stromentale, Haydn	¾	ditto	0	10
	Song, 'He was despised'	C	ditto	3	3
	Chorus, 'Worthy is the Lamb'	C	ditto	2	6
Larghetto	Air, 'Their sound is gone out', Messiah	C	ditto	1	4
	Chorus, 'Blessing and Honour'	C	ditto	0	7
	Chorus, 'Let us break their bonds'	¾	ditto	0	6
	Duetto, 'Deh quel pianto', Bach	¾	ditto	1	0
Adagio	Aria, 'Il consine della vita', Handel	C	ditto	2	10
	Sonata second, Op. 42, Haydn	2–4ths	ditto	1	6
	Fifth movement of the Passione Stromentale, Haydn	C	ditto	0	9
Lento	Middle movement of Sonata 1, Op. 25, Clementi	2–4ths	ditto	2	6
	Sixth movement of Passione Stromentale, Haydn	C	ditto	0	6
Andante	Duett, 'O Death', Messiah, Handel	C	ditto	0	6
	Air, 'Every Valley', Messiah, Handel	C	ditto	1	7
	Middle movement of a Sinfonia in C, Haydn	2–4ths	ditto	1	0
	Middle Movement of Overture Festino, Haydn	2–4ths	ditto	2	3
Andantino	Middle movement of Sonata ii, Op. 21, Kozeluch	6–8ths	ditto	1	6
	Ditto in Overture La Reine de la France, Haydn	C	Minim	2	8
Allegretto	Last movement of Sonata iii, Op. 21, Kozeluch	2–4ths	Crotchet	1	6
	Entre-act of the Overture to Henry IV, Martini	2–4ths	ditto	1	0
Allegro	Chorus, 'And the Glory of the Lord', Handel	¾	ditto	1	0

	Finale to the Fourth Sonata, Op. 17, Haydn	3/4	ditto	0	6
	Chorus, 'He trusted in God' ,Handel	C	ditto	1	5
	Air, 'Se il ciel mi divide', Piccini	C	ditto	0	8
Vivace	Second Oboe Concerto, Handel	3/4	ditto	1	6
	Overture, Roxalana, Haydn	3/4	ditto	0	5
Alla Breve	Chorus, 'And with His stripes', Handel	¢	Minim	1	2
	Chorus, 'Throughout the land', Solomon, Handel	¢	ditto	1	9
Presto	Last movement of La Chasse, Kozeluch	2–4ths	ditto	1	9
	Ditto of Sonata i Op. 25, Haydn	2–4ths	ditto	1	0
Prestissimo	Last movement of 'But who may abide', Handel	C	ditto	2	0
	Ditto of Sonata ii, Op. 17, Haydn	6–8ths	dotted crotchet	0	5

Tempo ordinario (common time), and *Tempo giusto* (proper time), are purposely omitted. The first varies with the fashion of the age, the last with the fancy or judgement of the performers.

Enough, it is presumed, has now been advanced, to show that the terms made use of are indefinite, or misapplied; and I shall now endeavour to prove, that it would be very easy to substitute definite characters. Loulie invented a machine, called a chronometer, to measure time, a description of which is given by Malcolm, and may be seen in the Encyclopaedia Britannica, under the article Chronometer. This machine is more complex, expensive and unwieldy than is necessary, and twice as long as that I made use of in my experiments, which was indeed merely a piece of tape and a plummet, graduated into English feet and inches; a measure more generally intelligible than the cyphers used by Loulie, which could only be understood by those possessed of one of his chronometers.

The time of music already composed may be obtained at the many judicious performances at the concerts of ancient music, at cathedrals and operas; and, allowing this time to be incorrect [*sic*] from having been traditionally handed down to us, it appears to me the only way of preventing it from becoming still more so. It will be easy for present and future composers to render the time of their works indisputable, by prefixing one of the notes to each strain with its duration expressed by the swing of a pendulum, as in the preceding table.

A very ingenious leader, previous to his conducting Graun's Te Deum, studied the time of the various movements, and observed by his watch, what were their respective durations (i.e. the overall performing time of the movement). This method appears to me tedious, and of no use at a rehearsal or concert, as each movement might be tried over very often before its real time could be obtained; and each succeeding leader would have the same experiments to make, which gave so much trouble to his predecessor.

The objections of Monsieur Diderot to the use of a chronometer are by no means insurmountable; and some of them are ingeniously answered by Rousseau.[1] M. Diderot remarks that, 'in a movement there are, perhaps, not two bars of the same duration!' Happily, however, we have no such music; it never existed out of France; and is at length banished its only asylum. He also remarks, that 'It is impossible for a leader to have his ear attentive to the sound of the pendulum, and his eye on the book, throughout the whole of a movement'. And this were an arduous task indeed!—but the objection does not apply to my proposal. The pendulum I recommend makes no noise; it is only to be set in motion before a movement begins at a rehearsal, or perhaps in the leader's own room, but certainly not at a performance. A leader

[1] Under the article Chorister, Rousseau recommends the use of a chronometer.

of the most ordinary abilities may remember and preserve the time of a piece of music he has ever heard.   But it is a very different and far more difficult thing to *discover* that time; which, indeed, can only be effected by repeated trials, great loss of time, and unnecessary trouble.   In songs, solos and all other performances of taste and execution, the time must be entirely regulated, as usual, by the principal performer.   But in all full pieces, I think, the time should be left to the direction of the composer.   What leader, playing at sight, could judge of the time of Gluck's Overture to Iphigenie?   Or what conductor could foresee, that in the chorus of 'Wretched Lovers', after its solemn beginning, which consists of slow notes, a rapid and animated counter-subject should burst forth, and totally alter the original character of the movement?

Some may urge, that the time of music is not of so much consequence as the expression; and that the attention will consequently be diverted from an important to an unworthy object. To this I answer that I have not the least wish that my plan should interfere with the expression, which I think of far greater importance than accuracy of time; I therefore wish all composers to retain the words *grazioso*, *spiritoso*, *cantabile*, *sostenuto*, *staccato*, *maestoso*, *agitato*, and all other terms of expression, as well as to adopt definite characters of time.

It may be urged, that, if the present terms convey but an obscure meaning, the proposed characters would convey none at all, unless a pendulum were at hand.   But that situation were forlorn indeed, where a string, a weight, and a scale of inches could not be procured; and should this scheme be approved and adopted, the chronometer would become as much an appendage to a musical instrument, as a desk is at present to a pianoforte, or a bow to a violin.

Finally, the chronometer would be found of the highest use to scholars; who, in the absence of their master, are frequently at a loss to discover, remember and retain the time of any movement.

I could advocate much more in favour of my plan; but am conscious, that I ought rather to apologise for having troubled you with so much already.   I therefore hasten to subscribe myself

Your humble servant

W.C.' [*sic*]

THE DOUBLE-DOT CONVENTION

It is an accepted fact that in eighteenth-century performance a note of a quaver or less in length which followed a dotted note or a rest was shortened, i.e. further delayed in its entry (the double-dot was not then known).   It was not, however, a strict rule to be universally applied.   C. P. E. Bach, writing in his *Versuch über die wahre Art des Clavier zu spielen*, says, 'A general method of treating dotted notes has arisen because of our inadequate notation.   This is to play the notes following the dotted notes as short as possible.   There are, however, many exceptions. . . .   A modification of the rule is necessary.   For example, music of a tender mood does not accord with the defiant effect of dotted notes.   In such cases, therefore, the player must shorten the dotted notes.'[1]   It is obvious that the convention was not observed where it was alien to the character of the music; in fact, the last sentence of the quotation indicates that it was often applied in reverse.

To observe the convention in all cases would often be a misrepresentation of the composer's intention.   It would surely be contrary to the *Affekt* to turn

---

[1] In der Schreibart der punctirten Noten überhaupt fehlt es noch sehr oft an der gehörigen Genauigkeit. Man hat daher wegen des Vortrags dieser Art von Noten eine gewisse Hauptregel festsetzen wollen, welche aber viele Ausnahme leidet . . .; bald ist ein flattirender Affekt, welcher das diesen punctirten Noten sonst eigene Trotzige nicht verträget, die Ursache, dass man bei dem Puncte etwas weniger anhält.

the smoothly flowing [♩. ♪♪♩] of the Pastoral Symphony, 'He shall feed His flock' and 'How beautiful are the feet' into [♩·· ♪♪♩]; the sorrowful [♪ ♩·♪ ♩·♪] of 'Behold the Lamb of God' into [♪♪♩·♪ ♩·♪]; or the solemn conclusion of 'All we like sheep' [♩. ♪♩] into [♩·· ♪♩].

But where this latter time relationship ([♩. ♪♩. ♪]) occurs in the *grave* of the Overture there is more room for individual interpretation. It is true that when Handel wanted the effect of a double-dotted crotchet followed by a semiquaver he wrote it with a tie [♩·_♪♪] (see the manuscript RM 20.g.7 (XIV) Folio 1 verso). It could be argued that he desired the same time relationship in the overture to *Messiah* but, expecting the performers to give effect to the convention, he wrote it as [♩. ♪]. Here, however, the mood of this music is reflective and for this I feel that the full quaver is better.

'The trumpet shall sound' is another case. Handel wrote

[♩·♪ | ♩ ♪ ♪♪·♪ | ♩]

The quaver (on the second half of the second beat) is often printed, or interpreted, as a semiquaver or a demi-semiquaver. I believe that this arises from a wrong conception of the music coupled with too fast a tempo. Handel, after some consideration, indicated both tempo and mood by *pomposo ma non allegro*. When the quaver in question is treated as a semiquaver or a demisemiquaver it gives a sense of superficial bravura to the air. Given its full quaver length it lends to the prophetic utterance the dignity which Handel's tempo indication suggests. The third beat dotted group alone is sufficient for the expression of the *Affekt*.

The convention has been applied to bars 3–6 of this air, Handel's [♩. ♪♪♪] being read as [♩·· ♪♪·♪]. It would be reasonable to argue that being in a hurry and having written the figure [♩. ♪♪·♪] in the first two bars Handel omitted to write the dot and the semiquaver-beam in the third beat in the following bars. On the other hand, the repetition of [♪·♪] on every third beat for six bars not only becomes monotonous but weakens the effectiveness of its use in bars 1 and 2. Handel frequently varied an odd beat or bar for this very reason: witness the greater effectiveness of the dotted groups in the following figure from the chorus 'But thanks be to God' resulting from the contrast with the even quaver group:

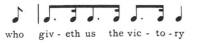

who giv - eth us the vic - to - ry

How much less effective would be

who giv - eth us the vic - to - ry

but if a passage is open to interpretation, editors often smooth out essential differences in their desire for a consistent reading.

The same argument is applicable to bars 1, 2, 9, and 10 of the chorus 'The Lord gave the Word'. Handel's ♩ is often printed or interpreted as ♩.

The air 'I know that my Redeemer liveth' is entirely a matter of interpretation, for Handel has written three variants of the characteristic four-note motif. It appears first as ♩ again as ♩ and yet again as ♩.

The following examples are from the Autograph score.

(a) The opening *ritornello*
(bars 5–9)

(b) The opening *ritornello*
(bars 12–14)

(c) The *ritornello*
(bars 66–70)

(d) The final *ritornello*
(bars 157–161)

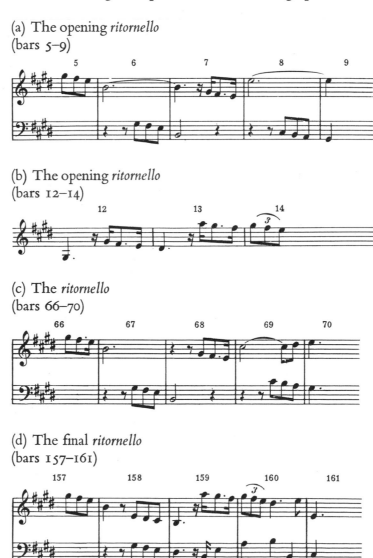

(e) Bar 55, violin in
unison with voice

Neither 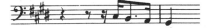 nor ⁣ ⁊ ⁊♪♪♩ arise from the convention of the dot for under the convention ⁣ ⁊ ♩♪♩ could only be interpreted ⁣ ⁊⁊♪♪ and Handel has not written this time-group anywhere in the air. Compare the first bar of Example (a) with the first bar of Example (c)—the last quaver of bar 5 has become a semiquaver in bar 66. Compare bar 55 in Example (e) with bars 7 and 8 in Example (a)—in the latter the first as well as the last note is a semiquaver. The *ritornello* bars 66–75 only are consistent, for the time-group in the violin is the same both times and contrast is obtained between violin and continuo by the continuo answering in even quavers. On the other hand, it could be argued that whatever the time-group of the violin it should be imitated exactly in the answering continuo; bars 5–9 of the introduction

would be consistent if the continuo in bar 8 were

Again it could be argued that he wrote ⁣ ⁊ ♪♪♩|♩. in the *ritornello* with the performing convention in mind, that when he wrote quavers it was because he was in too great a hurry to write the additional semiquaver rest, dot and semiquaver-beam, that he intended ⁣ ⁊⁊♪♪♩|♩. every time. This solution, theoretically so satisfying, is, however, untenable for the motif is repeated twenty-seven times; further, it is completely contrary to the *Affekt*.

A casual glance would suggest that where an interval of an octave or more separates the motif from the preceding note (see Example (b)) or where an interval of an octave or more separates the last two notes of the motif (see Example (a) bars 7 and 8) Handel's intention was ⁣ ⁊⁊♪♪♩|♩. Yet in such circumstances in bar 55 (where violin and voice are in unison) he wrote even quavers.

It is my opinion that with one exception he meant the violin part to sound as it is written (the responsive motif in the basso-continuo to echo exactly the preceding violin time-group); the exception being bars 10 and 11 ♩.♪♪.♪♪.♪ for wherever he repeated this figure for a number of beats the double dotted interpretation seems to accord with the *Affekt*.

The short note of the dotted groups in the choruses 'Glory to God', 'For unto us', 'Lift up your heads' and 'His yoke is easy', the duet 'O Death where is

thy sting' and the repeated violin figure [musical notation] from 'The
trumpet shall sound' must always be kept short, but the tempo usually takes
care of this.   There is, of course, no doubt that the convention would apply
in the chorus 'Surely He hath borne our griefs'.   Here, where the character of
the music clearly demands a demisemiquaver as the short note following the
rest, Handel wrote a semiquaver.   That the essential rhythmic unit is
[musical notation] is made clear by the later repeated groups [musical notation]
Equally certainly would the convention apply in 'Thus saith the Lord'.   In
bars 1, 5, 7, 8, 9, 25 and 27 Handel wrote [musical notation] but showed how he
wished the time-group to sound when he wrote [musical notation] in a subsequent
alteration to bar 3 (see pp. 55-6).

The convention has also been applied to bar 92 beat 2 of the air 'Rejoice
greatly'.

Handel here wrote:

Prout in England (1906)
Schering in Germany (1939) } print it so:
Coopersmith in America (1947)

If only the voice and basso-continuo parts were concerned this application of
the convention would be justifiable for it is in full accord with the *Affekt*.
But the fact that in the violin part, with the three remaining beats of bar 92
and the whole of bar 93 occupied with the dotted group, he wrote even quavers
on this one beat only, raises a reasonable doubt and leaves the interpretation
open.

THE COUNTER-TENOR VOICE

The counter-tenor was the usual alto voice in Handel's day.   When available
this voice ought to be used not only in the solos written for it but also in the
choral alto part.   However, as Handel wrote in *Messiah* for bass and counter-
tenor or contralto within the same compass of a twelfth between the notes
A and E (on the two occasions when he went lower, once down to G and once
down to F, he made the notes optional) these solos can be sung by either bass

or male or female alto. The real issue, however, is not one of compass but of *timbre*.

It must be emphasized that the late Baroque composer, although not over fastidious in some respects, had moved a considerable way from the Renaissance *da cantor o sonar* or 'apt for voyces or vyols'. He was conscious of *timbre* as well as register. Certainly when he wrote for the alto voice he wrote for the male alto with its characteristic octave-higher quality. Writing, say, the low G, he mentally heard not the sepulchral quality produced by a female contralto in that register but the upper-partial quality of the counter-tenor. See the chorus 'Hymen, fair Urania's son' from *Alexander Balus* where in the main statement the alto has the theme. It would take a disporportionate number of female altos to make the theme sing through the other parts. Even so the effect would be entirely different from that which Handel expected.

The use of the counter-tenor voice as choral alto has a distinct bearing upon Handel's optional notes at the octave. The upward limit for the average counter-tenor voice is c''. In the whole of *Messiah* this note occurs in the alto part only 21 times. The note d'' occurs only twice and in both of these cases he gave the optional lower octave. Where all parts in a unison melody encompass d'' he drops the alto to the lower octave.

('Hallelujah' chorus)

But when the alto is the highest melodic line and where the upper note maintains the shape of the original subject he obviously preferred the upper note.

('And with His stripes')

He made this clear in the orchestral part of the chorus 'Let all the angels' for although (in order to save himself the trouble of writing the notes) he had written in the second violin stave at bar 9 the instruction to the copyist 'ut A.' he wrote in bar 10 in the second violin stave just one note—the alto optional upper note. (See also 'All we like sheep', bar 65.)

In addition to the optional upper notes in the alto part there are three cases in other parts; two concern the tenor and one the soprano; all three are high As in their respective voices. In 'Let all the angels', bar 15 in the tenor on beat 3, Handel wrote the optional upper octave in the voice part in the same manner as in the above example, and (as with the alto in bar 10) after writing

'ut T' in bar 10 in order to save himself the trouble of writing the choral tenor
notes on the viola stave, he wrote on that stave just one note, in bar 15—the
tenor optional upper note. (See also the tenor in bar 27 of this chorus.)

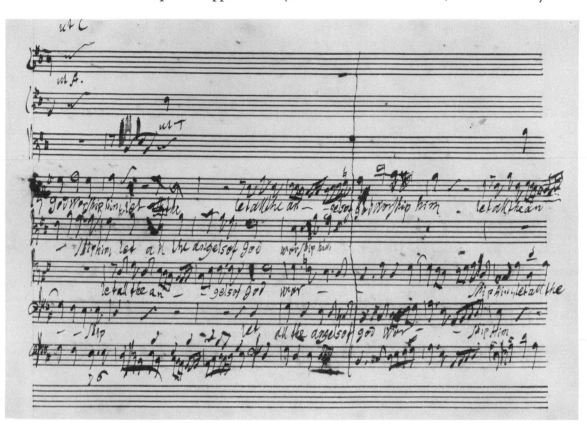

A striking and very clear indication that wherever Handel gave optional
notes in the soprano, alto, or tenor voice the lower note was, in fact, the optional
note, an option dictated by his practical knowledge not only of the capabilities
but also of the limitations of his singers, is given in the chorus 'He trusted in
God' in bars 52 and 53.

In the opening statement of the subject Handel set the words 'let Him deliver
Him' to a leap of a rising fourth:

The final soprano statement is set in the same key. Here, the realist Handel
wrote:

But, once again, having written 'ut Cant' for the copyist he troubles to write on the first violin stave at this point just the following ten notes:

Another case in point is the 'Hallelujah' chorus bar 29 in the soprano part.

Handel obviously wanted the soprano to echo the tenor's 'hallelujah' at the end

of bar 28  with He also wrote an

optional a'' in the second half of the bar but later smudged it out; the first, however, he did not smudge out. This is reasonable for there is purpose in the first but not in the second. It would seem that wherever he wrote an optional note in the soprano, alto or tenor voice, even though sometimes it was only a note head, he desired the upper note if it was possible.

There is one case where he omitted to write an optional upper note in the alto. I use the word 'omitted' for in writing the viola part he wrote the upper note and as that note preserves the shape of the theme (and again it is d'') he would naturally prefer it to be sung:

Viola

Alto

There is only one case where Handel wrote an optional note for the bass voice. It is in bar 8 of the air 'The people that walked in darkness'.

walk - ed in dark - ness

In this case it is fairly obvious that he would prefer the lower notes to be sung. It is of interest that in the Hamburg copy there are only the lower notes.

ORNAMENTATION

During the Baroque period, improvised ornamentation was an essential part of the art of performance. The composer's melodic line was regarded as a basic design to be enhanced in performance by the addition of *appoggiaturas* and passing notes; the long, sustained note as a seed to be developed by the performer's art into a more or less luxuriant growth; and the final cadence as the occasion for the cadenza, so that by means of a suitable flourish (during which the performer displayed his technique) the music would be brought to a conclusive ending.

Handel wrote with these performing conventions in mind. Here is an excerpt from a contemporary manuscript copy of his *Italian Cantata*, 'Dolce pur d'amor l'affanno':

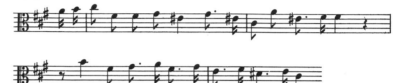

and here is the same passage showing the ornamentation which Handel himself added to it later.

(Cambridge, Fitzwilliam Museum. 30.H.2)

Ornamentation was not limited to secular works. Handel wrote many orchestral and vocal (choral and solo) trills, as well as both *appoggiaturas* and passing notes, in compositions expressly written to be sung in church. (See the following examples from the *Chandos Anthem*.)

(British Museum. RM 20.d.8)

See also the ten trills which he wrote in the first six bars of one of the most

Ornamentation added in pencil is to be found in some contemporary manuscript scores of *Messiah*, although it must be pointed out that the authorship of these additions has not been satisfactorily proved. But the manuscript harpsichord part of *Messiah* (RM 19.d.1) in the British Museum, said to have been written by Handel's friend and librettist, Jennens, contains many ornaments and some melodic deviations which are written in ink in the course of the manuscript, not as subsequent additions.

Ornamentation appeared later in printed editions. For example, the Schwencke Edition (Hamburg 1809) printed Handel's

Chrysander, the editor of the Handelgesellschaft, was fully aware of the need for ornamentation, for, after producing an *Urtext* of *Messiah*, he endeavoured to bring the *Urtext* to life by producing a separate performing

edition freely and copiously ornamented.   In this edition Chrysander printed
Handel's

as

These notes on ornamentation are not dogmatic.   Any serious student of
the period knows that sign, name, and interpretation of the ornaments were
constantly confused, and that the ornamentation varied from artist to artist,
and possibly from performance to performance with the same artist.   The
following suggestions are simply an indication of the kind of thing that
should be done if the composer's 'shorthand' is to be correctly translated into
sound.

The Vocal Line

In the examples below I have applied the performing convention of the
period to long, sustained notes and to the vocal line in general.

'Comfort ye', a fully ornamented vocal line

people saith your God saith your God

Speak ye com-fort-ab-ly to Je-ru-sa-lem speak ye

com-fort-ab-ly to Je-ru-sa-lem And

cry un-to her that her war - fare, her

war - fare is ac-com-plish'd, that her in-

i - qui-ty is par-don'd, that her in-

i - qui-ty is par - - - don'd

The voice of him that cryeth in the

wild-er-ness "Pre-pare ye the way of the Lord, make

straight in the des-ert a high-way for our God

'But who may abide'

(Bar 73)

Who shall stand when He ap-pear-eth

(Bar 120)

And who shall stand when He, when He ap - peareth And

who shall stand when He————————— ap - pear - eth

For He is like—— a re - fi - ner's fire—— And

who shall— stand when He —— ap - peareth, when He ap - peareth

'I know that my Redeemer liveth'

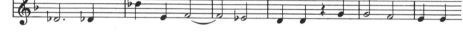

(Bar 92)

I know that my—— Re - deem - er liv - eth

And though worms de - stroy— this bo - dy yet

'If God be for us'

The Da Capo

In Handel's time a *da capo* unadorned was inconceivable to either composer, performer, or audience. Tosi's *Opinioni de' cantori antichi e moderni, o sieno osservazioni sopra il canto figurata* was published in Italy in 1723, translated into English by Galliard in 1742 (reprinted in 1743), and translated into German by Agricola in 1747. Tosi's book, therefore, is a reasonably safe guide to performing conventions contemporary with Handel. On the *da capo* air he writes:

> In the first part they require nothing but the simplest ornaments, of a good taste and few, that the composition may remain simple, plain and pure; in the second they expect that to this purity some artful graces be added, by which the judicious may hear that the ability of the singer is greater; and in repeating the air he that does not vary it for the better is no great master.

In the eighteenth-century *Messiah* manuscript known as the Goldsmith score, ornamentation for use in the *da capo* has been added to the air 'He was despised'. The following ornamented *da capo* of this air is based largely upon that in the Goldsmith score. But as ornamentation was not limited to voices (see part 5 on Instrumental Ornamentation) I have also suggested imitative ornamentation for the string parts for use in the *da capo*:

'He was despised', ornamented *da capo*

sor - rows, and ac - quainted with grief _____ A man of

sor-rows and ac-quaint-ed with grief

He was de-spi - sed

re-ject - ed   He was de - spi-sed and re-ject - ed of

men A man of sorrows and ac - quainted with grief _____ A

man of sorrows and ac - quaint-ed⎯ with grief He was de - spi-sed

re - jected A man of sorrows and acquaint-ed with

grief, and acquaint-ed with grief.⎯⎯⎯⎯⎯ A man⎯ of

sor - rows and ac - quaint - ed with grief.

'The trumpet shall sound', ornamented *da capo*

* Cadenza here. See page 110.

The Cadenza

The vocal cadenza was an essential part of any eighteenth-century performance. To omit a cadenza is a falsification of style and contrary to the composer's expectations.

The decline of the vocal cadenza was doubtless due to its abuse—Galliard in his translation of Tosi's *Osservazioni* complains that 'some, after a tender and passionate Air, make a lively merry *cadence;* and, after a brisk Air, end it with one that is doleful'—as well as to the general decline in vocal technique, for the vocal technique of the eighteenth century was instrumental in its virtuosity.

Whilst the ideal vocal cadenza is improvised in the moment of inspiration, there is no reason why a written cadenza should not be sung, as it were, spontaneously, always provided that the singer possesses the necessary technique and sense of style. An excellent improvisation need lose none of its excellence in being written down and later performed by other than its creator. It must, however, be performed spontaneously as an extension and in the mood of the air from which it stems or not at all.

The Tenbury–Dublin score has the following cadenza to 'Every valley' added in pencil:

It should be noted that it is not in the writing of Handel or the copyist. It appears to be a later addition. However, the figure

was used extensively by singers as an essential figure in the improvised cadenza, and moreover it was frequently written by Baroque composers as part of the vocal line—Handel himself used it many times (see the following example from Cleopatra's air 'Hark, hark he strikes the golden lyre' in *Alexander Balus*).

Chrysander, in his performing edition, doubtless uncertain of the contemporary public's reaction to the elaborate cadenza of the eighteenth century, wrote only a cadential flourish, e.g. in the air 'The people that walked in darkness' he wrote:

In the following cadenzas I have attempted something more elaborate, more in accord with eighteenth-century practice. These are, of course, purely personal, as the cadenzas of Handel's own singers, Frasi, Avolio, Galli, and Guadagni, were personal to them. They are, however, the result of an absorption in Handel's music and a close study of eighteenth-century vocal technique and style. They are offered as models. The musical seed of each is to be found in the air from which it arises. There is in them nothing in the way of rhythmic figuration of harmonic implication, whether it be the use of the chromatic harmony of the major on the flattened supertonic (with its melodic and harmonic consequences), or the influence of the Dorian mode in the minor key, that cannot be found in Handel's own hand.

'Every valley'

'But who may abide?'

- ner's fire

'O Thou that tellest good tidings'

is ris - en is ris -

- en up - on Thee

'The people that walked in darkness'

Up - on them hath the light shi -

- ned

'Rejoice greatly'

Be-hold thy King com-eth, com -

eth, com -

- eth un - to Thee.

'Thou shalt break them'

'The trumpet shall sound'

Various Vocal Ornaments

Various ornaments were added by the performer during the course of an air in order to add colour to the salient word, note or rhythmic group as well as to the many cadences occurring during the course of an air where any more conclusive flourish would interrupt the movement.

(a) In the falling cadence

(b) In the rising cadence

(c) Some general examples

The Appoggiatura

Georg Philipp Telemann provided clear evidence of the use of *appoggiaturas* in a table in his *Harmonische Gottesdienst* published in 1725:

But Handel did not write *appoggiaturas* only in recitative. Note his *appoggiatura* in bar 2 of 'Behold and see'.

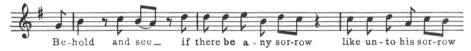

The following is offered as a logical extension of this indication in bars 7–9:

INSTRUMENTAL ORNAMENTATION

(a) The interpretation of Handel's own orchestral ornamentation in *Messiah*

In *Messiah* Handel used only the trill sign.   But Handel's trill sign signified not *merely* a trill but an ornament; the ornament most fitting in the particular context.   Here are some interpretations:

The overture

i.e. beginning on the principal note.

'Rejoice greatly' ($\frac{12}{8}$ setting)

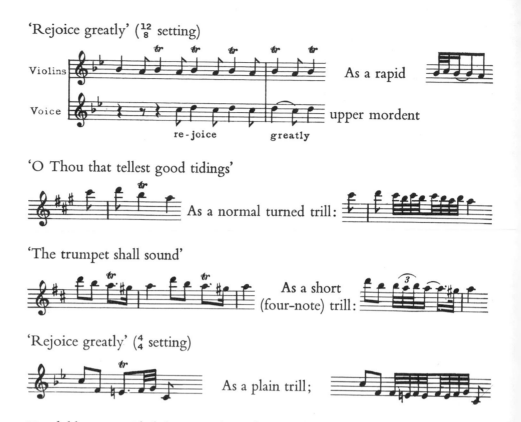

As a rapid upper mordent

'O Thou that tellest good tidings'

As a normal turned trill:

'The trumpet shall sound'

As a short (four-note) trill:

'Rejoice greatly' ($\frac{4}{4}$ setting)

As a plain trill;

Handel here provided the equivalent of a turned ending in the demisemiquavers.

Wherever the note to be trilled contains a fraction of a beat and is followed by a single note completing the beat, the short trill with its *point d'arrêt* effect is appropriate.

e.g. 'Thou art gone up on high'

as

In many cases the short note that follows a short trill needs to be further shortened. This is a matter of artistic judgement. It depends entirely on the *Affekt*. Compare the examples given above from 'The trumpet shall sound' and 'Thou art gone up on high'.

At a slower tempo the trill could begin with a full *appoggiatura*. e.g.

or the same with a rest to emphasize the final semiquaver.

'But Thou did'st not leave'

As a delayed upper mordent:

Pastoral Symphony

As a fully turned trill:

'O Thou that tellest good tidings'

 beginning on the principal note (whenever rein-
forcing a sustained or repeated melody note):

(b) Additional Orchestral Ornamentation

Handel's trill signs were indications of what he expected the performers to
add in similar contexts, for he often wrote only one *tr* in a complete movement. See, for example, the one trill in the *allegro* of the Overture, bar 2 beat 4;
the one trill in 'He was despised' on the fifth quaver of bar 2; the one trill in
'Lift up your heads', bar 7 beat 1; the one trill in 'Their sound is gone out'
(chorus setting) in bar 22; the one trill (the only choral trill in the whole
oratorio) in the choral bass, bar 43, beats 1 and 2, in the 'Hallelujah' chorus.
(The only argument against the addition of choral ornamentation today in
pre-nineteenth-century works is the decline in vocal technique. Both Handel
and Bach wrote trills in their choral voice parts.) That Handel intended
ornaments but did not indicate them is proved by a comparison of the bass
setting of 'Thou art gone up on high' in the Autograph score with the alto
(Guadagni) setting of the same words in the Tenbury–Dublin copy but in
autograph. The closing *ritornello* is identical in both settings, yet although
in the penultimate bar in the Tenbury–Dublin setting Handel wrote '*tr*' over
the violins' C♯, the same note in the Autograph score is without any indication.
    In view of the evidence I suggest:
    (i) Where Handel has once ornamented a motif, that some of the repetitions
        of that motif should be similarly ornamented. See 'He was despised'.
    (ii) Where a melody is repeated many times, that it should be varied by
        the use of appoggiaturas and passing notes, particularly when it is
        imitative of a vocal line which has itself been ornamented.
    (I know that my Redeemer liveth. Bars 115–119, violin.)

(iii) That the orchestral parts of the choruses, most certainly the introductions and codas, should have suitable ornaments added; note Handel's own instrumental trills against the voices in the chorus 'Behold the Lamb of God' (see p. 97). The conductor should not hesitate to ornament inner orchestral parts when they have a characteristic melodic and rhythmic figure. Here is an example in which Handel ornamented the second violin not only when in thirds with the first violin but against an unornamented first violin:

Neither should the conductor hesitate to ornament the instrumental bass whenever it has a figure which Handel has ornamented in another instrument; compare bar 14 of the first violin with bar 22 of the basso-continuo in the Overture.

Note also the trills in the bass of the Overture in the contemporary harpsichord part:

(iv) That where a complete instrumental movement is repeated, the salient
harmonic, melodic, and rhythmic points be heightened by additional
ornamentation. Here is the first violin part of the *grave* of the Overture
to *Messiah* ornamented by me for use in the repeat:

In performing the baroque trill it is not sufficient to begin on the upper
note; the important point is that the upper note, as the generally dissonant note
or note of colour shall be maintained as the accent throughout; therefore, the
trill must be measured. Whether the instrumental trills be in semiquavers or
demisemiquavers is a decision to be made beforehand by the conductor in
relation to the context, to both tempo and *Affekt*.

Harpsichord Style

The basso-continuo is often realized merely as a succession of chords, but
the evidence in favour of a more elaborate realization wherever the principal
burden of the accompaniment is left to the keyboard continuo is both weighty
and clear. Nor was this more elaborate style limited to the harpsichord, for
Praetorius (1571–1621), writing on continuo playing, gives advice on the
selection of organ stops suitable for rapid passage work as distinct from those
suitable for more sustained playing. The following realizations are offered
as an indication of style. There is room for further elaboration in many places,
but not for simplification if the performance is to be true to Handel.

E

(a) Airs

This obviously demands plain chords:

This by reason of its context, requires a flowing accompaniment:,

This, however, can support, and gains in interest from, the counter-melody derived from the *ritornello*:

(b) *Secco* Recitative

'There were shepherds'

And the An-gel said un-to them fear not for be-

hold I bring you glad tid-ings of great Joy Which shall

be to all peo-ple for un-to you is born this day In the ci-ty of

This ornamentation section is by no means exhaustive; it is simply an indication of what must be done if the composer's 'shorthand' is to be correctly translated into sound. Neither is it dogmatic. Evidence that sign, name, and interpretation of ornaments were constantly confused is given by C. P. E. Bach in his *Versuch über die wahre Art das Clavier zu spielen;* writing of the turn he says that it is often indicated by the sign for the trill or even the mordent, and that mordent and trill themselves are often confused. Handel himself used the trill sign for any ornament. Further, knowing that performers would themselves introduce ornamentation, composers often did not bother to indicate it. And, finally, the interpretation of the written ornament or the choice and placing of the unwritten ornament was governed by the *Affekt*. It follows, therefore, that after making a study of the style of ornamentation and the performing conventions of the period, the final decision belongs to musicianship. As Quantz expressed it, 'Good taste acquired by certain rules and refined by much experience and exercise.'

6 The Harmonic Structure

HANDEL'S KEY-RELATIONSHIPS

IT has been said that the recent attempts by German musicologists to discover key architecture in the music of Handel are hardly convincing. It is put forward as evidence against him that he was prepared to have his arias sung in any key. It is true that directions for the transposition of a number of the arias are to be found on the manuscripts in Handel's own hand—e.g. 'But who may abide' has the instruction 'Un tono piu alto ex E for Mr. Low in tenor cliff'—but this merely indicates that when forced by circumstances he was prepared to have his sense of key-relationship disturbed rather than omit the aria. Further, it must be remembered that individual arias were sung sometimes separately from the oratorio. On 27th April 1748, 'He was despised, by Mr. Handel' was sung by Galli at Hickford's Room in Brewer Street. The real evidence regarding his key-sense is to be found in the key-relationships in the original score. These prove, at the least, that his choice and change of key was ever exceedingly apt.

Consider the following examples. The change to the tonic major at 'Comfort ye' where the first chord with the third in the top part comes as ease after pain, following the *grave* quality of the E minor Overture (*grave* no less in the *allegro* than in the opening *Grave*). The introduction to 'Thus saith the Lord' in which the reiterated chord of D minor, following the long sustained penultimate chord of D major in the cadence of the previous chorus, strikes a note of dramatic tension. The recitative ending of 'Comfort ye' in which the modulations ending in a perfect cadence in D major make the opening E major harmony of 'Every valley' sound with the freshness and vitality of a distant key remove whereas it is the same key as the previous arioso; the change to the key of the supertonic minor, either directly as between the E♭ major 'He was despised' and the F minor 'Surely he hath borne our griefs' or by a chromatic passing-note as between the first section and the contrast section of 'Rejoice greatly'; the use of key to clarify essential form as in the choral triptych beginning with 'Surely he hath borne our griefs' where, after lightening the F minor of the first two choruses by the change to F major in 'All we like sheep' he unifies the group by reverting to the original minor for the *adagio* coda. Or again in the choice of C major for 'Let us break their bonds asunder' which, coming after the closing modulations and final E minor cadence of 'Why do the nations', emphasizes the fact that this air does not require a *da capo* because the following chorus completes the implied ternary form. And the keeping of the same key for two consecutive numbers where the thought is similar or derivative as in the case where the B♭ major

'His Yoke is easy' follows the B♭ major 'Take his yoke upon you' of the previous air.

The change to the submediant or flattened submediant major was of significance for Handel. His choice of E♭ major for 'He was despised' following upon the G minor of 'Behold the Lamb' was hardly accidental, possibly not of design but at least intuitive; similarly the choice of B♭ major for 'He shall feed his flock' following upon the final D minor cadence of the previous recitative (I refer, of course, to his original settings of both of these numbers for soprano); or the choice of F major for the chorus 'Lift up your heads' following upon the A major air 'But Thou didst not leave His soul in hell'.

The recitatives have an important bearing upon key progression. The dominant-remove had not as yet gained the stranglehold of later years but Handel used this remove with a definite purpose. He would end a recitative with a modulation to the dominant key of the succeeding number. It was not, however, really a modulation in itself, it was a preparation of the ear for the key of the next number by emphasizing the dominant harmony of that key. For example: 'Thus saith the Lord' modulates to A minor but ends with a *tierce de Picardie;* the following air is in D minor. Again, 'Behold, a Virgin shall conceive' modulates to A major; the following air is in D major. And 'He was cut off out of the land of the living' modulates to E major; the following air is in A major.

One of the functions of the recitative is to form a modulating link between airs and choruses; therefore it is often written without key signature.

There are twelve recitatives in *Messiah*, not counting the recitative endings to 'Comfort ye' and the shortened version of 'Why do the nations' or 'For behold! darkness shall cover the earth'. Of the twelve only two remain in the same key throughout ('There were shepherds' and 'Unto which of the angels'); four begin and end in the same key ('And lo!' and 'Then shall be brought to pass', in addition to the two listed above); and five are without key signature (one other being in the key of C major).

'Unto which of the angels', although in D minor throughout, is of course correct in being without signature for here Handel was following the convention from *Musica ficta* of writing the key signature with one symbol less than it properly contains, the unrecorded symbol occurring as an accidental in the course of the music. Handel was not, however, consistent, for while in *Agrippina* he wrote two flats for E♭ major and in *Il Trionfo* two sharps for A major, yet in *Messiah* he wrote the full three sharps for the chorus 'And the glory' and the full three flats for 'O death where is thy sting'; but in the recitative preceding 'O death', which begins and ends in B♭ major (with a momentary transition into E♭ major), he wrote only one flat in the signature.

Six recitatives have key signatures. 'Thus saith the Lord' (*accompagnato*) has a one-flat signature, is in D minor and modulates to A minor concluding with a *tierce de Picardie*. 'Behold, a Virgin shall conceive' has a two-sharps signature, is in D major, and modulates to and ends in A major. 'All they that see Him' has a three-flats signature, but begins in B♭ minor and remains firmly in that key for five and a half bars; it then moves directly into the key of the signature, E♭ major, and, apart from a momentary suggestion of B♭ major through the introduction of the chord of the diminished seventh on A natural, it continues in E♭ major for the remaining five and a half bars. 'He was cut off out of the land of the living' has a one-sharp signature but begins on a chord of B minor and remains in that key for two bars; over the remaining three bars it modulates to and ends in E major—another case where Handel observed the key signature convention.

Of the recitatives without a key signature the *accompagnato* 'Thy rebuke hath broken his heart' is of most interest. This recitative shows another lingering influence, that of the earlier baroque feeling for tonality without key. No sooner is one key suggested than, by the use of a Neapolitan sixth, a *tierce de Picardie* or a chromatic seventh, we move to another. Immediately after the suggestion of A♭ major by the first chord we find ourselves in F minor in bar 2, only to be taken by a chromatic minor-seventh harmony to G minor in bar 3; an enharmonic chromatic seventh on the third crotchet of bar 6 is leading us to E minor when we are turned away by a *tierce de Picardie* in bar 8, and so it continues to the end, all extremely *affekt*-ive and yet very unforced.

The recitatives in *Messiah* are perfect examples of the form. The relative time-values of the vocal line in *secco* and of the orchestral parts in *accompagnato* express the general mood; the melodic curves are the counterparts of the emotional curves; and the *affekt*-ive harmony is fitted to the *affekt*-ive word.

HANDEL'S CADENTIAL DISSONANCES

Editors have tended to soften Handel's dissonances. Even the Renaissance-form created by suspensions is often ignored in the keyboard accompaniments in vocal score. The dissonance arising from the previous linear conception of music was not softened by the revolutionary turn to a vertical conception which marked the change from basso seguente to basso-continuo—the distinguishing characteristic of the Baroque. On the contrary, dissonance was accentuated. Further, the corpus of early Baroque compositions shows not only that it was used as a means of emphasizing significant words by horizontal dissonant intervals in the voice and vertical dissonances with the bass, but also that it became a commonplace in cadences, the tonic and the leading note being struck together immediately before the final cadence chord. This characteristic, foreshadowed by frequent use of simultaneous false-relation, continued through the middle Baroque into the late Baroque. Handel frequently used it. A vocal cadence much used by him anticipates the tonic so:

 ('If God be for us'). Mozart-Hiller, copied by

Prout, altered it to and so evaded the clash between

the tonic and the leading note.   Others, while retaining the original melody, soften the dominant harmony by omitting the third of the chord so:

Yet, throughout the oratorio, Handel clearly shows that whenever in the final cadence the melody consisted of the progression of the supertonic to the tonic spread over three notes he wanted the tonic to be anticipated, with the resultant harmonic clash between leading note and tonic.   In the cadence of the chorus 'All we like sheep' he wrote:

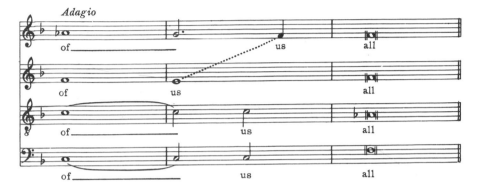

The clash between the E and F in the alto and soprano voices is further emphasized by the *adagio* tempo.   Similar examples both in his choral and orchestral writing are numerous and easy to find.   A particularly striking example is to be found in *Samson*, bar 27 of the chorus 'With thunder around', between the tenor and soprano:

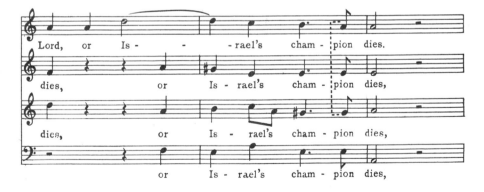

The chorus 'For unto us a Child is born' is the only case in the whole of *Messiah* where Handel repeats the supertonic in a final cadence.   However, in a middle cadence in bar 29 of the chorus 'But thanks be to God' he has repeated the supertonic.   Therefore, when in bar 37 of the same chorus he writes both terminations in two different parts at the same moment he raises a problem.

125

Ought we to alter the first violin in bar 37 to agree with the soprano note C and so fall into line with the cadence in bar 29, or ought we to alter the soprano to agree with the first violin note B♭ and so conform to Handel's more usual practice? The weight of evidence is in favour of the latter, with the resulting clash between the soprano B♭ and the tenor A. Moreover in the Tenbury–Dublin copy the soprano note is B♭.

HANDEL'S USE OF CHROMATICISM

Musica ficta, while leading to our present scale system, was in essence chromatic. It arose from a desire to soften the effects of the tritone, also of the whole tone when involved in a progression by step, either ascending or descending, followed by a return to the first note: in the latter case it is a foreshadowing of the chromatic mordent. This desire to colour the normal mode persisted and, statements to the contrary notwithstanding, the Baroque period and Handel in particular was no exception. The chords of the Neapolitan sixth (a lingering Phrygian influence) and of the augmented sixth were an integral part of Baroque harmony; while as such they in no way conflicted with the firm establishment of key in the late baroque, they were paradoxically a chromatic influence.

Certain it is that Handel wrote chromatically from his early Italian to his late English period, whether composing opera, oratorio or church music; here is an example from *Dixit Dominus* (1707):

And here is one from *Alexander Balus* (1747):

And here is a ground from *Susanna*, for the chorus 'How long, O Lord'

(1748); generally associated with Purcell because of his use of it in the most moving lament of Dido in the opera *Dido and Aeneas*, it was, in fact, common chromatic property:

(*Susanna*)

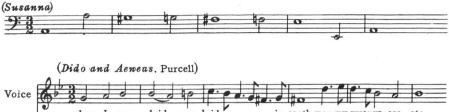

(*Dido and Aeneas*. Purcell)

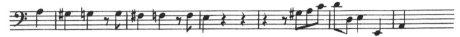

Handel used it in *Messiah*.   Here is the latter half of the introduction to 'Thou shalt break them':

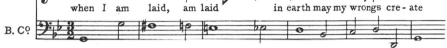

Later in the same aria he used the ascending chromatic scale:

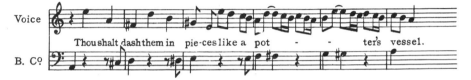

The influence of this ground is to be traced in the air 'The people that walked in darkness':

In this air Handel allowed the skill in word-painting that he shared with Bach to cause him to dwell upon the 'darkness' and the 'shadow of death', almost, if not quite, to the exclusion of the 'great light' that 'shined upon them'; this led naturally to chromatic writing.   The subject of *Messiah*, however, is so immense and yet so simple that chromaticism seems out of place, and whether by accident or design the fact remains that in both the arias and the choruses the melody and harmony are forthrightly diatonic.   The only exceptions are an occasional Neapolitan sixth (as in bar 42 of 'And he shall purify') or a raised subdominant (used to establish the dominant harmony, as the G♯ in the strings in bar 13 of 'Glory to God' and the E♮ in the vocal line bar 10 of 'Rejoice greatly') and the deliberate chromaticism of 'The people that walked in darkness' and 'Since by man came death'.

7 *The Basso-continuo Figuring*

COMPOSERS of the seventeenth and eighteenth centuries wrote for performance, not posterity. And as the composer himself usually directed the performances it was not necessary for him to write in his score the figuring for the realization of the continuo. The extent to which the score was so marked depended upon the type of man and the extent of his activities. Handel was anything but finnicky, he was extremely busy; therefore, his markings are relatively few.

It is instructive to analyse and to compare the figurings in the Autograph score and the conducting score, i.e. the Tenbury–Dublin copy, with the early printed editions, i.e. *Songs in Messiah*, published by Walsh and the full score published by Randall and Abell. When Smith wrote the Tenbury–Dublin copy he copied the Autograph score fairly meticulously; only occasionally did he omit any of Handel's figuring or rectify Handel's obvious errors. Similarly, although there are a number of differences (mostly without any significance) the figuring of the solos in the Randall and Abell score follows very closely the figuring in the *Songs in Messiah*.

It will be clearly stated in the following analysis where any figuring in the manuscripts is not written in Handel's own hand, and any significant differences will be discussed in detail.

In order to make this study I have collated the figurings in the Autograph score; the Tenbury–Dublin copy; *Songs in Messiah*, first edition (*circa* 1749); *The Songs in Messiah*, later edition, British Museum G. 160 P. (*circa* 1769); *The Songs in Messiah*, later edition, in the possession of Miss Joan Bernard; and the Randall and Abell full score.

In some cases two successive single figures indicate a suspension while in other cases the same two figures indicate two different harmonies; when enumerating I have counted these two figures in all cases as two figurings.

In the solo numbers, Handel wrote 278 figurings; Randall and Abell printed 2,273 figurings.

In the choruses, Handel wrote 438 figurings; Randall and Abell printed 1,847 figurings.

At least a third of Handel's figurings consist of the figure 6. Generally these do not seem to have particular individual significance but to be rather in the nature of a warning against a possible $\frac{5}{3}$ realization; e.g. to take two examples at random, the last quaver in bar 27 of 'His yoke is easy' and the third crotchet in bar 2 of 'I know that my Redeemer liveth'.

Handel generally wrote at least one or two figurings in each number, but in the following numbers he did not write any figurings:

'Every valley' (Randall and Abell print 179); 'The people that walked in darkness' (Randall and Abell print 42); 'Rejoice greatly' the $\frac{4}{4}$ setting (Randall and Abell print 189); 'The Lord gave the Word' (Randall and Abell print 19).

The absence of figuring in those parts of the score where the accompaniment consists either of continuo alone or continuo with an *obbligato* line for the violins throws an especial responsibility upon the keyboard-continuo player. In the air 'But Thou didst not leave His soul in hell' the sequence in bars 3 and 4 could well be realized sequentially as follows:

But whilst the first edition of *Songs in Messiah* does not positively differ from this solution, later editions and the Randall and Abell score change the figuring after the first group in bar 3:

Songs in Messiah 1st edition

Randall and Abell score (bars 3 and 4)

And in the comparable passage in the dominant key in bars 15 and 16 in Randall and Abell two of the $\frac{6}{4}$ figurings are declared as $\frac{4}{2}$:

The figuring that is given is often incomplete. Often when the orchestral parts contain some position of a chord of the seventh the discord figure is missing. In 'He was despised', bar 27, the minim C on beats 3 and 4 is figured ♮ but the second violin is holding the note B♭. There are so many instances of this that it might seem that Handel wanted the harpsichord player to strengthen the foundation triad and leave the discord to the orchestra.

On the other hand, with only the triad in the orchestral and vocal parts Handel on occasions figured the discord. In 'He trusted in God', bar 8 beat 3, with nothing but the root in the continuo and choral bass and the third in the choral tenor, he figured 7; and in the same chorus, bar 9 beat 1, with the root in the continuo and choral bass and nothing in the other voices or the orchestra, he figured $\frac{7}{\sharp}$. In 'O thou that tellest good tidings to Zion', bar 137 beat 1, with only the triad in root position in the voices and orchestra, he figured $\frac{6}{5}$ so by the addition of the sixth creating a supertonic secondary seventh harmony. In 'He shall feed His flock', bar 23 last quaver, with a second inversion of the major triad in the orchestra and solo voice, he figured $\frac{\flat}{6}$. In 'Glory to God', bar 11 beat 2, with a second inversion of a major triad in the orchestra and voices, he figured 6, so changing the harmony to the discord of the tonic major seventh. In these and many similar cases the responsibility for providing the essential colour of the harmony rests upon the keyboard-continuo player.

He must decide, for even the conventions were loosely applied. The figuring 2 could indicate either the last inversion of a chord of the seventh, a 4 3 suspension with the suspension in the bass, or a $\frac{7}{4}$ with the 9 8 suspension in the bass; the stroke across the figure 6 ($\cancel{6}$) could indicate the raising of the sixth by a semitone, merely a major sixth, on the supertonic a $\frac{6}{4}$, or on the leading note a $\frac{6}{5}$; the figuring $\frac{6}{4}$ could indicate either the second or the third inversion of a chord of the seventh; and the figure 6 in the figuring 7 6 could indicate either a $\frac{6}{3}$ or a $\frac{6}{4}$ but generally not a $\frac{6}{5}$.

There are many ambiguities in the figurings when the bass is considered by itself—ambiguities which are not explained by accepted conventions, for Handel wrote figurings that were either not covered by any convention or departed from the accepted conventions. In 'And He shall purify', bar 11 beat 3, he figured 5♮ for the fundamental concordant triad, but in 'Comfort ye', bar 16 beat 3, he figured 5♮ for the first inversion of the chord of the minor seventh; of course, a reference to what is happening in the orchestra and the solo tenor would make his intention clear, nevertheless it was considered necessary to clarify it in the Randall and Abell score as $\frac{6}{5}$, but the ♮ was omitted.

He was not consistent, for what he considered essential when writing one setting he completely omitted in the comparable bars in another setting of the same air. In the $\frac{12}{8}$ setting of 'Rejoice greatly', in bar 31 beats 3 and 4, Handel figured $\frac{4♮}{2}$ 6 and on the two following bars on the 2nd beats he figured a ♮; further, in bar 65 beats 3 and 4 (dotted crotchets), he figured 7 ♮; this he did in order to make clear the modulation to the dominant key. These figurings were equally necessary in the comparable bars in the $\frac{4}{4}$ setting, yet in the autograph of that setting he did not write a single figuring. In one matter, however, he was consistent, and that was in figuring the last inversion of a dominant seventh. If the augmented fourth from the bass note was diatonic he figured it merely $\frac{4}{2}$ but if it was chromatic he figured it either $\frac{4♮}{2}$ or $\frac{4}{2}$ according to the key.

Wherever Handel figured *bassetti* or *bassetgen* sections of the continuo in which the upper voices are singing alone and in contrapuntal style, it clearly indicates that the accompaniment usually printed, a simple reflection of the voice parts, is not what he would himself provide. Here are bars 84 to 90 of 'And the glory of the Lord' as written by Handel:

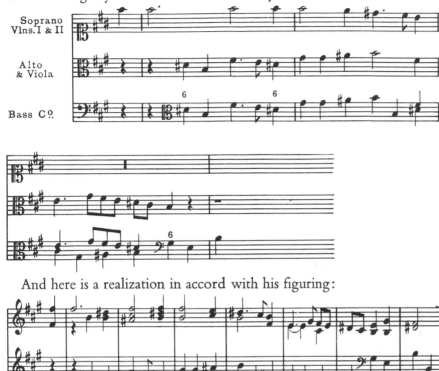

And here is a realization in accord with his figuring:

An examination of the non-autograph figuring throws an interesting light upon the realization practice of the period.

1. Handel's known dislike of the use of the second inversion of the dominant seventh when the root does not form part of the previous harmony has been mistakenly extended to the avoidance of the seventh in all cases where the discord is not in the vocal or orchestral parts. As I have already instanced, Handel himself figured the discord when the parts contained only the notes of the fundamental triad. But the *Songs in Messiah* and the Randall and Abell score contain numerous figurings of 7 where today we play consonant triads. For example, in 'If God be for us', bars 101 to 104, which are almost invariably realized as simple common chords and unfigured in the Autograph score, have the figuring 7 on each chord with the following result:

Another class of exception is suggested by the figured rests to be found both in the first edition of *Songs in Messiah* and in Randall and Abell. The following example is taken from *Songs in Messiah*, 'How beautiful are the feet', bars 8 and 9:

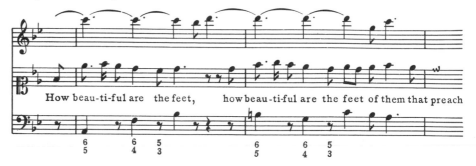

And here is another example taken from Randall and Abell, 'If God be for us', bar 104:

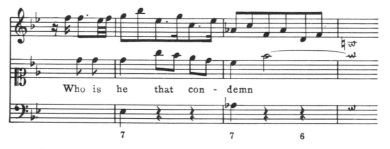

2. Cadential ornamentation is a practice that is accepted by all students of the period. Further supporting evidence is to be found in the figuring in these first printed editions where, at cadence points with the third from the root in the melody, the figuring is either 4 3 or $^6_4\,^5_3$. The 4 or $^6_4$ is an editorial anticipation of the cadential ornamentation. Here is an example from 'I know that my Redeemer liveth', bar 34:

In a similar cadence at bar 74, beats 2 and 3, the figuring is $^6_4\,^5_3$. This example is of particular significance as evidence that the practice of ornamenting a melodic line was not confined to singers, for this is a *ritornello* cadence.

3. Considerable discussion has raged concerning the air 'The people that walked in darkness'. Did Handel intend it to be performed *tasto solo* (or more accurately *all' unisono*) or did he intend the bass to be realized? In the

first place it is not strictly an *aria all' unisono*. Then, Handel troubled to
mark with the words *tasto solo* all the other passages that could be performed
in that manner—see the choruses 'Glory to God', 'Hallelujah', and 'Amen'.
Further, in the first edition of *Songs in Messiah*, as well as in the Randall and
Abell full score and in the later editions of *The Songs in Messiah*, the first
note of this air has the figuring ♯ and this is repeated in the comparable
bars 4, 19, and 34; this in itself is a clear indication that it was the custom in
Handel's lifetime for the keyboard-continuo player to realize the bass in the
unison sections of the aria, as well as in the other sections (which contain some
39 figurings). Finally, in the eighteenth-century manuscript harpsichord part
(British Museum RM 19.d.1) the *unisono* section is copiously figured. As
this manuscript is declared by Professor Larsen to be in the handwriting of
Jennens, the librettist of *Messiah*, there can be little doubt about general contemporary practice regarding this air. Indeed, it is reasonable to assume
with Professor Bukofzer that all *all' unisono* airs were supported by keyboard
harmony unless otherwise indicated by the composer.

Before leaving this matter one other point needs to be referred to: it concerns the Pastoral Symphony. In general keyboard-continuo players leave
this number unrealized. In *Songs in Messiah* and the Randall and Abell
full score there is not a single figuring, but in the Autograph score Handel
wrote just one figuring. He figured a ♯ under the second dotted minim in
bar 15. This represented a chromatic harmony leading to a transition into
the relative minor; hence his need to figure it. It follows that it was his
custom to realize the bass throughout the Pastoral Symphony.

4. The practice of keeping a harmony alive by keyboard repetition in one
form or another is indicated by Handel himself in the recitative 'Behold a
Virgin shall conceive' (the Autograph score) in which in bar 3 he repeats the
$\frac{4}{2}$ figuring of the previous bar under the tied note D which is sustained for
three and a half bars. It is also indicated in the first edition of *Songs in
Messiah*, 'He was despised', bars 36 to 37, where the $\frac{7}{5}\flat$ figuring for the
diminished seventh harmony sustained by the strings for six crotchet beats is
figured no less than three times.

5. Neither Handel nor Smith nor Smith's copyists were completely
accurate. For instance, there are a number of cases where a figure intended
for the note after a rest is written under the rest. There is, however, one case
regarding the position of a figuring that deserves special consideration. In
'O Thou that tellest', bar 135, Handel scored in orchestra and voices the
harmony of the tonic minor seventh; the root is D and the minor seventh
discord C natural is in the choral alto and the violins. On the last quaver of
the previous bar (134) Handel scored the plain common chord of D. To
reserve the change to the chromatic harmony for the final 'Glory' might well
be regarded as another touch of Handel's craftsmanship; but in the Autograph
score Handel's own figuring 7♮ is not merely clearly to the left of the bar
line that separates bar 134 from bar 135, but it is slightly to the left of the last

quaver in bar 134 to which it clearly refers.

In the Tenbury–Dublin copy, however, Smith placed it under the first quaver of 135.

6.   The practice where there are rests in the continuo stave for the keyboard-continuo (in common with the orchestral continuo instruments) to be silent (except at, say, the third entry in a fugue which begins with the upper voices), clearly has exceptions.   First an obvious exception.   In 'Thou shalt break them', bar 10, Handel wrote:

This bar is both the lead into the voice and the final cadence bar, for Handel did not write out the coda but merely indicated a repeat of the instrumental introduction.   It is obvious that Handel intended the violins to drive straight on to the second beat descending octave leap.   In view of this the pause over the first beat of the basso-continuo makes nonsense of the rest on the second beat of that stave.   Unquestionably Handel expected the bass to continue and to support the violin on the second beat.   Also, the octave leap suggests emphasis and demands keyboard reinforcement of the second beat.

It should be noted that the figurings in *The Songs in Messiah* (*circa* 1769 edition) (copy G.160.P in the British Museum) and those in the Randall and Abell full score (1767) are generally in agreement; but the rare copy of *Songs in Messiah* (*circa* 1749) in the William C. Smith collection differs somewhat from these.

Appendix B sets out seriatim the variations in figuring that are to be found. The differences will be referred to in detail only where they are of some significance.

The statement that certain of Handel's and of Smith's figuring was 'in error' is essentially true; but the use of the word 'error' is open to question.   Even to say that the basso-continuo was figured carelessly would not be strictly exact, for the keyboard-continuo player of the period was expected to be a thorough musician, so well versed in the science of his art and with an ear so sensitive that neither figures nor their inflexions were really necessary.

8 Handel's Treatment of English

THE ITALIAN INFLUENCE

HANDEL's vocal compositions in English reflect the influence of his stay in Italy in his elision of syllables—the gliding from the final vowel of one word into a following word that begins with a vowel or an h—gliding so rapidly that, as far as rhythmic impact is concerned, they become one syllable. The understanding of this is of vital importance, for if a composer has written

| ♩ ♩ ♩ | and in performance it becomes | ♩ ♩ ♩ ♩ | the rhythmic shape of the whole passage, and therefore its musical meaning, is misrepresented.

In 'Comfort ye', bar 31 appears as follows in the Autograph:

[musical notation: "cryeth in the"]   in Randall and Abell   [musical notation: "cry - eth in the"]

Prout (the standard English edition until 1958) unfortunately copied Randall and Abell, although in the preface to his edition Prout discusses syllable elision and gives the excellent example of 'glorious', normally a three-syllable word, being treated as a two-syllable word.

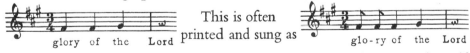

Thy glo - rious deeds in - spired my tongue

(from Samson)

In the chorus 'And the glory of the Lord', bar 13 in the alto part appears as follows in the Autograph:

[musical notation: "glory of the Lord"]   This is often printed and sung as   [musical notation: "glo-ry of the Lord"]

Handel intended the rhythmic impact of three crotchets. He himself gave proof of this when, forgetting the original words, he wrote

glo - ry of God

in the bass in bar 35.

In the same chorus, bars 106–110 in the soprano part appear as follows in the Autograph and the copy RM 18.e.2:

and the glory- and the glo - ry, the glory of the Lord

This was changed almost immediately by Smith in the Tenbury–Dublin copy, copied some eighteen years later in the Hamburg, and printed later still in the Randall and Abell score with the following word alteration:[1]

and the glo - ry, the glo - ry, the glory of the Lord

I submit that Handel did not hear these bars as a three-part phrase but as a two-part phrase:

and the glo -ry and the glo - ry, the glo -ry of the Lord

He used the Italian technique of elision in order to avoid any break in bar 107.

The failure to understand Handel's musical purpose in using elision technique has resulted in a complete misreading of bars 23–24 in the tenor part and bars 26–27 in the alto part in the 'Hallelujah' chorus.

These bars appear as follows in the Autograph. Handel did not write unnecessarily. He used the sign ∻ whenever a word or phrase was to be repeated. Note the tie over the bar-line of the third bar, third stave

[1] The dotted slurs and brackets are the author's.

and similarly in the alto part.

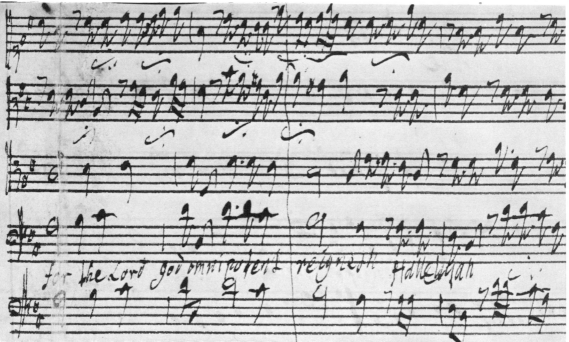

But in the Randall and Abell, and over 130 years later in the Prout edition, Handel's tie over the bar-line was ignored; an exciting figure became pedestrian.

In one of the secondary manuscript copies, RM 18.b.10, the tie has been erased—apparently with a knife; the syllables were incorrectly written and the music was altered to fit the words! This misreading of the Autograph is strange, because Handel drew very solid ties over the bar line in both the tenor and alto staves, and the Autograph was correctly interpreted in the Tenbury–Dublin copy, the Hamburg copy and RM 18.e.2 copy as:

It has been assumed that Smith took some part in the publication of the Randall and Abell score, but this and other major misinterpretations in that score lead one to question the extent of his co-operation.

The opening phrase of 'Blessing and honour' from the chorus 'Worthy is the Lamb' provides a '–ry and' elision similar to those in 'And the glory'. Handel here wrote in bars 24–25:

Bless-ing and hon-our glo-ry and pow'r be un - to him be un - to him

It is completely wrong to break up Handel's reiterated quavers by singing the last quaver in bar 24 as two semiquavers.

THE GERMAN INFLUENCE

In spite of his experience in setting to music Italian, French, and English texts Handel's mother tongue asserted itself quite strongly at times. For instance, he knew well that the English words 'these', 'those', and 'were' were monosyllables, the final e being silent, and often set them so; yet he often set them as disyllables as though they were German words.

(a)

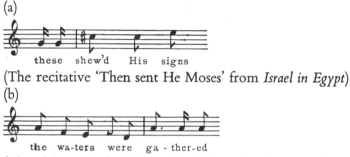

these shew'd His signs

(The recitative 'Then sent He Moses' from *Israel in Egypt*)

(b)

the wa-ters were ga - ther-ed

(The chorus 'And with the blast' from *Israel in Egypt*)

Sometimes he set them correctly and incorrectly in the same sentence. This explains the one note too many in both 'There were shepherds' and 'And lo, the Angel of the Lord'. As he wrote he heard respectively:

(1)

there we - re shep - herds

(2)

and they we - re sore a - fraid

In RM 18.e.2, Smith corrected example (1) by adding the word 'and' at the beginning of the sentence. He had support for this in the original Greek and the Authorised Version where this sentence begins with 'and'. In Randall and Abell the correction was effected by omitting the first note. However, this error is of little importance.

But example (2) is of considerable importance. This was first correctly interpreted in the harpsichord part RM 19.d.1 (*circa* 1750) and some ten years later by Smith in RM 18.e.2, by turning the repeated quaver D into a crotchet:

and they were sore a - fraid

In Randall and Abell the correction was made to the detriment of the vocal shape by omitting the note C:

and they were sore a - fraid

This misinterpretation was repeated by Prout in 1902, by Coopersmith in 1946, and by Watkins Shaw in 1958.

SYLLABIC RHYTHM

The distribution of the syllables, their relation to the music, is to vocal music very much what bowing is to stringed and tonguing is to wind instruments, and obviously it is a very important part of the composer's craft. Of itself, quite apart from the measure, the mode, the melodic contour or the rhythm created by the changing harmonies, syllabic rhythm suggests a general as distinct from a detailed *Affekt*.

Although Handel's setting of English often results in extremely false accentuation, his placing of the syllables invariably creates the syllabic rhythm which exactly expresses the spirit underlying the text. He was extremely sensitive to this syllabic rhythm. For example, as will be seen below, in bar 14 of the air 'Thou shalt break them' he first wrote:

rod   of   i - ron

then simply by extending 'rod' by a quaver and reducing 'of' from a smooth couplet to a single quaver he gave added force to the whole passage:

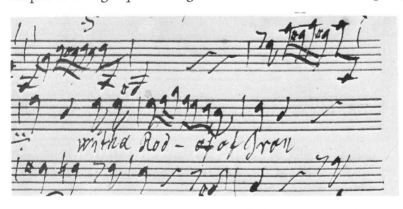

Similarly in 'The trumpet shall sound', bars 38–40:

he first set the word 'rais'd' to six quavers:

Ex.169 rais'd   incor-rup - ti - ble

He then altered it to the more vigorous and (followed by a further alteration in the next bar) rhythmically 'disturbing' syllabic grouping of the notes in a sequence of 4–2–3.

Ex.170 rais'd——— in - cor - rup - ti - ble

The resulting accents upon 'cor—' and '–tible' are, of course, ludicrous to English ears.   But the attempted solution by the copyist of RM 18.b.10:

raised   in - cor - rup - ti - ble

repeated in the Randall and Abell full score and in practically all editions to this day, runs completely counter to Handel's purpose in making the alteration, i.e. to break the six quavers into two contrasted time groups.   In the final result, although this attempted solution restores correct accent to the word, it takes the vigour out of the phrase.   Incidentally, Handel's final word arrangement is unaltered in the Tenbury–Dublin and Hamburg copies.   In the following arrangement I have provided an acceptable accent and at the same time maintained Handel's grouping of the quavers:

rais - ed in - cor - rup - ti - ble

Whatever fresh arrangement of the words is made, Handel's syllabic rhythm must be maintained.

In the air 'If God be for us', the voice part bars 25–29, appears as follows in the Autograph:[1]

If God be for us who can be a-gainst us

These bars were first copied exactly by Smith in the Tenbury–Dublin copy but they were altered later to:

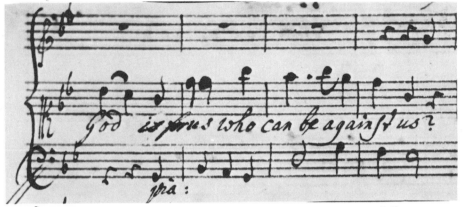

The alteration was a well-intentioned attempt to improve Handel's treatment of the language—to balance the first beat accent on 'against' in bar 29 with a similar accent on 'for' in bar 27. Handel obviously felt the rhythmic impact of three crotchets to be essential to the *Affekt* for in bars 37–41 he again wrote:

If God is for us who can be a-gainst us

These bars also were first copied exactly in the Tenbury–Dublin copy and later altered:

[1] In bars 25 to 27 Handel wrote 'If God *be* for us' but in bars 37 to 39 he wrote 'If God *is* for us'.

In bar 26 the word 'is' has been scraped out from its original position under the second crotchet in bar 26 and written under the third crotchet. The word 'us' was first written at the beginning of bar 27 and so left little room for the insertion of the word 'for'. Further, the words 'is for' are thickened and the ink has spread as the paper was roughened by erasure; note the thick slur in bar 26. The additional crotchet in bar 27 made necessary by the altered word distribution is squeezed in between the note against 'us' and the bar line. The note against 'us' was from its size quite obviously first a minim; observe also the spacing between the notes in this bar. The writing in the alteration differs considerably from Handel's hand; Handel's 'i' is practically vertical whereas the same letter in the Tenbury–Dublin alteration slopes to the right; Handel's 's' is a clear two-way hook, whereas in the Tenbury–Dublin alteration it is extended by a diagonal connecting stroke. The two crotchets on the first and second beats in bars 27 and 39 as altered in the Tenbury–Dublin copy were not part of Handel's conception; this is proved by the instrumental introduction in which the corresponding bar (bar 3) has a minim.

Bars 7–10 in the 'Amen' chorus present an interesting case. They are written as follows in the Autograph score:

Yet in many editions the vocal bass is printed so:

a - men,   a - men,   a - men, a - men

The tension which Handel obtained by the extension of the one syllable over the detached notes and the rests is lost when each group of three beats is sung as a complete 'Amen'. As Handel wrote it, it is one phrase driving towards the final bar, and broken by the syllable 'men' at the end of bar 9 only in order to give greater force to the final bar.

There are other cases where Handel's word arrangement has been unnecessarily altered and often to the detriment of his vocal line.

In bar 9 of 'He shall feed His flock' Handel wrote this word distribution:

It is often printed

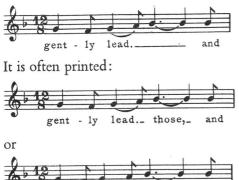

The smoothly flowing quality of Handel's word distribution is disturbed in the last example, by the impact of the word 'his' on the last quaver, an impact that is emphasized by the articulation of the final consonant of the word 'with' on the preceding semiquaver.   In bar 21 Handel wrote:

It is often printed:

or

Handel began to write it as in the last example but then smudged out the syllable slur over the first two notes.

The line after the word 'lead' is Handel's continuation mark; when he desired a sentence or part of a sentence to be repeated he wrote a different sign.

In bar 28 Handel wrote:

The alteration in the Tenbury–Dublin copy is unquestionably not for the better:

Smith was uncertain about the word distribution for when he first made the copy he wrote only the first syllable of 'unto' and then nothing until the word 'that' in the next bar; 'to him all ye' were written in a different ink which has now faded to a very light brown.   The flowing character of Handel's word distribution is completely changed by the syllable-for-note alteration. The fact that the alteration is in the Tenbury–Dublin copy does not lend it any authority. It is simply an example of well-intentioned contemporary meddling.

In bar 34 Handel wrote:

It is sometimes printed:

Words or no words, Handel conceived this musical phrase with a rest at the beginning of the fourth dotted crotchet beat, for he first wrote bars 4–6 as:

He then wrote a crotchet f¹ running its stem through the first rest and also ran his pen through the second rest.

In bars 34–35, Handel's word arrangement over the bar line is:

It is sometimes printed:

Not only is the word 'that' less singable than the original 'are' but the absence of the slurred syllable 'are' over the first two notes in bar 35 disturbs the comfort and confidence which underlie this air.

'I know that my Redeemer liveth' has been subjected to many alterations. In two cases the alterations are a reversion to a word arrangement that Handel had previously discarded. In bars 125 to 129 he first wrote:

He then altered it to

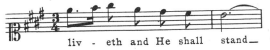

Note the filling of the former minim head against 'them' and the addition of the crotchet for the word 'of'. Handel's discarded first thought was copied in RM 18.e.2, printed in the Randall and Abell score, and repeated by Prout.

The phrase in bars 133–137 has suffered similar treatment. Handel's discarded first thought was copied into RM 18.e.2, printed in the Randall and Abell score, and repeated by Prout.

In the final phrase, bars 149–153, Handel's alteration was ignored by Smith, who made an alteration of his own in the Tenbury–Dublin, Hamburg, and RM 18.e.2 copies. Smith's alteration, which was printed in the Randall and Abell score, was repeated by Chrysander.

I have not been able to work on the Goldschmidt copy[1] but on a loose sheet of white paper in the Tenbury–Dublin copy there is evidence that the Goldschmidt copy contains another word arrangement differing from Handel's and Smith's. The paper reads:

different reading in Mr. Goldschmidt's score from that of Sir Frederick Gore-Ouseley's[2] Part III Air 'I know that my Redeemer liveth' bars 57 and 58.

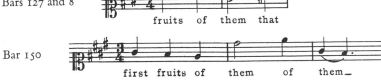

Bar 107 Vln. Pian, Bar 115 Violins *f*.

Bars 127 and 8

Bar 150

All these alterations in adapting words are corrections in the same writer's hand as that of the score.

But, on another sheet of paper in the Tenbury–Dublin copy there is a statement (referring to the 'Hallelujah' chorus) signed by Otto Goldschmidt which reads, 'In the score in Smith's handwriting, which I possess, the three

[1] See p. 8.
[2] I.e. the Tenbury-Dublin copy.

unison Ds in Alto, Tenor and Bass have the words "and Lord of Lords" substituted in Handel's writing'.

The Goldschmidt alterations, whoever made them, are repeated in the Prout and the Coopersmith editions.

The Aylesford copy in the Newman Flower collection has numerous alterations to Handel's word arrangements: with the exception of the last two examples the word alterations are written above the stave.

Bars 29–35:

Bars 49–53:

Bars 57–65:

Bars 109–115:

Bars 149–153

These alterations, consisting of frequent repetitions of short groups of words, arranged to give opportunity for the frequent taking of breath, would seem to have been made at the suggestion of a singer. Their syllable-for-note character cancels out the long curving line of Handel's single-vowel phrases. The use in bars 112–115 of words other than those associated with the *motif* of the air seems, to say the least, quite meaningless. And the addition of a single passing note in bars 33, 51, and 61 robs both the rhythm and melodic shape of the original melody of its character. If singers will think horizontally in terms of *line* rather than vertically in terms of bar-lines they will find that many word arrangements which look wrong on paper often fit the voice perfectly and sing themselves.

Consider, for example, bars 149–153 of this air. They constitute one unbroken phrase; the note D♯ both in itself as the leading note and as part of a harmonic discord demands unbroken progression to the following note E; this E sinks naturally into G♯ which as the 6 of a $\frac{6}{4}$ demands resolution on the fifth (F♯), and the F♯ as part of the first two cadence chords continues into the tonic.

The Goldschmidt distribution is a typical singer's arrangement. It provides an opportunity for taking breath between the two notes in bar 151, and so enables the singer to pause on the D♯ for as long as is considered 'effective', to sing the remaining notes *molto adagio* and to sustain the last note without anxiety. But musically this arrangement cuts the phrase in half, and the syllable-for-note treatment of the first four notes is not conducive to a true vocal *legato*.

Contrast this with Handel's word distribution, in which the slurring of the word 'first' over two notes suggests continuing movement, and where the unimportant preposition 'of' (containing one excellent singing vowel) placed on the bar line and sustained for a whole bar carries the phrase as on a wave over to the final cadence.[1]

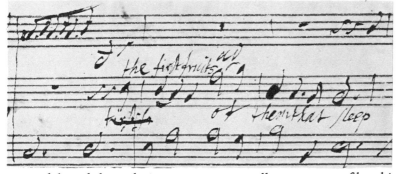

Handel used the technique, common to all composers, of breaking a sentence in the middle in order to give greater emphasis to the words by repetition and to obtain greater impetus in the drive towards the climax. The opening of the first chorus is a clear example:

[1] The 'ad' over the second stave is an abbreviation of adagio.

147

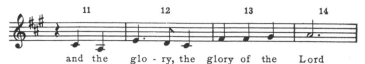

and the glo - ry, the glory of the Lord

The comma after 'glory' in bar 12 must be made aurally obvious (by a fine break, not a breath) if the music is to make its full effect. There are many examples of this throughout the work, but an outstanding example is to be found in the chorus 'For unto us a Child is born'. The tenor in bars 61–3 and the soprano in bars 63–5 were printed in the Randall and Abell score, have been repeated through the years and as late as 1902 in the Prout edition:

and the Gov - ern-ment shall be up-on his shoul - der

Yet in the Autograph these bars appear:

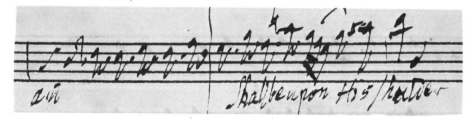

Handel's obvious intention was to break the sentence after 'be' on the first note in bar 64 and, by beginning again upon 'shall', to bring the word 'shoulder' on the final octave leap[1].

It must ever be remembered that whatever fresh arrangement of words is made, Handel's syllabic rhythm must be maintained. For although his accent may at times be false his syllabic rhythm is vital to the *Affekt*—it is the *Affekt*.

[1] In passing, observe the time-group in bar 64 beat 3. Handel's vigorous ♫♩ was replaced, in the 'Smith' copy RM 18.b.10, *circa* 1760, by the less vigorous ♩♫. This misreading was repeated throughout the years, even as late as 1946 by Coopersmith. It must, however, be pointed out that the word distribution is correct in the Coopersmith edition. Coopersmith errs in good company, for this passage is similarly printed with incorrect time group (but with correct word distribution) in Breitkopf's 1922 issue of the Chrysander-Seiffert 'performing' edition.

9 *A Critical Evaluation*

In the summer of 1720, in the private theatre on the estate of James, Duke of Chandos, at Cannons, Edgware, outside London, Handel presented *Haman and Mordecai*—a masque with scenery, and costume and action.   Some twelve years later he announced his intention of presenting the masque in London but, according to Burney, the Bishop of London forbade the presentation of a sacred story in the theatre.   As the work contained but little stage action Handel reshaped it as *Esther, an Oratorio,* and in the advertisement in the *Daily Journal* of 19th April, 1732, of the performance at the King's Theatre, Haymarket, announced:

there will be no action on the stage but the house will be fitted up in a decent manner for the audience.   The music to be disposed after the manner of the coronation service.

This may truly be said to be the seed from which *Messiah* grew, for, after the failure of *Deidamia* in February, 1741, Handel finally renounced opera and turned back to the epic form of *Esther,* with its emphasis upon the importance of the chorus, and within the twenty-four days between 22nd August and 14th September of the same year he composed *Messiah.*

Messiah is unique.   It would be fruitless to attempt to compare it with other oratorios, either Handel's or those of other composers.   However, no masterwork, even if it be unique, merely happens.   Rather does it result from the play and interplay of many forces consciously or subconsciously experienced. It is interesting to speculate what Handel oratorio owes to Cavalieri's *La rappresentazione di Anima e di Corpo,* the first oratorio so called (in reality a mystery play without the speaking-voice), with its siciliano-like *ritornelli* and the alternately homophonic and contrapuntal choruses of *Piacere e Compagni;* to Monteverdi's *Combattimento di Tancredi e Clorinda* (sometimes described as the first secular oratorio), with its addition of the epic to the dramatic by the use of the *testo;* to Schutz's tableau-like *Historia von der Geburt Gottes und Mariens Sohn Jesu Christi,* or his dramatic, many-voiced, concerto-like and at times very florid writing in *Symphoniae Sacrae;* to Carissimi's *Jephtha* with its emphasis on the chorus as protagonist; or to the Hamburg Biblical operas the form of which (complete with *recitativo secco* and *da capo aria*) was established in the church by the beginning of the eighteenth century.   Certain it is that, like all oratorio, Handel oratorio owes much to Italy and particularly to Italian opera.   It is indeed opera transferred to the concert platform and with some of its conventions discarded, but with the chorus no longer merely decorative or ejaculatory but elevated to a dominant role.

F

Handel did not write sacred or secular oratorio, he wrote concert oratorio; *Messiah* must be judged as such. It was not performed in church till some nine years after it was composed. Until the performance in the Chapel of the Foundling Hospital in May 1750, it had been heard only in the theatre or other places of entertainment. Jennens, the compiler of the libretto, used the word 'entertainment' in a letter to a friend. In Faulkner's *Dublin Journal* there appeared an announcement on 6th December 1743, which began, 'The said Society having obtained from the celebrated Mr. Handell, a copy of the Grand Musical Entertainment, Called the Messiah. . . .' And Lord Kinnoul, after hearing *Messiah*, congratulated Handel upon 'a great entertainment'. True, Handel is reported as having replied, 'I should be sorry if I only entertained them; I wished to make them better.' But no matter how God-inspired Handel may have felt—'I did think I did see all Heaven before me, and the great God himself'—*Messiah* was not conceived as church music, not even as non-liturgical church music.

It has been said that Handel suggested the subject of *Messiah* to Jennens—that the idea was born of his love for his sister then dead, whose favourite text was 'I know that my Redeemer liveth'. This could be, but it is not likely; although Handel may have rebuked archbishops with, 'I have read my Bible very well and will choose for myself', and have damned the iambics of Morell, his attitude towards Jennens as shown in their correspondence was that of an artist towards his patron. In a letter dated 19th July 1744, nearly three years after *Messiah* was composed, he wrote to Jennens, '. . . be pleased to point those passages in the *Messiah* which you think require altering.' It would seem that we owe *Messiah* not to any embitterment which Handel may have felt on account of his operatic failure, nor to any seeking after spiritual solace, nor to his love for his dead sister, but simply to the fact that Jennens had presented him with the libretto.

The authorship of the libretto has been questioned. Hone (1780–1842) in his *Table Book*, named one Pooley (said to be curate and secretary to Jennens) as the author. But a thorough search by various scholars of contemporary records, including the clergy lists, has failed to produce any proof of Pooley's existence. It has been suggested that Pooley has been confused with Matthew Poole, the compiler of the *Synopsis Criticorum Biblicorum*, but Poole died in Holland in 1679.[1] It has also been suggested that Jennens's neighbour, Dr. Bentley, of Nailstone, was co-author, but again there is no proof. In the absence of such proof and with the evidence of the letters that passed between Jennens and Handel it is reasonable to ascribe the authorship to Jennens.

In a letter to an unknown friend and correspondent of 30th August 1745, Jennens said,

I shall show you a collection I gave Handel, call'd Messiah, which I value highly, and he has made a fine Entertainment of it, tho' not near so good as he might and ought to have done. I

[1] M. Edwards, of Oswestry, in a letter to the *Radio Times*, 2nd February 1951.

have with great difficulty made him correct some of the grossest faults in the composition, but he retained his overture obstinately in which there are some passages far unworthy of Handel but more unworthy of the Messiah.

The continuity of spiritual and musical idea throughout the oratorio is remarkable, e.g. between the solo ending 'For He is like a refiner's fire' and the following chorus, 'And He shall purify'; the solo ending 'Take his yoke upon you' and the following chorus, 'His yoke is easy' and between the Christmas recitatives and the chorus, 'Glory to God'. For this unity of conception the librettist must be given credit.

Libretto and music in themselves and in relation to each other form a satisfying unity. Yet Zelter, who led the orchestra at the Berlin performance of *Messiah* (sung in Italian), conducted by Hiller in 1786, was of the opinion that *Messiah* was not conceived as a whole but was merely a number of occasional pieces strung together. To which Goethe, a great lover of the oratorio, replied, 'I am not disinclined to accept the idea that it is a collection, a compilation from a rich source of supply; since fundamentally it does not matter in the least whether the unity is formed at the beginning or the end; it is always the spirit that produces it in either case and here the unity was implicit in the Christian purpose of the work from the very outset'.[1]

It must be said that Jennens did not merely compile a selection from the Sacred Writings, he made several alterations without damaging the original text, and one of considerable importance. The important alteration is to the text of the *accompagnato* 'Thy rebuke hath broken his heart'. In the Authorized Version, Jennen's source, the passage reads: 'Reproach hath broken my heart; and I am full of heaviness: And I looked for some to take pity, but there was none; and for comforters, but found none'. Jennens changed it from the first person to the third: 'Thy rebuke hath broken *his* heart'. By this simple change he makes the listener part of the action, an integral part of the drama, and, by the suggestion of *testo* and *turba*, heightens a sense of resemblance at this moment to passion music itself.

Messiah was conceived and composed as a unity and as such it should be performed. There is nothing in it that can be omitted without damaging it and nothing that need be omitted on musical grounds. Examine the numbers most frequently omitted and what do we find?

'The Lord gave the Word'
Here is a chorus that is structurally well balanced, the harmonic basis of which is secure, the polyphonic texture of which flows easily and logically. The opening musical statement is arresting in its simplicity, and its later repetition is given fresh interest by the succeeding *divisions*. These *divisions* rise to a rhythmic climax and, being in all four voices at the one time, give a sense of a 'great company'.

[1] *Goethe and Handel*, by Stanley Godman, English Goethe Society, Vol. XXIII, 1954.

'Let all the angels of God worship Him'

After the arresting quaver-crotchet relationship of the opening 'Let all', the instruments followed by the voices give out the theme both normally and in *diminution* at one and the same time; the soprano part encompasses both forms for, after beginning naturally, it suddenly changes and begins all over again, but in *diminution*.   This is continued not in any academic manner but freely, with vitality and brilliance.

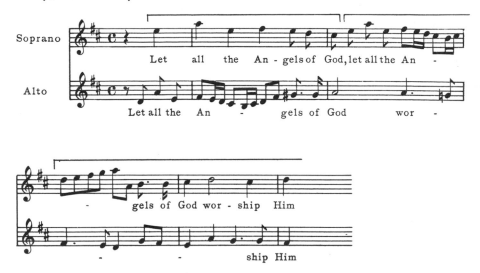

'Thou art gone up on high'

The instrumental introduction is of itself sufficient to commend this air to the informed musician and the uninformed music-lover alike. The opening violin theme with upward leaps of a seventh and descending scale passages, culminates in the following exciting cadence:[1]

The character of the opening vocal figure is essentially the same in the bass, alto (Guadagni) and soprano settings; but in the soprano and alto settings it is the more interesting because of the rhythmic contrast between the second and fourth bars of the figure; however, in the soprano and bass settings the melodic line gains considerably by the upward leap of a fourth on the word *up*, in the fourth bar, not merely as word painting but as the expression of the general *Affekt*.

[1] Note, bar 10, beat 1: a time-group Handel often uses for this *Affekt*. Cf. 'For unto us', bars 62 and 64, beat 3; often incorrectly given as

152

The air is further varied and yet unified in all three settings first by the use of one part of the introduction for the first *ritornello* and another part for the second *ritornello*, and then by using some section or figure as an instrumental counterpoint against the voice. This is particularly effectively accomplished in the bass setting.

Note also the rapid key transitions effected by the use of the chromatic major third and the minor seventh discord.

'If God be for us'

The original form of the opening vocal figure as written by Handel in the Autograph score (i.e. with a syllable to each note, the form in which it must surely ever be sung) has a forthright quality. This quality gains additional strength from the modal character of the theme, the trilled violin figure with its vigorous preliminary semiquaver, and the broken-arpeggio violin figure which, after descending, sweeps upwards over some two octaves towards its cadence.

The character of the trilled violin figure finds an echo in the vigour of the dotted group in the vocal *division;*

and the sweep of the broken-arpeggio figure is carried on in the even quaver bars of the vocal *division,* which is given increased rhythmic impetus by the fragment of the broken-arpeggio played by the violin against the sustained note in the voice:

'O Death where is thy sting' and 'Thanks be to God'

The evenly flowing quaver movement of the basso-continuo in the duet is an excellent foil to the broken and syncopated vocal theme.   The admonitory note of the Italian text of the original duet, *Se tu non lasci amore mio cor ti pentirai* (see p. 160), is not very far removed from the mood of the English text which Handel later set to music.   Certain it is that the broken iambics of the repeated 'O Death' and the syncopation caused by placing the questioning 'where?' on the second beat create a fitting musical expression of the text.

O Death, O Death where, where is thy sting, O Death where is thy sting

The Chorus is the complement of the duet which flows into it, moving, by just one passing note in the basso-continuo, from C minor into the original key, Eb. The connexion between duet and chorus is strengthened by the first choral entry, a statement of the duet theme by the choral basses (completed by the altos in bar 3), supported by the upper voices.   There is a further link in the rhythm of 'the sting of death is sin' from the duet and 'who giveth us the victory' in the chorus.   This duet-chorus movement is another example of Handel's effective and musically satisfying tripartite structures which, beginning with the solo voice (or voices), conclude with a chorus:

In truth there is nothing in *Messiah* which need be omitted on musical
grounds and nothing which can be omitted without damaging the work as
a whole. For example, the chorus 'Lift up your heads' is incomplete and
lacking in purpose unless it is followed by the joyful adoration of 'Let all the
angels of God worship Him'; so in like manner is 'How beautiful are the feet
of them that bring the Gospel of peace' when taken out of its situation as the
centre of a ternary structure bounded on one side by 'The Lord gave the
Word' and on the other by 'Their sound is gone out into all lands'; again,
'The trumpet shall sound' is less meaningful if we are denied the promise of

immortality expressed in the air's middle section, and so is the implied antithesis between 'the law' and 'love' in 'O Death, where is thy sting' and the joy in victory in 'But thanks be to God who giveth us the victory'; finally, 'Worthy is the Lamb that was slain' is the natural corollary of the faith that Handel expressed so convincingly in 'If God be for us'.

That *Messiah* was conceived as a whole is evident in countless ways; the structure of the whole work; the balance between the twenty-three choruses and the solos; the contrast obtained by *recitativo secco*, *recitativo accompagnato*, arioso and air and the variation of homophonic and polyphonic styles in the choruses; the unerring skill in placing subsidiary and principal climaxes (note in this connection the emphasis laid upon the idea of resurrection and ascension by following the chorus 'Lift up your heads' with another chorus, 'Let all the angels of God worship Him', separated by only five bars of *recitativo secco*); the linking up of air and chorus (a) in *Affekt* as in 'But who may abide' and 'He shall purify', 'He shall feed His flock' and 'His yoke is easy', and (b) by using the same melodic *motif* for two distinct numbers as in the duet 'O Death, where is thy sting' and the following 'But thanks be to God'; the reservation of the *da capo* air for moments of special emphasis; the use of key—witness the effect of the E major arioso 'Comfort ye' immediately following the E minor key of the overture, and of the opening of 'Thy rebuke hath broken his heart' that results from the A♭ major harmony after the C minor cadence of the previous chorus, an effect further heightened by the sudden transition into F minor; and the momentary touch of drama provided by the *turba* chorus, 'He trusted in God that He would deliver him'.

Handel's craftsmanship is consummate. And it is craftsmanship, for a close examination of the Autograph shows that many of the touches that one would regard as having been inspired, as having been written at white heat, are, in fact, Handel's second thoughts. The brilliant sounding tenor opening statement of the subject 'And cast away' in the chorus 'Let us break their bonds asunder' he at first gave to the bass: see p. 156.
The first form of the subject of the 'Amen' chorus was

Compared with its present form bars 5 and 6 of this example are almost unbelievable. The $\frac{4}{2}$ on the bass note G, in bar 84 (the fifth bar from the end) of the 'Amen' chorus, which leaves us as it were emotionally suspended in mid-air, he at first wrote as a plain $\frac{5}{3}$ on A. Here is the original choral bass from bar 80:

(It will be observed that the bass in bars 80–82 was at first an octave lower.) The beginning of 'Since by man' with the awe-full solemnity of the soprano line gradually rising from the low E was first

Much has been made of Handel's plagiarisms, particularly in *Israel in Egypt*, where something more than forty per cent of the thematic material is said to have been taken from other composers (see Sedley Taylor's *The indebtedness of Handel to works by other composers* and Percy Robinson's *Handel and his orbit*). But even when he used another composer's music without altering it in any way, he did in effect alter it by the very fitness of the new context in which he set it. In *Messiah*, however, Handel used no thematic material but his own, apart from the subject of 'And with His stripes', which is common to almost countless composers, and of the Pastoral Symphony, which is a tune used by the Italian Pifferari and is acknowledged by Handel in the Autograph by the word 'Pifa' at the beginning of the movement.

It could reasonably be expected, however, that, in treating a subject so sacred as *Messiah*, Handel would have used, as in *Esther*, some material from his own earlier works *La Resurrezione* (Rome, 1708), or the *Brockes Passion* (London, 1716), but he did not. The only reference to the past is the instrumental motive of 'Comfort ye' used by him thirty-two years earlier in *Agrippina* which, there, is so slight that its later use can scarcely be regarded as a quotation. Not until he used it in *Messiah* did the *motif* have musical significance. He did, however, quote from the immediate present. The Italian duet *Nò di voi non vo' fidarmi*, dated London, 3rd July 1741, was the seed of 'For unto us a Child is born';

The duet *Quel fior ch'all' alba ride*, dated London, 1st July 1741, was the seed of 'His yoke is easy'.

The third movement of the same duet was the source of 'And He shall purify':

and the early duet *Se tu non lasci amore mio cor tu pentirai, lo so ben io* was the seed of the duet 'O Death, where is thy sting' and the following chorus 'But thanks be to God'.

Some music composed to words has a quality of its own apart from the
words; a quality that according to its treatment—a slight change in the
rhythmic or melodic shape, in the accompaniment, in the harmonization or
even in the style itself—can express different, sometimes markedly different
ideas. The *divisions* in 'Thus saith the Lord' from *Messiah* are almost terrifying.

Yet, in the opening chorus of the 'Ninth Chandos Anthem', the same music sounds completely different. Robbed of its former recitative style by the change in the accompaniment, and of the sense of tumultuous outpouring by the alteration of the time relationship in the first group of the division itself (note the steadying effect of the quaver), it loses its sense of awe and takes on the mood of joyful praise.

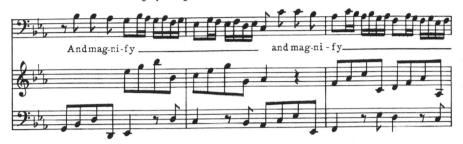

Handel's use in *Messiah* of material from his own works has suffered an amount of criticism. The instance in *Messiah* for which he has been most criticized is that in which he used material from one of the Italian duets (written for Princess Caroline a few months before he began *Messiah*) for the chorus 'All we like sheep have gone astray'; this music derives from the third movement of a duet in the Autograph in the British Museum RM 20.g.9 and is to be found on folio 41 verso. This duet is also the source for the 'Hallelujah' chorus (see bar 1 in Ex. (a)).

This chorus as often performed has a certain levity hardly consonant with confession. Rochlitz, discussing the unity of conception of *Messiah*, justified this apparent levity as a necessary relief from tension; he likened it to the facetious comments of the Fool in Shakespeare's *King Lear;* on these lines, of course, one could justify it by quoting Greek drama. Certain writers have found less justification for its use. The late Professor Edward Dent said, '*Messiah* incorporates some of Handel's own chamber duets, the melodies of which were more suitably illustrative of their original Italian words than of the sentences from Scripture to which he adapted them'.[1] There is, however, no necessity to attempt to justify; the fault for any seeming incongruity is in ourselves. When Handel wrote the duet he first wrote the tempo indication *andante.* Then, crossing out *andante,* he wrote *allegro.* When he used the material in *Messiah* he wrote at the top of the chorus *allegro moderato.* Some music is of such quality that it is acceptable *qua* music at different tempi. Beethoven marked the Funeral March from the 'Eroica' Symphony as $\flat = 80$. But Koussewitsky conducted it at $\flat = 62$ and Toscanini at $\flat = 52$. The late Dr. Percy Scholes, commenting on this, says,[2] 'But everybody would agree that the composer's marking is too fast'. It is, however, possible that had we, living in Beethoven's time, heard it at his tempo, we would have accepted it as the *just* tempo. Whether the tempo has speeded up or slowed down is not material to the present argument; what is pertinent is that certain music sounds *just* at different tempi. And Beethoven himself said 'Man muss die Tempos fühlen.' Handel first thought of the music which he ultimately used for 'All we like sheep' as *andante,* then as *allegro,* and finally as *allegro moderato.* If this chorus is sung with Handel's *moderato* in mind, I do not believe that it will be found to be incongruous.

As for the music from folio 37, verso, in the same volume for 'And He shall purify' (see p. 159), from folio 39, recto, for 'For unto us a Child is born' (see p. 158), from folio 36 recto for 'His yoke is easy' (see p. 159), only the bias resulting from a knowledge of the original Italian words can find anything unfitting in the wedding of the music to the biblical text.

The case of the duet in *Messiah,* 'O Death, where is thy sting', is interesting. The source is an early Italian duet, to be found in two manuscripts, one in the volume RM 20.g.9, folio 65 recto; the other RM 19.e.7, folio 77; this latter consists of 86 bars plus an *allegro* in $\frac{3}{4}$ of 81 bars. These must not be confused with the trio setting of the same words RM 18.b.11, folio 81 verso, which, in spite of a slight resemblance at one point, is very different music.

The *motif* as used in *Messiah* is unexceptionable, but as written to the original words the music *as music* would be quite unsuitable in *Messiah;* the reason being that the many syllables of the Italian text create a dancing rhythm that although suitable for that text is at variance with the thought underlying the biblical text (see p. 160).

One cannot think of Handel searching through his various manuscripts in order to find something he could use in order to save time. The music was in

[1] *Handel,* Edward J. Dent. Duckworth, 1934.
[2] *The Oxford Companion to Music,* Percy A. Scholes. Oxford University Press, 1938.

his mind in its *essential* melodic and rhythmic shape and if in essence it was suitable he wedded it to the words on the paper in front of him.

No one listening to the 'Slumber Song' in Bach's *Christmas Oratorio*, without previous knowledge of its source, would suspect that in its original situation in *The Choice of Hercules* it was an incitement to revel in the joys of the flesh. So with those numbers in *Messiah* that derive from the Italian duets. They must be judged where and as they stand in *Messiah* without any backward glances at their origin. It is difficult to conceive of a setting of *Messiah* by any other composer of the period—even Bach; many writers have attempted to evaluate one composer against the other but, as Professor Bukofzer has written, 'They are only equal where they are incomparable.' How compare Bach's tightly woven and logically developed Germanic contrapuntal style with Handel's alternating solid blocks of harmony and loosely woven Italianate counterpoint (to be picked up or dropped according to the dictates of the 'situation')? But to those who would underestimate Handel's contrapuntal skill, the eighty-one bars of the 'Amen' chorus is a more than sufficient answer.

There were many influences at work in Handel. His grounding in the science of the art under Zachau in Halle during the early years stood him in good stead till the end, although it was the least evident influence. His Italian experience added to his academicism a graciousness and freedom of expression obvious in his operas. And his English experience added a certain strength and directness of expression that is particularly in evidence in the oratorios.

But all the influences—Carissimi, Keiser, Scarlatti, Purcell, the Italian Cantata, the English Verse-Anthem, the Jacobean harmonic twist or hemiola-like rhythm, the masque or the ceremonial ode—he assimilated each thoroughly and by some alchemy made them all unquestionably his own.

Appendixes

APPENDIX A

ALTERNATIVE SETTINGS

I

Table of Manuscript Sources and their Contents

A COMPLETELY detailed description of the alternative settings of the text of *Messiah* is to be found in the chapter on alternative settings. This table is simply concerned with listing the manuscript sources of these settings. It should be understood that, with three exceptions to be referred to later, the various settings of any one text that are listed in this table are different musical settings, even although they stem from an identical *motif*. For example, the setting of 'How beautiful are the feet' listed as an alto solo in C minor is not, as has been stated elsewhere, a transposition of the soprano *da capo* air in G minor; it is a different musical setting. Again, the so-called 'duet' version of 'He shall feed His flock', in which the first stanza only was transposed down into F for alto, the second stanza remaining in the soprano key of B♭, is regarded as an alternative setting because of the change in vocal timbre and in key within the one air.

The first exception is the all-alto solo version of 'He shall feed His flock' with both stanzas in F major. This is a simple transposition. But its inclusion in the Table is justified because of its significance in relation to other alternative settings (see page 43). Further, it is the only version of this air to be found in the Mann 'Dublin' and the recently discovered Townley Hall manuscripts. The remaining two exceptions are the abridged versions of the $\frac{12}{8}$ 'Rejoice greatly' and the duet 'O Death'; both abridgements were made by Handel.

Not revealed by the table but worth noting are:

(1) the unexpected transposition of 'He was despised', a fifth higher and written in the soprano C clef, to be found in the Hamburg–Schoelcher manuscript;

(2) the transposition of 'If God be for us', a fourth lower and written in the alto C clef, to be found in the early (*circa* 1744) Granville, also the Needler, the Aylesford (Barclay Squire), and the Townley Hall manuscripts, not as an alternative but as the only version;

(3) the Chapel Royal setting of 'How beautiful' for alto-duet and chorus, differing from the alto-duet and chorus setting in the appendix to the Autograph score, to be found in a volume in the British Museum, shelf mark RM 20.g.6;

(4) the source of Handel's alteration in 'The trumpet shall sound' from the original *da capo* indication to *dal segno*. In the Autograph score he made clear his intention of a literal *da capo* by writing, on the third beat of the final bar of the middle section, the first two notes of the opening *ritornello*, in the G clef and followed by the words *da capo*. Smith copied this into the Tenbury–Dublin manuscript but Handel altered this to the note for the voice together with the first word of the text: 'The', added

the words *dal segno* and wrote the sign at the first entry of the voice;

(5) the absence from some manuscripts and editions of the chorus or the arioso setting of 'Their sound is gone out'. This is not without reason. When first composing *Messiah*, Handel used this text for the middle section of the air 'How beautiful'. Neither the chorus nor the arioso setting was then composed. It was only when the middle section of the air was omitted that the need arose for a separate setting of 'Their sound'. The word book of the first performance shows that even though a different setting of 'How beautiful' was then sung (the alto-duet and chorus setting, which did not include the text of 'Their sound') it was followed immediately by the air 'Why do the nations'. The chorus and arioso settings of 'Their sound' are not an integral part of the Autograph score, but are additions bound in at the end of the volume.

It is also of interest to note that the indication in 'Why do the nations' of *da capo* (held by the majority of Handelian authorities to be incorrect—certainly it is not in the Autograph) was written in the Needler, Aylesford (Barclay Squire), Marsh–Matthews, Rowe and the 'Smith' copies in the British Museum, shelf marks RM 18.b.10, and RM 18.e.2.

II

Table of Contents of the Principal Editions from 1749 to 1854

To list the contents of all the editions of *Messiah* published during the second half of the eighteenth and the first half of the nineteenth century would be tiresomely repetitive and of questionable value. Randall used Walsh's plates; Preston and Wright used both Randall's and Walsh's; Clementi, Collard and Collard used Peck's plates[1]; and John Bishop, in a preface, referred to Edward J. Rimbault's 'high opinion' of his (Bishop's) work to the extent of copying it. I have therefore selected the following *representative* publications:

1. The Walsh *Songs in Messiah* (*circa* 1749), the first *Messiah* music to be published.

2. The Randall and Abell full score (*circa* 1767)—the first published full score.

3. The Arnold full score (*circa* 1787)—the only eighteenth-century printed full score to contain the recitative setting of 'But who may abide'.

4. The Harrison and Co. New Musical Magazine edition 'With Choruses' (1784), an early equivalent of the present-day vocal score and a reasonable guide to the versions generally sung at that time.

5. Peck's edition (1813), which puts a date to the omission in performance of the middle sections both of 'He was despised' and of 'The trumpet shall sound'—in the body of the volume only the first sections of these airs are printed, the middle sections being placed in the Appendix.

6. Two of the various editions made by John Clarke (Clarke-Whitfeld) for a number of different publishers between the beginning of the century and

[1] Although the title-page declares 'Printed by Clementi, Collard & Collard 26 Cheapside', yet at the foot of the final page is 'Peck engraved 1813', just as it is in 'Peck's Edition of Handel's *Messiah*. . . . Printed and Sold by James Peck, 47 Lombard Street 1813'.

his death in 1836, namely the early Button, Whittaker and Beadnell edition and the edition published by 'Jones & Co. (Temple of the Muses), Finsbury Square, MDCCCXXXV'. The former has an appendix containing most of the various alternatives and is therefore almost complete. The latter is a general-purpose edition without alternative settings, and its contents therefore are a reasonably reliable indication of what constituted a *Messiah* performance in the early part of the second quarter of the century.

7. Two of the various editions prepared for R. Cocks and Co. by John Bishop (1817–1890), an organist of Cheltenham—not to be confused with Sir Henry Bishop (1786–1855), Professor of Music in the University of Oxford, who also edited the oratorio. John Bishop's editions included the Centenary Edition (1841), Library Edition (1852), People's Edition (1855), Students' Edition (1855), and Festival Edition (1857), and of these I have selected the Centenary (a popular edition without choice of alternative settings) and the Library (a very complete edition containing, in addition to all the alternatives, the Mozart arrangements of 'The trumpet shall sound' and 'If God be for us'). The Centenary Edition is noteworthy on two counts; it shows that the performance of the G minor soprano air 'How beautiful' without the middle section was becoming the general practice by 1841, and it precedes the later 'duet' version of 'He shall feed His flock' (the first stanza for alto) with the recitative at the original soprano pitch. The Library setting shares with the 1787 Arnold edition the distinction of including 'But who may abide' in the recitative setting. It also shares with the Arnold the questionable distinction of indicating *da capo* at the end of 'Why do the nations'—perhaps a pardonable peccadillo, as the 1749 *Songs in Messiah* also indicates *da capo* for this air.

8. The Rimbault Edition, published in 1850; although prepared for the English Handel Society it does not contain any of Handel's alternative settings, but finds space for the 'Mozart' versions of 'The trumpet shall sound' and 'If God be for us'; it includes the original all-$\frac{3}{8}$ setting for bass of 'But who may abide' and the setting for soprano of 'Thou art gone up on high' to the exclusion of the later Guadagni settings of these airs (both in autograph and written for Handel's favourite male alto, Guadagni); it gives only the first section of the G minor air 'How beautiful'; and sins with the rest in indicating *da capo* for 'Why do the nations'.

9. There remains one other edition chosen for this list—that edited by Sir George Elvey (1816–93), Organist of the Chapel Royal, Windsor. Elvey's claim on our attention is that he studied under Crotch, who in turn had studied under John Randall (1715–1799), who sang the name-part in the 1732 performance of *Esther*, later becoming Professor of Music in the University of Cambridge, where he was responsible for performances of Handel's works. Elvey's edition, dated 1854 and advertised 'as performed by the London Sacred Harmonic Society', was published by J. Surman, conductor of that society. In view of Elvey's direct succession from Handel and of the later publication by the Sacred Harmonic Society of the facsimile of the Autograph

score one might reasonably expect this to be a complete and scholarly volume. But this is not so. The edition is, however, exceptional in one respect; although 'He shall feed His flock' is printed in the 'duet' version (i.e. with the first stanza transposed for alto into F major), it is preceded by the recitative neither in Smith's transposed alto-pitch version from the Tenbury–Dublin manuscript nor in Handel's soprano-pitch original from the Autograph score, but in yet another version. Now, a favourite transition of Handel's is to the submediant, usually not to the relative minor but from a minor key to its submediant major: e.g. the B minor of 'The people that walked in darkness' to the G major of 'For unto us a Child is born'—the D major of 'Glory to God' to the B♭ major 'Rejoice greatly'—the G minor of 'Behold the Lamb of God' to the E♭ major of 'He was despised'—the C minor of 'He trusted in God' to the A♭ opening of 'Thy rebuke'. The relationship between the recitative 'Then shall the eyes of the blind' and the following air 'He shall feed His flock' is such a case. In the Autograph, where Handel wrote both stanzas of the air in B♭ major, he ends the preceding recitative with a perfect cadence in D minor. When Smith, in the Tenbury–Dublin manuscript, transposed the first stanza of the air down, for alto, into F major, he also transposed the recitative so that it ended with a perfect cadence in A minor and so preserved Handel's key-relationship. If Elvey knew of Smith's transposed recitative or of Handel's key scheme, he obviously did not approve of either, for he wrote a transposition of his own. Inserting a signature of two flats, he began the vocal line on the note F and so ended with a perfect cadence in C minor. This apart, the edition is just another general-purpose publication without alternative settings, the settings selected being those established by general usage at that time—settings that continued generally to be sung for another hundred years.

APPENDIX B
VARIATIONS IN FIGURING

Overture

In the 37 bars in the Autograph score (bars 38–98 inclusive are missing from the Autograph score) there is not a single figure. In the Tenbury–Dublin copy there is just one figuring, a $^{4+}_{2}$ in bar 95 beat 4. In Randall and Abell there are 158 figurings.

Bar 7, beat 4 in Randall and Abell is figured 5; in *Songs in Messiah* (first edition) it is $^{6}_{5}$; although the 6 is not raised it implies the addition of D♯ to the harmony.

Bar 24, beat 4 in Randall and Abell is figured $^{4+}_{6}$; in *Songs in Messiah* it is 4. The harmony is $^{6}_{4}$.

Bar 26, beats 1 and 2. Note the implication of the figuring in all three publications of $^{4}_{2}$.

Bar 51, beat 4. Note the implication of the figuring in all three publications of $^{6}_{5}$. Although the 5 is not lowered it implies the addition of F♮ to the harmony.

Bar 71, beats 1 and 3, in the Randall and Abell score are figured $^{5}_{4}$ $^{5}_{♯}$, in *Songs in Messiah* they are $^{6}_{4}$ $^{5}_{♯}$. The $^{6}_{4}$ implies a note G in the harmony. This is possible as the F♯ is in the violin II° and there is not a tenor F♯ in the orchestra.

'Comfort ye'

In the 37 bars in the Autograph score there are 6 figurings.
          in the Tenbury–Dublin copy there are 8 figurings.
          in Randall and Abell there are 43 figurings.
The pages containing bars 1–13 are missing from the Autograph score.

'Every valley'

In the 84 bars in the Autograph score
      in the Tenbury–Dublin copy } there is no figuring.
      in Randall and Abell there are 179 figurings.

A number of $^{6}_{5}$ figurings and one 5 figuring in Randall and Abell are 6 in *Songs in Messiah*.

Bar 32 in *Songs in Messiah* figures 6 on the 6th quaver for 6, but on the 7th quaver the 6 stands for $^{6}_{5}$.

Bar 35 the 3rd quaver Randall and Abell and *Songs in Messiah* figure 6 for $^{6}_{4}$.

Bar 40, beats 3 and 4, *Songs in Messiah* figures 4♯ for $^{6}_{4}$ $^{5}_{♯}$.

Bar 69 the 5th quaver, note the implication of the $^{6}_{5}$ in *The Songs in Messiah*.

171

'And the glory'

In the 138 bars in the Autograph score ⎫
                in the Tenbury–Dublin copy ⎬ there are 7 figurings.
                in Randall and Abell there are 97 figurings.
Handel's figuring of the *bassetti* should be noted.

'Thus saith the Lord'

In the 30 bars in the Autograph score there are 8 figurings.
                in the Tenbury–Dublin copy there are 7 figurings.
                in Randall and Abell there are 39 figurings.
    N.B.—In *The Songs in Messiah* there are also 39 figurings, but in *Songs in Messiah* there is not a single figuring.

'But who may abide' (bass setting)

In the 136 bars in the Autograph score there are 51 figurings.
                in the Tenbury–Dublin copy there are 47 figurings.
                In Randall and Abell there are 134 figurings.

'But who may abide' (Guadagni setting)

In the 158 bars the Autograph manuscript in the Tenbury–Dublin copy has 30 figurings
    The Randall and Abell score has 192 figurings.
    This Guadagni setting is not printed in *Songs in Messiah*.
    Bar 7, beat 3: Handel figured $\frac{4+}{2}$ in error for $\frac{4+}{3}$.
    Bar 121, beat 3: Handel figured 6 in mistake for $\frac{6}{\flat}$.
    Bar 147, beat 1: The Autograph manuscript has 3 for $\frac{4+}{3}$. But there may have been other figures there originally, for the page has been trimmed before binding.

'And He shall purify'

In the 58 bars in the Autograph score ⎫
                in the Tenbury–Dublin copy ⎬ there are 25 figurings.
                in Randall and Abell there are 139 figurings.
    N.B.—In bar 4 Handel figured a 6 on the 4th quaver; the Randall and Abell engraver placed it against the 5th quaver. Chrysander realized the 5th quaver as $\frac{5}{3}$, but it is generally realized as $\frac{6}{3}$.

'Behold, a Virgin shall conceive'

In the 6 bars in the Autograph score there are 5 figurings.
                in the Tenbury–Dublin copy ⎫
                in Randall and Abell ⎬ there are 7 figurings.

The additional two figurings in the Tenbury–Dublin copy are under the first two chords in the cadence bar.

Bars 2 and 3: in the Autograph score Handel repeated the $\frac{7}{4}$ figuring of bar 2, beat 3 in bar 3 beat 1 under the sustained note d (see The Basso-continuo Figuring, p. 133).

'O Thou that tellest' (air and chorus)

In the 130 bars in the Autograph score there are 17 figurings.
in the Tenbury–Dublin copy there are 15 figurings.
in Randall and Abell there are 140 figurings.

In bar 39 the 4th quaver is generally realized as a $\frac{5}{3}$. In Randall and Abell it is figured 6, but in *Songs in Messiah* it is 6♯. If it is to be a 6, obviously it must be sharpened. Many $\frac{6}{5}$ figurings in the Randall and Abell score are 6 in *Songs in Messiah*.

'For behold, darkness shall cover the earth'

In the 23 bars in the Autograph score there are 14 figurings.
in the Tenbury–Dublin copy there are 11 figurings.
in Randall and Abell there are 36 figurings.

'The people that walked in darkness'

In the 63 bars in the Autograph score
in the Tenbury–Dublin copy } there is no figuring.
in Randall and Abell there are 42 figurings.

N.B.—The figuring ♯ under the first note and the last quaver in bars 4, 19, and 34; and in bar 23 in *Songs in Messiah* and Randall and Abell 6 5 ♯, in *The Songs in Messiah* $\frac{6}{3♮}$ 5 ♯, and in RM 19.d.1 $\frac{6}{♮}$ ♯.

'For unto us a Child is born'

In the 99 bars in the Autograph score
in the Tenbury–Dublin copy } there are 22 figurings.
in Randall and Abell there are 113 figurings.

Single basso-continuo notes, as on beats 1 and 3 of bars 21, 22, and 23, are often erroneously played unharmonized. Handel made it clear that they should be harmonized by the figuring ♯ that he wrote under beat 1 bar 22 and the figuring ♮ that he wrote under beat 3 of bar 58.

The Pastoral Symphony

In the 21 bars in the Autograph score
in the Tenbury–Dublin copy } there is 1 figuring, a ♯ under the second minim in bar 15.
in Randall and Abell there is no figuring.

'There were shepherds abiding in the field'

In the 4 bars in the Autograph score

     in the Tenbury–Dublin copy } there are 2 figurings.

     in Randall and Abell

  In *Songs in Messiah* there is only 1 figuring: a $\frac{7}{2}$ at bar 2, beat 3.

  In the Tenbury–Dublin copy, in the last bar, there is a meaningless $\frac{4}{3}$; but against the 4 is a blunt pencil mark (the 4 is in ink). This may have been an attempt to alter the 4 to 5, or an intended suspension may inadvertently have been written vertically instead of horizontally, as inversely in 'He shall feed His flock', bar 23 in *Songs in Messiah* where the cadential $\frac{6\ 5}{4\ 3}$ was figured $\frac{6\ 4}{5\ 3}$.

'And lo!' (recitative *accompagnato* setting)

In the 7 bars in the Autograph score

     in the Tenbury–Dublin copy } there are 4 figurings.

     in Randall and Abell

'But lo!' [*sic*] (arioso setting)

In the 31 bars in the Autograph score there are 5 figurings.

     in Randall and Abell there are 54 figurings.

'And the angel said unto them'

In the 9 bars in the Autograph score

     in the Tenbury–Dublin copy } there are 4 figurings.

     in Randall and Abell there are 6 figurings.

'And suddenly'

In the 8 bars in the Autograph score there are 5 figurings.

     in the Tenbury–Dublin copy there are 3 figurings.

     in Randall and Abell there are 7 figurings.

  Bar 2, beats 1 and 2, are generally printed incorrectly as $\frac{6}{2}$; Handel's harmony in the strings is $\frac{6}{4}$. The note on the second and third semiquavers in violin II° is generally printed as E; in the Autograph score Handel clearly wrote D; further, he figured it $\frac{6}{4}$. This $\frac{6}{4}$ was written by Smith in the Tenbury–Dublin copy and printed in *Songs in Messiah*. However, in Randall and Abell and *The Songs in Messiah* it was printed as $\frac{6}{2}$.

'Glory to God'

In the 49 bars in the Autograph score there are 36 figurings.

     in the Tenbury–Dublin copy there are 32 figurings.

     in Randall and Abell there are 47 figurings.

Handel's figuring of 6 in bar 11, beat 2, is generally realized as $^6_4$. This is a mistake. Handel often used the discord of the major seventh.

'Rejoice greatly' ($^4_4$ setting)

In the 108 bars in the autograph setting in the Tenbury–Dublin copy there is not a single figuring.[1]

In Randall and Abell there are 189 figurings, only 16 bars being left unfigured.

'Rejoice greatly' ($^{12}_8$ setting)

In the 117 bars in the Autograph score there are 8 figurings.[1]
             in Randall and Abell there are 235 figurings.
(The Tenbury–Dublin copy contains only the $^4_4$ setting.)

'Then shall the eyes of the blind be opened'

In the 8 bars in the Autograph score there are 3 figurings.
          in the Tenbury–Dublin copy there are 4 figurings.
In Randall and Abell there are 8 figurings.

'He shall feed His flock'

In the 56 bars in the Autograph score
         in the Tenbury–Dublin copy   } there are 12 figurings.
         in Randall and Abell there are 98 figurings.
The Autograph score and the Tenbury–Dublin copy differ in the last quaver in bar 23. The Autograph score has $^♭_6$. Smith, in copying the Tenbury–Dublin manuscript, omitted the necessary ♭. The $^♭_6$ is here used for $^6_{4♭}$.

Bar 30: Randall and Abell and *The Songs in Messiah* figured $^6_4$ $^5_{3♮}$ on the 4th and 6th quavers respectively; but *Songs in Messiah* has only a ♮ against the 4th quaver.

'His yoke is easy'

In the 51 bars in the Autograph score there are 25 figurings.
         in the Tenbury–Dublin copy there are 22 figurings.
         in Randall and Abell there are 96 figurings.
Bar 2: the 3rd quaver usually figured 6 is figured 5 in the Autograph score.

'Behold the Lamb of God'

In the 32 bars in the Autograph score
         in the Tenbury–Dublin copy   } there are 7 figurings.
         in Randall and Abell there are 53 figurings.

[1] See The Basso-continuo Figuring, p. 130.

'He was despised'

In the 68 bars in the Autograph score there are 16 figurings.

       in the Tenbury–Dublin copy there is no figuring.

       in Randall and Abell there are 120 figurings.

In the Tenbury–Dublin copy many pages of this air are missing; only 30 bars remain.

Bars 36 and 37: in *Songs in Messiah* the $^7_5{}^\flat$ is printed three times under the diminished seventh harmony which is sustained by the strings for six slow crotchet beats (see introductory notes to the section).

Bar 27, beat 3: Note the figuring $\natural$ for $^7_\natural$.

Bar 31, beat 2: Note the figuring 6 for $^6_{5\flat}$.

Bar 47, beat 3: In *Songs in Messiah* (first edition) this is figured $6\flat$, but in the later edition it is figured $^6_4{}^\flat$.

This air provides examples of Handel's use of 3 for 7 and 6 for $^6_5$.

'Surely He has borne our griefs'

In the 26 bars in the Autograph score there are 39 figurings.

       in the Tenbury–Dublin copy there are 40 figurings.

       in Randall and Abell there are 71 figurings.

Bar 25, beat 1: As Handel used the one flat less key signature convention the 6 in this figuring requires to be flattened. Handel, in the Autograph score, wrote it incorrectly as $^6_{5\flat}$. Smith copied it so in the Tenbury–Dublin copy, but it was printed correctly in Randall and Abell as $^6_5{}^\flat$.

Bar 14, beat 1: in the orchestral and vocal parts the harmony is $^9_3$. Handel figured it 7.

Bar 25, beat 2: The harmony in the orchestra is 6; Handel figured it $^6_{5\flat}$ for the keyboard continuo player.

'And with His stripes'

In the 91 bars in the Autograph score there are 15 figurings.

       in the Tenbury–Dublin copy there are 11 figurings.

       in Randall and Abell there are 94 figurings.

'All we like sheep'

In the 92 bars in the Autograph score   ⎱
    in the Tenbury–Dublin copy   ⎰ there are 6 figurings.

       in Randall and Abell there are 99 figurings.

Bars 90 and 91: Note the figuring $4\natural$ for $^{6\flat}_4\ ^5_\natural$.

'All they that see Him'

In the 11 bars in the Autograph score   ⎱
   in the Tenbury–Dublin copy   ⎰ there are 6 figurings.

       in Randall and Abell there are 17 figurings.

'He trusted in God'

In the 63 bars in the Autograph score
       in the Tenbury–Dublin copy   } there are 36 figurings.
       in Randall and Abell there are 133 figurings.

    Bar 8, beat 3: with only E♮ and G in the orchestra and voices on the beat but with the tenor moving to the note C on the second quaver Handel here figured 7.

    Bars 8 and 9, beat 1 is indicative that where a choral voice has a rest on an accent followed by a descending step of a second from the note before the rest and where Handel did not trouble to write out the notes in the orchestral staves but merely wrote the direction to the copyist 'Ut Cant', etc., it was his intention that in the orchestral parts there should not be a rest but that the previous note should be tied over.

    Bar 26, beat 1: On the first quaver of the beat the harmony is in doubt for the only notes in orchestra and voices are B♭ and G. On the second quaver the alto moves to the note E♮ and so provides a root to the harmony. Handel figured this beat $\frac{6}{5}$. I suggest that this is in error for $\frac{6}{4}\!\!\!_{3}$.

    Bar 42, beat 2: In the choral alto Handel cancelled out the sharp of the previous bar by using a natural but in the figuring indicated it erroneously by raising the sixth ♯6. Smith copied it so in the Tenbury–Dublin copy, but it was corrected to 6♮ in Randall and Abell.

    Bar 45, beat 1: Handel here figured $\frac{4}{2}$ in error for $\frac{4\sharp}{2}$. Smith copied it so into the Tenbury–Dublin copy; but it was corrected in Randall and Abell.

'Thy rebuke hath broken His heart'

In the 18 bars in the Autograph score
       in the Tenbury–Dublin copy   } there are 20 figurings.
       in Randall and Abell there are 21 figurings.

    Handel's regard for the key progression in this accompanied recitative is shown by the unusual trouble he took in figuring the bass.

    In 18 bars he wrote 20 figurings. He figured all but two of the changes of harmony, those in bars 12 and 15.

    In Randall and Abell and *The Songs in Messiah* the figuring $\frac{7}{\natural}$ was added for bar 12, but in *Songs in Messiah* it was figured 5.

'Behold and see'

In the 15 bars in the Autograph score there are 18 figurings.
       in the Tenbury–Dublin copy there are 17 figurings.
       in Randall and Abell there are 29 figurings.

    Bar 3, the second quaver. This bar as Handel first wrote it was the same as bar 5 except that it consisted only of the vocal melody and the basso-continuo. Handel then altered the first two quavers in the voice part and the second quaver in the basso-continuo but failed to remove the ♯ figuring which now was incorrect. On many occasions Smith copied Handel's errors into the Tenbury–Dublin copy but in this case he corrected the error by omitting the sharp.

Bar 12, the third quaver is figured 6 in Randall and Abell and *Songs in Messiah* (first edition and *circa* 1769 edition) but has been realized by a modern editor as $\frac{6}{\sharp}$. It is unfigured in the Autograph.

'He was cut off out of the land of the living'

In the 5 bars in the Autograph score
   in the Tenbury–Dublin copy } there are 6 figurings.
   in Randall and Abell there are 7 figurings.
Bar 1, beat 3: Handel figured this $\frac{7\sharp}{2}$ in error. (He used here the one sharp less key signature.) It was copied so in the Tenbury–Dublin copy and printed in *Songs in Messiah* but it was corrected in Randall and Abell and *The Songs in Messiah*.

'But Thou did not leave His soul in hell'

In the 43 bars in the Autograph score
   in the Tenbury–Dublin copy } there are 4 figurings.
   in Randall and Abell there are 128 figurings.
Bar 14 : Handel figured only a ♯ in this bar and Smith copied it so in the Tenbury–Dublin copy. In the Randall and Abell and *The Songs in Messiah*, however, there is a $\frac{6}{4}$ under the first quaver, although the third from the bass is in the voice, and $\frac{5}{\sharp}$ under the third quaver; this is an editorial anticipation of cadential ornamentation.

Songs in Messiah is not consistent, for while bar 14 is figured ♯, the essentially identical bar 37 is figured 4 3.

Bar 4 the third quaver and bar 16 the second quaver. *Songs in Messiah* differs from *The Songs in Messiah* in figuring 6 as against $\frac{6}{4}$.

Chrysander realizes bar 4, 3rd quaver, as $\frac{6}{3}$ and bar 16, 2nd quaver, as $\frac{6}{3\sharp}$.

Prout realizes bar 4, 3rd quaver, as $\frac{6}{2}$ and bar 16, 2nd quaver, as $\frac{6}{4}$.

'Lift up your heads'

In the 77 bars in the Autograph score there are 58 figurings.
   in Randall and Abell there are 114 figurings.
In the Tenbury–Dublin copy the pages containing bars 18–60 inclusive are missing from the manuscript. For the remaining bars the figuring in that copy is identical with the figuring in the Autograph score with the exception that Smith omitted to copy in the Tenbury–Dublin copy the four figurings of 6 in bar 11

'Unto which of the angels'

In the 5 bars in the Autograph score there are 3 figurings.
          in the Tenbury–Dublin copy there are 2 figurings.
          in Randall and Abell there are 3 figurings.

'Let all the angels'

In the 37 bars in the Autograph score there are 8 figurings.
          in the Tenbury–Dublin copy there are 7 figurings.
          in Randall and Abell there are 52 figurings.
Note the figuring ♯ in the *bassetti* bar 15 beat 2.

'Thou art gone up on high' (bass setting)

In the 124 bars in the Autograph score
in the Tenbury–Dublin copy } there are 2 figurings.
in Randall and Abell there are 121 figurings.
   The two figurings in the Autograph score occur in bar 53 beats 1 and 3: they are respectively ♯ and 6. Having written the sharp fortuitously (for there are many other places where an indication of the quality of the third is much more necessary), he wrote the 6 in order to guard against a realization of the C♯ as a $\frac{5}{3}$.
   Bar 123, beat 1: Note the figuring 6 in the Randall and Abell score. This is generally realized as a $\frac{7}{3}$.

'Thou art gone up on high' (Guadagni alto setting)

In the 116 bars in the autograph manuscript in the Tenbury–Dublin copy there are 12 figurings.
   In Randall and Abell there are 192 figurings.
   Bar 31: In this bar the basso-continuo consists of a crotchet note on the first beat followed by two crotchet rests. Under the note is the figuring 5 and under the following rest is the figuring 6. There are several indications throughout the manuscripts that Handel played not only over *bassetti* but in certain cases even over rests in the basso-continuo.

'The Lord gave the word'

In the 25 bars in the Autograph score
in the Tenbury–Dublin copy } there is no figuring.
in Randall and Abell there are 19 figurings.

'How beautiful are the feet' (G minor *da capo* air setting)

In the 33 bars in the Autograph score there are 2 figurings.
          in the Tenbury–Dublin copy there is no figuring.
          in Randall and Abell there are 113 figurings.

The two figurings in the Autograph score are both the same, a ♯ in bars 33 and 35. They merely mark the modulation to D minor which had already been made very clear in bar 30 by the music itself.

Bar 1, 10th quaver: The figuring 2 (Randall and Abell) is used here and elsewhere throughout this air not for $\frac{4}{2}$ but for the 4 3 suspension with the suspension in the bass $\frac{5}{2}$.

Bar 21, 6th quaver, is figured $\frac{6}{4}$ in Randall and Abell ($\frac{6}{4}$ in *The Songs in Messiah*) for $\frac{4}{2}$.

'How beautiful are the feet' (alto duet and chorus setting)

In the 161 bars in autograph in the Appendix to the Autograph score there are 2 figurings.
In the Randall and Abell score there are 126.

'Their sound is gone out' (chorus setting)

In the 38 bars in autograph in the Appendix to the Autograph score there are 5 figurings.

In the Randall and Abell score there are 46 figurings.

This chorus is not in the Tenbury–Dublin copy. (See chapter on alternative settings.)

Bar 5, beat 4: The string harmony on this beat is the first inversion of F minor. But the soprano and first oboe part (clearly an ornamental resolution of a dissonant E upon D) lends authority to the figuring $\frac{6}{5}$ in Randall and Abell.

'Their sound is gone out' (arioso setting)

In the 23 bars (in the Appendix to the Autograph score, but not in Handel's writing) there are 19 figurings.

In Randall and Abell there are 40 figurings.

This setting does not exist in autograph. (See chapter on alternative settings.)

'Why do the nations'

In the 96 bars in the Autograph score
in the Tenbury–Dublin copy } there are 4 figurings.
in the Randall and Abell copy there are 113 figurings.

Bar 95 in the Autograph Score the Tenbury–Dublin copy, and *Songs in Messiah* is figured 4 ♯; but in the Randall and Abell score and in *The Songs in Messiah* it is figured simply ♯. When, in the Tenbury–Dublin copy, Handel wrote the accompanied recitative alternative ending, he harmonized it in the strings as follows:

'Let us break their bonds asunder'

In the 67 bars in the Autograph score there are 8 figurings.
in the Tenbury–Dublin copy there is 1 figuring.
in Randall and Abell there are 48 figurings.

Bar 57, last quaver, and bar 61, first quaver: the harmony, unfigured in the Autograph, is a plain triad, but Randall and Abell figure $\frac{6}{5}$ and 7 respectively.

'He that dwelleth in Heaven'

In the 4 bars in the Autograph score and in the Tenbury–Dublin copy there are 4 figurings. In Randall and Abell there are 6, one for each harmony.

'Thou shalt break them'

In the 74 bars in the Autograph score and the Tenbury–Dublin copy there is just 1 figuring. In Randall and Abell there are 87.

Handel's single figuring is a ♯ in bar 66, beat 1.

Bar 20, beat 1: The Randall and Abell figuring of 6 is incorrect; the figuring for the bar should be 7 6♯.

Bar 29, beats 2 and 3: Handel has given the third of the harmony to the voice on beat 2 (the root is in the basso-continuo), but in Randall and Abell the figuring is $\frac{6}{4}\frac{5}{3}$, another case of editorial anticipation of cadential ornamentation.

'Hallelujah'

In the 94 bars in the Autograph score there are 17 figurings.
in the Tenbury–Dublin copy there are 13.
in Randall and Abell there are 138.

The Tenbury–Dublin copy may have contained more figurings; the pages containing bars 6, 14, 34, and 35 have been trimmed prior to binding.

Bar 38, beats 3 and 4: in the Autograph score figured $\frac{6}{4}\frac{5}{3}$, in the Tenbury–Dublin copy $\frac{4}{5}\frac{5}{3}$.

Handel was in error in figuring $\frac{5}{3}$ for $\frac{6}{4}$, and Smith added to this the error of figuring the third beat $\frac{4}{5}$ with the sixth from the bass in trumpet I°, violin I°, and choral alto. Both Handel and Smith were doubtless confused by the almost identical bar 34, in which on the fourth beat Handel first wrote the note A in the basso-continuo, afterwards altering it to G. The Randall and Abell score has the figuring correctly as $\frac{6}{4}\frac{4}{2}$.

'I know that my Redeemer liveth'

In the 164 bars in the Autograph score
in the Tenbury–Dublin copy } there are 8 figurings.
in Randall and Abell there are 152.

Bar 2, beat 3: Handel figured this as 6, but in Randall and Abell and

The Songs in Messiah it was figured 6 5, the 5 representing the semiquaver passing note. In *Songs in Messiah*, however, it was figured just 6. It would appear that at the harpsichord Handel was content with a crotchet chord, leaving the passing note to the *obbligato* instrument.

Bar 14, beats 2 and 3: The second beat is the root position of the dominant harmony, with the third from the root in the *obbligato* violins, but in the Randall and Abell score this beat is figured 4 and the following beat 3. This is of particular interest as evidence of instrumental cadential ornamentation. Both the first edition and *circa* 1769 edition of *Songs in Messiah* figure 4 on beat 2.

Bar 34, beats 2 and 3: This is another case where with root and third in the parts Randall and Abell figured 4 3 in editorial anticipation of cadential ornamentation. (See also bars 74, 87, and 160.) In bar 74 in Randall and Abell the figuring is not just 4 3 (which could be $\frac{5-}{4\,3}$) but $\frac{6}{4}\,\frac{5}{3}$.

'Since by man came death'

In the 6 bars there is only one basso-continuo note and that is not figured in the Autograph score or any copies or editions.

'By man came also'

In the 10 bars in the Autograph score
  in the Tenbury–Dublin copy } there is no figuring.
  in Randall and Abell there are 17 figurings.

'For as in Adam'

In the 6 bars there is only one basso-continuo note and that is figured ♮ in the Autograph score, the Tenbury–Dublin copy and the Randall and Abell score.

'Even so in Christ'

In the 15 bars in the Autograph score
  in the Tenbury–Dublin copy } there are 16 figurings.
  in Randall and Abell there are 25 figurings.

'Behold I tell you a mystery'

In the 8 bars in the Autograph score
  in the Tenbury–Dublin copy } there is no figuring.
  in Randall and Abell there are 6 figurings.

'The trumpet shall sound'

In the 213 bars in the Autograph score there are 9 figurings.
  in the Tenbury–Dublin copy there are 10 figurings.
  in Randall and Abell there are 162 figurings.

The additional figuring in the Tenbury–Dublin copy, a ♯ in bar 76 beat 3, is without significance.

Bar 27, beat 2: With a $\frac{5}{3}$ in the orchestra the figuring in the Randell and Abell score is 4 followed on the 3rd beat by 3. A notable case of editorial anticipation of instrumental cadential ornamentation, as it concerns not merely the harpsichord and violin I° but also violin II°.

Bar 37, beat 1, usually realized as a $\frac{5}{3}$, is figured in Randall and Abell as 6.

Bar 190, beat 1, figured 6 in Randall and Abell, is often realized as 5. The sixth must, of course, be raised. In bar 193, beat 1, Randall and Abell again figures 6 without indicating the sharp; but *The Songs in Messiah* prints it correctly as ♯.

'Then shall be brought to pass'

In the 5 bars in the Autograph score
      in the Tenbury–Dublin copy } there are 2 figurings.
      In Randall and Abell there are 3 figurings.

In bar 3 it almost looks as if Handel in figuring a diatonic augmented 4th departed absent-mindedly from his usual practice and raised the figure 4 so: $\frac{4}{2}$.

'O Death, where is thy sting'

In the 41 bars in the Autograph score
      in the Tenbury–Dublin copy } there are 6 figurings.
      in Randall and Abell there are 112 figurings.

Bar 32, beats 3 and 4: In the Randall and Abell score the only figuring is a ♮ on the 3rd beat; but in *The Songs in Messiah* the figuring is $\frac{6}{4}$ $\frac{5}{♮}$ on the 3rd and 4th beats respectively. Another case of editorial anticipation of cadential ornamentation, this time with two singers.

'Thanks be to God'

In the 91 bars in the Autograph score
      in the Tenbury–Dublin copy } there are 2 figurings
      in Randall and Abell there are 101 figurings.

'If God be for us'

In the 178 bars in the Autograph score
      in the Tenbury–Dublin copy } there are 18 figurings.
      in Randall and Abell there are 169 figurings.

Bar 72, beats 2 and 3: With the 3rd of the dominant harmony in the violin and the root in the basso continuo the figuring is 4 3. Another case of editorial anticipation of instrumental cadential ornamentation. (See also bar 106 where the Randall and Abell figuring is 4 ♮.)

'Worthy is the Lamb'

In the 71 bars in the Autograph score there are 51 figurings.
> in the Tenbury–Dublin copy there are 48 figurings.
> in Randall and Abell there are 119 figurings.

The discrepancy between the Autograph score and the Tenbury–Dublin copy is accounted for in one instance by the trimming of a page and in the other two instances sheer forgetfulness on the part of Smith.

'Amen'

In the 88 bars in the Autograph score there are 47 figurings.
> in the Tenbury–Dublin copy there are 39 figurings.
> in Randall and Abell there are 109 figurings.

Bar 17, beat 4: with only the notes E in the soprano and C♯ in the tenor Handel figured the C♯ in the *bassetti* 7.

SERIATIM LIST OF TEXTUAL VARIANTS

OVERTURE

Bar 4, last note, violin II°

In the Autograph score this note d' is without cancellation of the ♯ against the previous d' on the fourth quaver of the same bar. The note is, however, unquestionably natural for according to the practice followed by Handel each note is diatonic unless it is expressly marked otherwise. There are many similar cases.

Bar 21, 3rd quaver, violin I°

In Autograph score c''

In Tenbury–Dublin copy ⎫
   Hamburg copy ⎬ c''♯
   RM 18.e.2 copy ⎭

This is obviously an error of omission in the Autograph score. Cf. violin II° bar 18.

Bar 22, beat 2 2nd quaver, violin I°

In Autograph score ⎫
   Tenbury–Dublin copy ⎪
   Hamburg copy ⎬ c''
   RM 18.e.2 copy ⎭

As the note c'' is purely a decoration of the note d'' this could be regarded as an error of omission similar to that in bar 21; but less certainly so.

Bar 36, beat 2, viola

In Autograph score ⎫
   Tenbury–Dublin copy ⎪
   Hamburg copy ⎬ e'
   RM 18.e.2 copy ⎭

In Randall and Abell ⎫
   printed score ⎬ d'

Although in the Autograph score the notehead spreads down completely into the d' space, it is Handel's usual pointed shape for notes on a line. Yet in the equivalent place, bar 87 (bars 32 and 34 are not equivalent), in the Tenbury–Dublin copy (the page containing bar 87 is missing from the Autograph), the 2nd beat is harmonized as a $\frac{5}{3}$ with the third of the chord in the viola. Chrysander prints e' in the viola part, but d' in the keyboard realization.

Bar 37 to the end

The pages containing these bars are missing from the Autograph. Bars 1 to 55 are missing from the Tenbury–Dublin copy also.

Bar 64, beats 2 and 3, viola

In Tenbury–Dublin copy ⎫
   Hamburg copy ⎬ e'
   RM 18.e.2 copy ⎭

In Randall and Abell ⎫
   printed score ⎬ d' with $\frac{6}{5}$ figuring

The reading d¹ would seem to be in error, for bars 64 and 65 are basically a harmonic sequential repetition of bars 62 and 63; the harmony of the first of each two bars is in the root position, that of the second in the first inversion. In the Hamburg copy this is one of several cases of notes 'corrected' in pencil. These notes are pencilled through and in the margin are the letters 'DD'. The remaining corrections and copyist's errors will not be referred to unless they have a bearing upon other evidence.

Bar 67, beat 4, viola	In Tenbury–Dublin copy	Only a minute spot of ink remains, with the faint outline of a sharp.
	In other MSS.	a'♯

Bar 85, Violin I°	In Tenbury–Dublin copy	The first part of this bar is in bad condition

'COMFORT YE'

Bars 1–13 inclusive	The pages containing these bars are missing from the Autograph.

Bar 15, beat 4, basso-continuo	In Autograph score	Both quavers are A

	In Tenbury–Dublin copy
	   Hamburg copy
	   RM 18.e.2 copy
	   Randall and Abell
	      printed score
		Both quavers are B

Smith was guilty of several copying errors. Once made, there is no safeguard against the repetition of the error (cf. 'Every valley', bar 14, the 1st quaver, viola). Chrysander's argument in the preface to the Handelgesellschaft *Messiah* volume, 'the last two quavers almost look like A; yet G [Goldsmith], O [Tenbury–Dublin] and H [Hamburg] agree in giving B, which will be right', is not securely founded. Handel clearly wrote the notes A, and there can be no argument against them.

Bar 22, beat 4, voice, the note for the word 'is'	In Autograph score
	   Tenbury–Dublin copy
	   Hamburg copy
	   RM 18.e.2 copy
		d'♯

What both Chrysander and Prout state to be the note f'♯ in the Autograph is not a note but an ink-soak from the other side of the page where Handel has inked in a minim head somewhat heavily when turning it into a crotchet. The sharp pointed note head across the line d¹ is clearly to be seen below the blot.

Bar 31 | In Autograph score
Tenbury–Dublin copy
Hamburg copy
RM 18.e.2 copy

In *The Songs in Messiah*

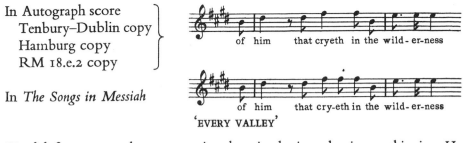

'EVERY VALLEY'

Handel first wrote eleven, not nine, bars in the introduction to this air. He later crossed out two bars, one (a) between bars 5 and 6 and the other (b) between bars 7 and 8.

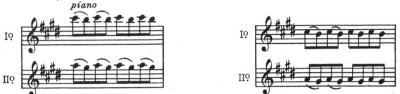

These deletions do not show in the Sacred Harmonic facsimile of 1868. It would seem to have escaped notice that in the Autograph score there are also pencil deletions in the form of wavy lines at bars 70 and 71 to reduce these two bars to one in conformity with the deletions in the introducion.

These wavy lines indicate that the 5th, 6th, 7th and 8th quavers of bar 70 and the 1st, 2nd, 3rd and 4th quavers of bar 71 are to be cut. The vocal semibreve in bar 70 has had a stem added to it. The effect is to make a bar out of the first half of bar 70 and the second half of bar 71. Although this cut has not been observed it is a natural corollary to the cut in the introduction.

Bar 14,
1st quaver,
viola | In Autograph score
Randall and Abell
printed score } c''♯

In Tenbury–Dublin copy
Hamburg copy
RM 18.e.2 copy } b' in error

In the Hamburg copy the notes b' are pencilled through and the letters 'CC' written above.

Bars 26 and 41,
viola | What in the Autograph appears to be a tie over the second and third quavers is intended as a *louré* bowing indication.

Bar 33,
2nd quaver,
viola

In all the MSS.

In Randall and Abell } e¹
  printed score

Some modern editors print d¹. Handel clearly wrote E and in view of the immediately preceding bars there is no reason for reading D.

Bar 35, voice

In Autograph score

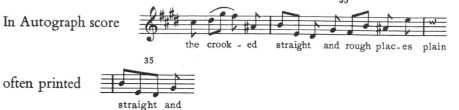

the crook - ed straight and rough plac-es plain

often printed

straight and

Although Handel omitted the word 'the' his grouping of the quavers makes it quite clear that this was in error.

Bar 63,
1st quaver,
violin I°

In Autograph score   Handel clearly wrote *tr* over this note.

In Tenbury–Dublin copy
  Hamburg copy
  RM 18.e.2 copy } Smith omitted to copy the *tr*. The omission has been repeated in subsequent editions

'AND THE GLORY'

Bar 27,
choral alto

In the Autograph Handel first wrote:

shall be re - veal - ed

He then altered the crotchet note a¹ to a minim (the crotchet note-head with stem is still to be seen) with the following word distribution:

shall be re - veal'd, shall be

In Tenbury–Dublin copy
Randall and Abell
  printed score
Arnold
Chrysander
Prout

shall be re - veal - ed be

Bar 35,
choral bass

In Autograph score
  RM 18.e.2 copy

glo-ry of God

In Tenbury–Dublin copy
  Hamburg copy
  Randall and Abell
    printed score

glo-ry of the Lord

Handel's word change was obviously a slip of the pen, but it was a further proof of his desire for three firm crotchets in this bar of the theme, of his intention that 'ry of' should be sung as one syllable when both syllables occur on the second beat.

Bar 54,
basso-continuo

In Autograph score

In Tenbury–Dublin copy
  Hamburg copy
  RM 18.e.2 copy
  Randell and Abell
    printed score

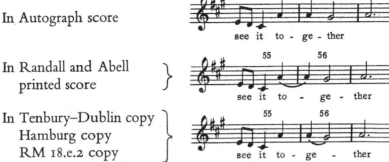

Handel often maintains a sustained basso-continuo against a moving choral bass.

Bars 55 and 56,
choral alto

In Autograph score

In Randall and Abell
  printed score

In Tenbury–Dublin copy
  Hamburg copy
  RM 18.e.2 copy

Handel failed to make clear his syllable distribution. In one of the secondary MS. copies, RM 18.b.10, the two a's over the bar-line were originally tied, but the tie has been erased, apparently with a knife, and a slur drawn over the two notes in bar 56.

Bar 56,
choral bass

In Autograph score
  Tenbury–Dublin copy
  Hamburg copy

In Rm 18.e.2 copy
  Randall and Abell
    printed score

The ♩ ♩ is clearly Handel's intention, for he first continued the tenor in unison with the bass and wrote that also as a minim followed by a crotchet.

Bar 56,
basso-continuo

In Autograph score
  Tenbury–Dublin copy
  Hamburg copy

In RM 18.e.2 copy
  Randall and Abell
    printed score

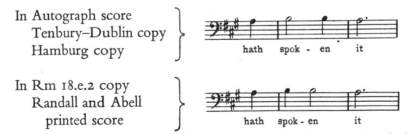

Bar 96, the note d[1],
basso-continuo,
viola and choral
tenor

In Autograph score
Tenbury–Dublin copy } The necessary ♯ is omitted
Hamburg copy

The viola is *without* the necessary ♯ although it is
inserted in the basso-continuo

In RM 18.e.2 copy   The tenor is written without the ♯
Randall and Abell } All three parts have the ♯
printed score

Bar 107,
choral soprano

In Autograph score
RM 18.e.2 copy }

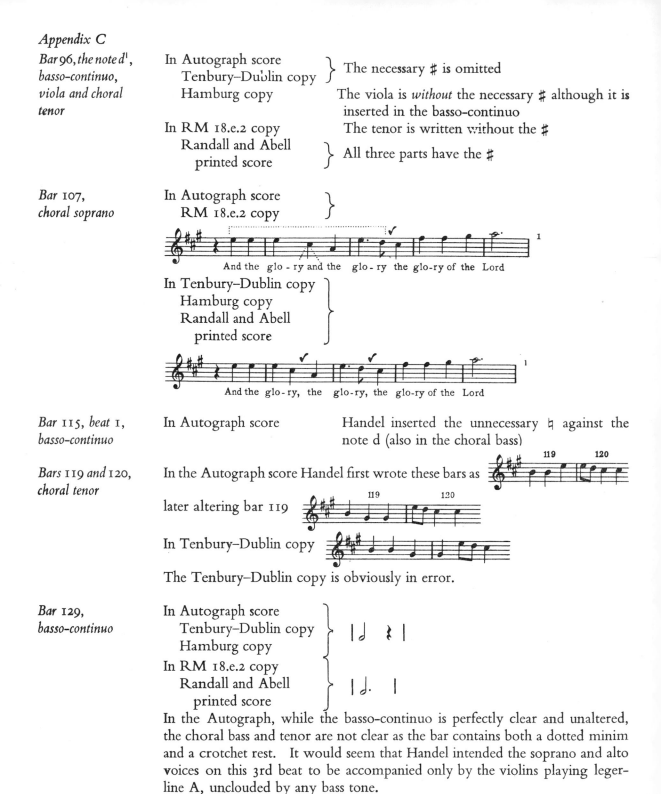

And the glo-ry and the glo-ry the glo-ry of the Lord

In Tenbury–Dublin copy
Hamburg copy
Randall and Abell
printed score

And the glo-ry, the glo-ry, the glo-ry of the Lord

Bar 115, beat 1,
basso-continuo

In Autograph score   Handel inserted the unnecessary ♮ against the
note d (also in the choral bass)

Bars 119 and 120,
choral tenor

In the Autograph score Handel first wrote these bars as

later altering bar 119

In Tenbury–Dublin copy

The Tenbury–Dublin copy is obviously in error.

Bar 129,
basso-continuo

In Autograph score
Tenbury–Dublin copy }
Hamburg copy

In RM 18.e.2 copy
Randall and Abell }
printed score

In the Autograph, while the basso-continuo is perfectly clear and unaltered,
the choral bass and tenor are not clear as the bar contains both a dotted minim
and a crotchet rest. It would seem that Handel intended the soprano and alto
voices on this 3rd beat to be accompanied only by the violins playing leger-
line A, unclouded by any bass tone.

[1] The brackets and phrase marks are editorial.

Bar 136, viola	In the Autograph this bar is not accounted for. Handel obviously omitted to write the necessary dotted minim note a¹.

'THUS SAITH THE LORD'

Bars 1, 5, 7, 8, 9, 25 and 27	In the Autograph score [musical notation]
Bar 3	In the Autograph score [musical notation]
Bar 3, beats 3 and 4, basso-continuo	In Autograph score / RM 18.e.2 copy } [musical notation] In Tenbury–Dublin copy / Hamburg copy } [musical notation]

In the Autograph score Handel first wrote these beats as they appear in the Tenbury–Dublin and Hamburg copies.   He later blotted out the first note and replaced it by a quaver and a semiquaver rest.   When making the Tenbury–Dublin copy, Smith failed to copy Handel's correction of the basso-continuo, and continued the mistake in the Hamburg copy.

Bar 9, beat 1	Handel is often charged with lack of care for detail. Yet at this point having written [musical notation: the sea and the dry land] he then turned the quaver of the word 'sea' into a crotchet and crossed out the quaver rest in order to prevent the descending octave leap from being broken.

Bar 14, beat 1, basso-continuo	In Autograph score / Tenbury–Dublin copy / Hamburg copy } E RM 18.e.2 copy / Randall and Abell printed score } C in error

This mistake has been repeated by later editors.   Handel first wrote e in the third space of the bass stave.   He later ran it through in ink and clearly wrote E on the first leger-line below the stave.

Bar 23, the last quaver, voice	In Autograph score g In Tenbury–Dublin copy / Hamburg copy / RM 18.e.2 copy / *The Songs in Messiah* } f♯

'BUT WHO MAY ABIDE'

Bar 7, 3rd quaver, basso-continuo   Handel wrote $\frac{4}{2}$ in error for $\frac{4}{3}$.

Bar 111,   This bar appears in autograph (in the Tenbury–Dublin copy) **so**:

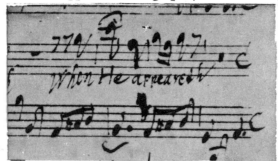

The pause should not be observed in performance.

Handel first wrote   The hook to the stem of the first note is obviously added as is the crotchet stem which he drew through the quaver hook of the second note.   As the pause completely nullifies the time relationship ♪ ♩ that Handel sought in making the alteration, it would appear that he forgot to remove it.

Bars 134 and 135 voice   In Autograph score

The erroneous repetition of the word 'He' and the absence of the tie is due to bar 134 ending one folio and bar 135 beginning the next in the Autograph score.

Bar 146, voice   In Autograph in the Tenbury–Dublin copy Hamburg copy RM 18.e.2 copy

In Randall and Abell printed score

Bar 147 to the end   In the version transposed for soprano, folio 26 verso, in the Hamburg copy:

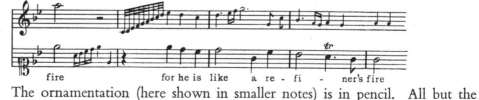

The ornamentation (here shown in smaller notes) is in pencil.   All but the

opening six notes are written on the empty violin I° stave. It is quite possibly Chrysander's writing.

'AND HE SHALL PURIFY'

Bar 5, beat 3,
viola

In the Hamburg copy b'♭ in error; see also bar 38, 3rd quaver, c' in error.

Bar 10, beat 1,
choral alto

In Autograph score
   Tenbury–Dublin copy

The Tenbury–Dublin copy is obviously in error. The comparable notes in the original statement of the *subject* in the soprano and the succeeding *answer* in the bass are even quavers. That the bass has a dotted group in bar 10, beat 1, is no reason for altering the alto *answer*. In the tenor stave bar 27 Handel first wrote a dotted group and then altered it to even quavers.

Bars 15–16,
violin II°, viola
and
basso-continuo

In the following music example the ordinary sized notes show what Handel wrote in the Autograph score. The small sized notes and rests and thin stems and hooks show what Handel inserted in the Tenbury–Dublin copy when he added the *ripieno* instructions. Smith did not copy any of these additions into either the Hamburg copy or RM 18.e.2.

Bar 19, last
quaver, choral
bass

In Autograph score
   Tenbury–Dublin copy
   Hamburg copy
   RM 18.e.2 copy
   Randall and Abell
     printed score } g

In Chrysander
   Prout } b♭

In the Hamburg copy the g has been crossed out in pencil and in the margin is written the letter 'b'.

Bar 23,
3rd quaver,
choral tenor

In Autograph score
   Tenbury–Dublin copy
   RM 18.e.2 copy
   Randall and Abell
     printed score } e'♭

In Hamburg copy b'♭

I have not found the Hamburg reading in any other manuscript and have found it in only one printed edition, the Chrysander Handelgesellschaft.

Bar 24, beats 3 and 4, basso-continuo

In Autograph score
   Tenbury–Dublin copy
   Hamburg copy
   RM 18.e.2 copy
In Randall and Abell
   printed score

The Randall and Abell error has been copied by later editors.

Bar 27, 2nd quaver, choral alto

In Autograph score   c'
In Tenbury–Dublin copy   First copied as c' then altered to the note a'♭
In Hamburg copy
   RM 18.e.2 copy } a'♭

Irrespective of the question of the consecutive perfect fifths with the bass the alteration to the note a'♭ preserves the shape of the theme. The c' could easily be a slip of the pen. One can hardly doubt that Handel intended the note a♭.

Bar 30, 2nd quaver, choral bass

This b♮ is often printed at the lower octave, due to a misreading of an alteration in the Autograph score.

Examination of the Autograph score shows that Handel's first idea for the choral bass was

He later made many alterations. These are hard to decipher, but what might have been the lower octave B is definitely smudged out and written over by Handel. In the basso-continuo the only note on the second quaver is the upper octave b.

In Tenbury–Dublin copy
   Hamburg copy
   RM 18.e.2 copy
   Chrysander } B
In Prout   b
The basso-continuo in all MSS. is

Bar 40, 1st note, choral alto

In Autograph score   c'

In RM 18.e.2 copy   d'
A copyist's error, for, according to Handel's usage, the harmony here is $\frac{5}{3}$ and not $\frac{6}{4}$. Moreover, both violin II° and viola have c''.

Bar 41, beat 3,
1st quaver, viola

In Autograph score
    Tenbury–Dublin copy
    Hamburg copy
    RM 18.e.2 copy   } d'

In Randall and Abell
    printed score   } g'

The note g' agrees with the *subject*, and as the viola is doubling the choral tenor, which at this point is singing g', the note d' would seem to be in error.

Bar 55, beat 2,
viola

Handel first wrote this bar in the Autograph score

He then joined the first two notes together as quavers but omitted to add the necessary additional beat. Later ink was spilled in quantity over the whole of this page, following which a copyist rewrote it endeavouring to imitate Handel's handwriting. On this additional page (non-autograph), inserted in the Autograph score, this bar was given as   But

Handel's time values for the last two beats, now clearly to be seen through the faded ink, were and remain unaltered. Obviously it is the second beat that Handel omitted to add.

Here is the reading in the Tenbury–Dublin copy, the Hamburg copy, and RM 18.e.2:

'O THOU THAT TELLEST'

In the 1st, 2nd and 3rd editions of [*The*] *Songs in Messiah* this air was printed an octave higher, i.e. for counter-tenor voice.

In the Randall and Abell edition of the full score, published some eighteen years later, it was printed at the lower octave, for contralto voice. In the Autograph score what looks like the name 'Mrs. Cibber' is written in pencil. The Tenbury–Dublin copy has 'Sig^ra Galli', 'Guadagni' and 'Young'.

Bar 12, violin I°   In Autograph score

Although written by Handel over the 4th quaver of the violin part, this pause should be observed on the 5th quaver and only in the closing *ritornello*. I believe that Handel first intended the introduction to end on a crotchet d''.

Having written a *fine* pause over, as it was then, the crotchet note d'', he did not trouble to write out the coda in full, but simply wrote the instruction '*Il ritornello da capo si scriva*'. When he afterwards altered the crotchet to two quavers he omitted to alter the position of the pause. Some editors believe that Handel intended two quavers without a pause in the introduction and a crotchet with a *fine* pause at the coda.

This might have been so had he first written the two quavers and altered them to a crotchet. But, as it appears that he first wrote the crotchet and altered it to two quavers, I believe that he wanted the octave leap in both cases. Cf. the octave leap ending in the autograph versions of 'Thou art gone up on high' (bass and alto) and 'Thou shalt break them'.

Bars 27–28,
basso-continuo

In Autograph score Handel first wrote

He then crossed through the ties in ink of the same thickness. It would appear that he wanted the beats to be marked and the harmony to be kept moving. Smith failed to observe Handel's alteration for these bars appear

In Tenbury–Dublin copy
    Hamburg copy   with the ties that Handel had crossed out. This
    Randall and Abell   error has been repeated by later editors.
       printed score

Bar 29,
voice

In Autograph score
    Tenbury–Dublin copy
    Hamburg copy
    Chrysander

            get thee up

In RM 18.e.2 copy
   The Songs in Messiah
   Prout

Bar 49,
basso-continuo

Handel first wrote
In Autograph score

He later altered it in the Autograph score and it was correctly copied in the

Tenbury–Dublin and Hamburg copies

It was given incorrectly
In RM 18.e.2 copy
   Randall and Abell
     printed score
   and repeated by later
     editors

Bar 103, 11th *semiquaver*, *violin I°*	In Autograph score Tenbury–Dublin copy Hamburg copy	a¹
	In RM 18.e.2 copy and repeated by later editors	c''♮

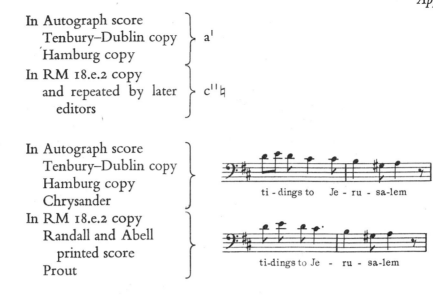

Bar 110, *choral bass*	In Autograph score Tenbury–Dublin copy Hamburg copy Chrysander
	In RM 18.e.2 copy Randall and Abell printed score Prout

'FOR BEHOLD, DARKNESS SHALL COVER THE EARTH'

Bar 5, *2nd quaver*, *violin I° and II°*	In Autograph score Tenbury–Dublin copy RM 18.e.2 copy Randall and Abell printed score	♫
	In Hamburg copy Chrysander	♪. ♪

'THE PEOPLE THAT WALKED IN DARKNESS'

Handel's *V unis e viol* written against the violin stave in the Autograph score indicates that he wanted the timbre of the viola in the violin register, except where it was beyond the normal technique of the period. This is further supported by the Foundling viola part the notes of which (apart from four obvious copyist's errors in bars 29, 31, and 33) are printed in my edition of the score in the Hallische Händel-Ausgabe.

Handel's indication is also often interpreted as a *tasto solo* instruction for the harpsichord continuo player. Much has been written both in favour of and against any realization of the basso-continuo in this air. It is also argued that while the major section and the cadence bars of the minor section may be realized, the minor section itself must be *tasto solo* or *al unisono* throughout. The evidence is:

   in the first edition of *Songs in Messiah*
   (a) the major section has four figurings;
   (b) the cadence bars of the minor section where violins and basses are not in unison have the necessary cadential figuring;

(c) bar 23, halfway through the minor section, still in unison, is also figured;

(d) the opening note of each minor section is figured with a sharp; in the first section twice, in the introduction and at the entry of the voice.

Finally, in the eighteenth-century manuscript harpsichord part of *Messiah* in the British Museum, shelf mark RM 19.d.1 (said to be in the hand of Jennens, Handel's friend and the librettist of *Messiah*) the bass is figured throughout. Here is the first phrase:

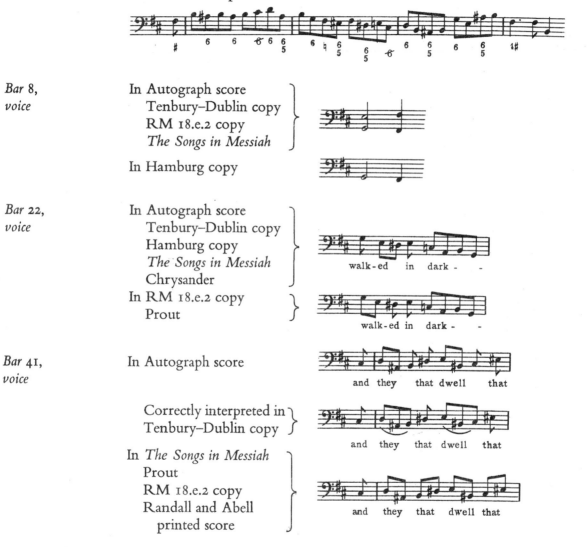

Bar 8,
voice

    In Autograph score
      Tenbury–Dublin copy
      RM 18.e.2 copy
      The Songs in Messiah

    In Hamburg copy

Bar 22,
voice

    In Autograph score
      Tenbury–Dublin copy
      Hamburg copy
      The Songs in Messiah
      Chrysander
    In RM 18.e.2 copy
      Prout

Bar 41,
voice

    In Autograph score

    Correctly interpreted in
    Tenbury–Dublin copy

    In *The Songs in Messiah*
    Prout
    RM 18.e.2 copy
    Randall and Abell
    printed score

'FOR UNTO US A CHILD IS BORN'

Bar 7,
basso-continuo

The lower octave G was added to the Tenbury–Dublin copy by Handel when he added the *ripieno* instruction.

198

Bar 8, beat 3,   In Autograph score
violin II°   Tenbury–Dublin copy
                          Hamburg copy   } d¹
                          RM 18.e.2 copy
                     In Randall and Abell
                          printed score   } g¹
                          and repeated by
                          later editors

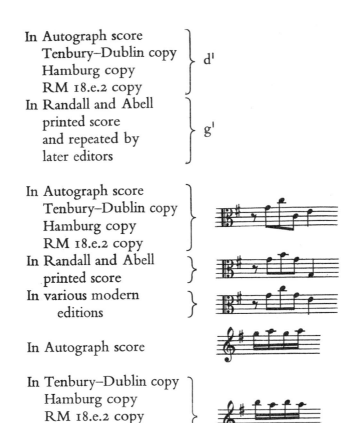

Bar 9,   In Autograph score
viola   Tenbury–Dublin copy
                          Hamburg copy
                          RM 18.e.2 copy
                     In Randall and Abell
                          printed score
                     In various modern
                          editions

Bar 51, beat 3,   In Autograph score
violin II°

                     In Tenbury–Dublin copy
                          Hamburg copy
                          RM 18.e.2 copy
                          Randall and Abell
                          printed score

In bars 35 and 70 the root of the harmony is in the choral and basso-continuo therefore it is obviously correct for the violin II° to have the third of the harmony so continuing the violin passage in thirds. In bar 51 it is the third of the harmony which is in the choral and basso-continuo. There is reason, therefore, in Handel breaking the passage in thirds in order to have the root of the harmony in the violin II°. His omission of the root and doubling of the third of the harmony in bar 87 runs counter to the foregoing argument. But I suggest that this was forced upon him by the difficult context.

Bars 61–63,   In Autograph score
choral tenor   Tenbury–Dublin copy
     and   Hamburg copy
Bars 63–65,   Chrysander
choral soprano

And the Gov-ern-ment shall be, shall be up-on —— his shoul - der

In RM 18.e.2 copy

And the Gov-ern-ment shall be up-on his shoul - - - der

In Randall and Abell
   printed score
  Prout

And the Gov-ern-ment shall be up-on his shoul - - - der

Smith copied the words incorrectly in RM 18.e.2, advancing the word 'shoulder' to halfway in bar 62 (64) instead of bringing it on the octave leap in bar 63 (65). It was printed in the Randall and Abell score with the same incorrect word arrangement as in RM 18.e.2 and an additional mistake: Handel's time group bar 62 (64) beat 3 ♪♪♩ was printed in reverse ♩♪♪. In Chrysander's performing edition the time-group is incorrect (as Randall and Abell) but the word arrangement is correct.

Bar 77, beats 3 and 4, viola	In Autograph score
	  Tenbury–Dublin copy ⎫ Time value ♩. ♪
	  Hamburg copy
	In RM 18.e.2 copy
	  Randall and Abell
	    printed score ⎬ Time value ♩ ↯♪
	  and later editors

It is a feature of Handel's writing in $\frac{4}{4}$ time to have a half-beat rest for the first half of the second beat and a dot continuation for the first half of the fourth beat. They are almost, if not completely, invariably in this order—not the reverse.

Cf. the basso-continuo in this bar.

Bar 79, choral bass	In Autograph score Handel wrote in error 'a Son *was* given'. Earlier, in bar 42, he first wrote 'was' and then crossed it out and substituted 'is'.

Bar 82, 1st note, choral alto	In Autograph score this is much altered
	In Tenbury–Dublin copy ⎫
	  Hamburg copy
	  RM 18.e.2 copy ⎬ f'♯
	  Chrysander
	In Prout a'

Bar 91, beat 3, (1st semiquaver), violin 1°	In Autograph score
	  Tenbury–Dublin copy ⎬ b'
	  Hamburg copy
	In RM 18.e.2 copy
	  Randall and Abell ⎬ g'
	    printed score
	  and later editors

THE PASTORAL SYMPHONY

Handel first wrote the Pastoral Symphony without the middle section and the consequent *da capo*. He later wrote a middle section (after two attempts), altered the basso-continuo dotted minim C in bar 11 to a crotchet and added the three notes leading to the middle section. In the Foundling score the Pastoral Symphony is without a middle section and the orchestral parts stop at bar 11.

Handel made clear his intentions regarding balance and timbre by the orchestral layout in the Autograph score:

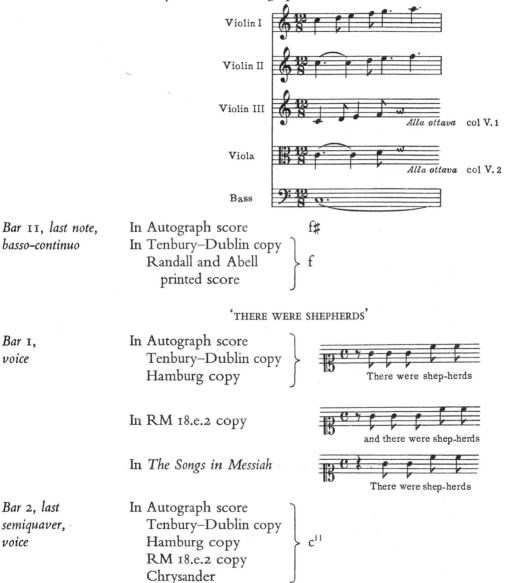

| *Bar 11, last note,* *basso-continuo* | In Autograph score | f♯ |
| | In Tenbury–Dublin copy Randall and Abell printed score | } f |

'THERE WERE SHEPHERDS'

Bar 1, *voice* — In Autograph score, Tenbury–Dublin copy, Hamburg copy

There were shep-herds

In RM 18.e.2 copy

and there were shep-herds

In *The Songs in Messiah*

There were shep-herds

Bar 2, last semiquaver, *voice* — In Autograph score, Tenbury–Dublin copy, Hamburg copy, RM 18.e.2 copy, Chrysander } c^{11}

In *The Songs in Messiah*
Prout
} b^{I}

'AND LO! THE ANGEL OF THE LORD'

Bar 6,
voice

In Autograph score
    Tenbury–Dublin copy
    Hamburg copy
    Chrysander

And they were sore a - fraid

In RM 18.e.2 copy
    RM 19.d.1 copy

And they were sore a - fraid

In Randall and Abell
    printed score
    Prout

And they were sore a - fraid

Bar 6, last quaver,
violin II°

In all the MSS.   a^{I}
Sometimes printed incorrectly as g^{I}

Bar 6, beat 4,
violin I° and II°,
viola, 'celli

There is no authority for the practice sometimes followed of substituting rests for Handel's notes in the last beat and three-quarters of the accompaniment in bar 6.

'AND SUDDENLY THERE WAS WITH THE ANGEL'

Bar 2, 2nd, 3rd,
6th and 7th
semiquavers,
violin II°

In Autograph score
    Tenbury–Dublin copy
    Hamburg copy
} d^{II}

In RM 18.e.2 copy
    Randall and Abell
        printed score
    and later editors
} e^{II}

The note is clearly d^{II} in the Autograph score. Moreover in the following bar where Handel wanted the second from the bass he figured it, but in this bar he figured just $^6_4$.

Bar 6, beat 2,
last semiquaver
violin II°

In Autograph score
    Tenbury–Dublin copy
    Hamburg copy
} d^{II}

In RM 18.e.2 copy
    Randall and Abell
        printed score
    and later editors
} e^{II}

Bar 7, beat 2, last semiquaver, violin II°	In all the MSS. Randall and Abell printed score	} e''
	Sometimes printed as	c''♯

Bar 8, beat 2, 3rd semiquaver violin I°	In Autograph score Tenbury–Dubiin copy Hamburg copy	} d''
	In RM 18.e.2 Randall and Abell printed score and repeated by later editors	} e''

'GLORY TO GOD'

Handel wrote '*Da lontano e un poco piano*' not at the head of the score but expressly between the two trumpet parts. He first wrote '*In disparte*' but crossed it out.

Handel's *piano* in bar 7 is the first general dynamic mark in this chorus. A study of his other scores clearly proves that it was meant as a contradiction of a previously understood *forte* at the beginning of the chorus.

Bar 35, trumpets	In Autograph score Tenbury–Dublin copy Hamburg copy RM 18.e.2 copy Randall and Abell printed score	The two notes occur on beats 1 and 2
	Sometimes printed on beats 3 and 4	

Bar 35, 2nd trumpet, beat 2	In Autograph score Tenbury–Dublin copy Hamburg copy	} f'♯
	In RM 18.e.2 copy Randall and Abell printed score	} g'

On beats 1 and 2 Handel wrote in the *bassetti* stave

Bars 44–47	In the Autograph, over the bar-line between bars 44 and 45, Handel wrote '*pian*' against the two violin and the viola staves; in bar 46 over the viola stave he wrote '*pian p*' (*piu piano*); and over the basso–continuo stave overlapping

bars 46 and 47 he wrote '*pian pian*', interpreted by Smith in the Tenbury–Dublin copy as *pianissimo* in bar 47. Handel variously used '*pian pian*' and '*pianiss*' for the same dynamic indication.

'REJOICE GREATLY,' $\frac{4}{4}$ SETTING

This $\frac{4}{4}$ setting, although in Handel's autograph, is contained not in the Autograph score but in the Tenbury–Dublin copy.

Bar 8, beats 3 and 4, basso-continuo

In the Tenbury–Dublin copy
RM 18.e.2 copy
Randall and Abell printed score

In Hamburg copy but corrected in pencil by a modern hand to agree with the Autograph MS.

Sometimes printed by later editors

Bar 34, beat 4, voice

With two syllables to three notes, Handel here clearly drew a syllable slur over the last two notes. He thus made clear his intention to divide the beat into a short syllable followed by a long one. This has been overlooked by most editors. Indeed, in the most recent English edition Handel's division has been reversed. The syllable slur is over the first two notes.

Bars 34 and 35, voice

In Autograph
Tenbury–Dublin copy
Hamburg copy
RM 18.e.2 copy

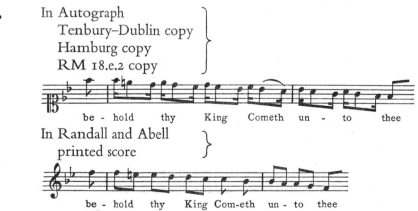

be - hold thy King Cometh un - to thee

In Randall and Abell printed score

be - hold thy King Com-eth un - to thee

The even quaver version is not to be found in any of the MSS. The syncopated time group is an example of Handel's own decoration of a melodic line for in the corresponding bar in the previously composed $\frac{12}{8}$ setting he wrote

be - hold thy King Cometh un - to thee

Bars 35, beat 3, *voice*	In Tenbury–Dublin copy RM 18.e.2 copy Randall and Abell printed score Prout	
	In Hamburg copy Chrysander	

Bar 42, beats 3 *and 4, violin*	In Tenbury–Dublin copy RM 18.e.2 copy	

The Hamburg copy has not the grace notes.

Bar 76, *last half-beat, voice*	In the Tenbury–Dublin copy, much blotched but looks like	
	In RM 18.e.2 copy Randall and Abell printed score	
	In Hamburg copy	

Bar 92, *beat 2 till bar 94, beat 1, violin*	In the Tenbury–Dublin copy these notes are without ornamentation; but in the comparable bars in the first setting of this air (the $\frac{12}{8}$ setting) Handel wrote the indication *tr* over the first note of each of these beats.

Bar 92, *beat 2*	In the Tenbury–Dublin copy, Handel wrote two even quavers in the violin part on this beat, although on all other beats in this and the following bar he wrote the dotted group. Further, in both voice and basso-continuo on this beat he wrote a quaver rest followed by a quaver note.

Bar 101, *last semiquaver, violin*	In the Tenbury–Dublin copy Hamburg copy RM 18.e.2 copy	the ♮ is omitted, in error; c.f. bars 2 and 11

Bar 107, *beat 4 violin*	In the Tenbury–Dublin copy	
	But in the comparable bar 8 Handel wrote	

'HE SHALL FEED HIS FLOCK'

Bar 11, *3rd and 4th notes, voice* Bar 19, *first two notes, voice*	In the Autograph Handel drew a syllable-slur over these two notes, in error.

Bar 20,
last quaver,
violin II°

In Autograph score the note is G.   The violin II° is playing in unison with the singer from the last quaver in bar 10 until bar 23, with the exception of this note g'' which is a tone above the voice.

In the alto transposition in the Tenbury–Dublin copy, and in the Hamburg copy and RM 18.e.2 copy this note is similarly a tone above the voice.   It would seem to be in error.   Possibly when writing the violin II° part Handel had forgotten the vocal line and was still thinking in thirds with the basso-continuo.

In the Hamburg copy this note is marked in pencil with a cross.

Bars 21 and 22,
voice

In Autograph score
Tenbury–Dublin copy
Hamburg copy

In *The Songs in Messiah*
Chrysander

In RM 18.2.2 copy
Prout

Bar 24, beat 4,
violin II°

In Autograph score
RM 18.e.2 copy
Randall and Abell
printed score

The corresponding notes in the alto transposition would be
But in the alto transposition in the
Tenbury–Dublin copy
Hamburg copy

Bar 25, last
quaver, violin II°
and viola

In the Autograph score in the original all-soprano version in B♭ major the *ritornello* which occurs immediately before the first statement of the words 'Come unto Him all ye that labour' ends in bar 25 with a perfect cadence in B♭ major; the basso-continuo note B♭ being sustained to the end of the bar (and through bar 26).   It was natural, therefore, for the first vocal note of the second stanza (the note f'', the last quaver in bar 25) to be harmonized with B♭ major harmony; Handel gave the third of the chord d'' to the violin II° and doubled the root b'♭ at the fifteenth in the viola.

But the copyist when transposing the first stanza of this air down into F major for contralto ended the transposition of the violins and viola parts at the 11th quaver of bar 25 (the soprano begins to sing the second stanza on the 12th quaver of that bar). The sheet bearing the transposition was inserted in the Tenbury–Dublin copy in front of the complete two-stanza all-soprano copy in which the sign $ was written at the 12th quaver in bar 25 to show the link with the last note of the alto transposition.

Unfortunately, as the basso-continuo note is sustained to the end of the bar there resulted, from the combination of the transposed bass note and the untransposed violin II° and viola parts on the last quaver, a harmonic progression not intended by Handel. There is no doubt that according to Handel's practice the basso-continuo note F on the last quaver of bar 25 should be harmonized not as a $\frac{6}{4}$ but as a $\frac{5}{3}$ or $\frac{7}{3}$; cf. the harmonic progression across the bar line of bars 23–24 and 30–31. Note especially Handel's use of dominant harmony on the last quaver of bar 10 although the tonic is in the bass at that point. The weight of evidence is in favour of dominant harmony on the last quaver of bar 25.

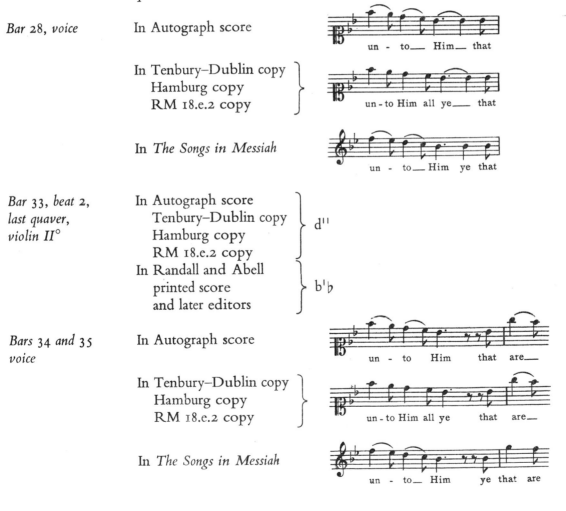

207

Bar 36, beat 2,
violin I° and II°

In Autograph score
   Tenbury–Dublin copy
   Hamburg copy

In Randall and Abell
   printed score

In RM 18.e.2

Handel did not write out the violin I° part but simply the instruction to the copyist *colla parte* (i.e. the voice); and the voice part here clearly consists of even quavers. (Equally clearly Handel wrote the dotted group in the violin II°.)

Bar 50,
voice

In Autograph score
   Tenbury–Dublin copy
   Hamburg copy
   RM 18.e.2 copy
   Chrysander

ye____ shall find rest,____ and

In *The Songs in Messiah*
   Prout

ye shall find__ rest,____ and

Handel first drew a slur over the third and fourth notes but then definitely crossed it out.

'HIS YOKE IS EASY'

Bars 2 and 9,
beat 3, choral
soprano and bass

In Autograph score
   Tenbury–Dublin copy
   Hamburg copy

In RM 18.e.2 copy
   Randall and Abell
      printed score

Bar 9, beat 3
(2nd note),
choral bass

In Autograph score
   Tenbury–Dublin copy
   Hamburg copy
   Randall and Abell
      printed score
   Chrysander

f

In RM 18.e.2 copy
   Prout

d

The note f in the Autograph score is obviously in error for d, as in all other statements the demi-semiquaver is a tone or semitone below the previous note. Further in bar 42, in the Autograph Handel first wrote f'' in soprano and 1st violin and then smudged it out, replacing it with d''.

Bar 11, beats 3 and 4, violin I° and II° and viola

In the following example the ordinary sized notes show what Handel wrote in the Autograph score. The small sized rests and thin stems show what Handel inserted in the Tenbury–Dublin copy when he added the *ripieno* instructions. Smith did not copy these Autograph additions into either the Hamburg copy or the RM 18.e.2 copy.

Bars 14–15, violin I° and II° and viola

(See note on bar 11.)

Bar 24, beat 2, basso-continuo

In Autograph score
    Tenbury–Dublin copy
    Hamburg copy
    RM 18.e.2 copy
In Randall and Abell
    printed score

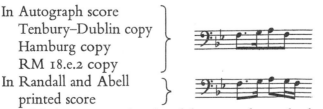

Handel first wrote the choral bass exactly as the basso-continuo. He later altered the last quaver f to two semiquavers, but left the basso-continuo unaltered. This cannot be considered to be an oversight for it is evident from the basso-continuo in bars 8 and 15, and particularly bar 30, that in this chorus he desired the customary instrumental simplification of the choral bass: in bar 30, beat 1, Handel first wrote in the basso-continuo and then altered it to

Elsewhere where the *Affekt* demanded it he did not hesitate to reverse the conventional practice and, against a quaver movement in the choral bass, write passing semiquavers in the basso-continuo. Cf. the chorus 'He trusted in God' bars 3 and 4.

Bars 25–26,
 choral bass
	In Autograph score
	    Tenbury–Dublin copy
	    Hamburg copy
	    Randall and Abell
	     printed score
	
	 In RM 18.e.2
	
	 In Chrysander
	
	 In Prout

The basso-continuo does not provide any evidence because it is in the more usual simplified form of the period

In bar 25 of the Autograph the Alto is

Bar 30, beat 1, *basso-continuo*	See note on bar 24.
Bar 31, *choral bass*	In Autograph score

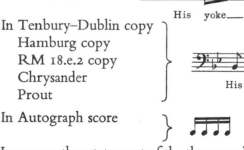

	In Tenbury–Dublin copy
	   Hamburg copy
	   RM 18.e.2 copy
	   Chrysander
	   Prout

Bar 32, beat 3 *choral bass*	In Autograph score

In every other statement of the theme and in the source-duet *Quel fior ch'all'alba ride* this group is

Bars 37 and 38,
 choral, soprano
	In Autograph score
	   Tenbury–Dublin copy
	   Hamburg copy
	
	 In RM 18.e.2 copy
	   Randall and Abell
	   printed score

Bar 42, beat 3, *the semiquaver* *basso-continuo*	In all the MSS a In Randall and Abell printed score g, in error

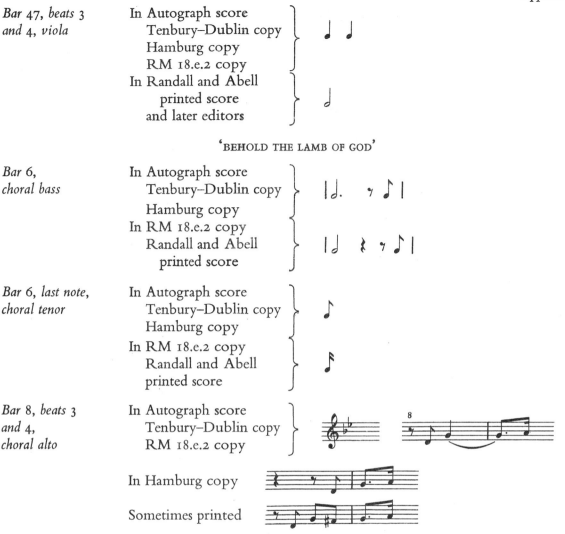

Bar 47, *beats* 3 and 4, *viola*

In Autograph score
Tenbury–Dublin copy
Hamburg copy
RM 18.e.2 copy

In Randall and Abell
printed score
and later editors

'BEHOLD THE LAMB OF GOD'

Bar 6,
choral bass

In Autograph score
Tenbury–Dublin copy
Hamburg copy

In RM 18.e.2 copy
Randall and Abell
printed score

Bar 6, *last note,*
choral tenor

In Autograph score
Tenbury–Dublin copy
Hamburg copy

In RM 18.e.2 copy
Randall and Abell
printed score

Bar 8, *beats* 3
and 4,
choral alto

In Autograph score
Tenbury–Dublin copy
RM 18.e.2 copy

In Hamburg copy

Sometimes printed

In the preface to the Chrysander score it is stated that the Autograph score and the Tenbury–Dublin and Goldschmidt copies are as in the first music example above. But this note then continues, 'but the correction in H (i.e. the Hamburg copy) is, in any case, to be regarded as right'. This in spite of the fact that the Hamburg copy contains numerous copyist's errors, many of which have been pencilled through and the correction noted in the margin.

Bar 12, *beat* 2,
violin I°

In all the MSS and the
Randall and Abell
printed score

This may reasonably be
regarded as being an error
by oversight for as in

every other repetition of this vocal phrase the violins and viola play the dotted group. In this bar, against the violin I° crotchet a' Handel wrote in the viola

Bar 12,
basso continuo

In Autograph score
Tenbury–Dublin copy
Hamburg copy

In RM 18.e.2 copy
Randall and Abell
printed score

Handel often sustains the basso-continuo against a phrasing rest in the upper parts.

Bar 14, beat 4,
viola

In Autograph score
Tenbury–Dublin copy

Hamburg copy
RM 18.e.2 copy

Handel wrote the viola part carelessly in this bar on both beats 3 and 4

Bar 18, beat 2,
choral soprano

In Autograph score
Hamburg copy

In Tenbury–Dublin copy
RM 18.e.2 copy
Randall and Abell
printed score

[*sic*]

Bar 25, beats 1
and 2, *choral
alto and tenor*

In Autograph score
Tenbury–Dublin copy

In RM 18.e.2 copy
Hamburg copy

In Randall and Abell
printed score

In the Autograph score the viola playing the same notes as are in the choral tenor has the time groups . It would seem that Handel wrote the even quavers in the tenor on beat 1 in error.

'HE WAS DESPISED'

In the first printed edition this air was printed an octave higher (for counter-tenor) with the instruction that it was to be sung an octave lower.

In the Tenbury–Dublin copy the pages containing from the last half of bar 18 to bar 33 are missing.

It must be recorded that in the Schwenke edition published at Hamburg 1809 the following recitative is printed between the air 'He was despised' and the following chorus 'Surely He hath borne our griefs'. An interpolated recitative is usually substituted for the preceding air; but the words taken from Isaiah LIII, 11 would seem more suitable as a substitute for the following chorus. It is numbered separately in the Schwenke edition and so could have been regarded as a preparation for the following chorus. The source is the same in both the English Authorized Version and the Lutheran Bible. 'He shall see the travail of his soul, and shall be satisfied; by his knowledge shall my righteous servant justify many; for he shall bear their iniquities.'

This recitative is without any authority.

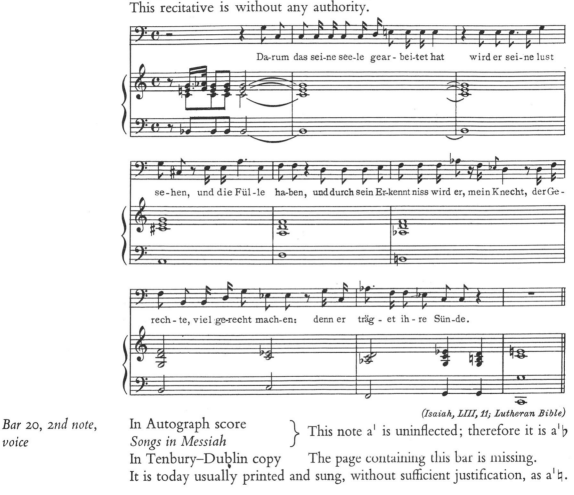

(Isaiah, LIII, 11; Lutheran Bible)

| Bar 20, 2nd note, voice | In Autograph score *Songs in Messiah* | } This note a¹ is uninflected; therefore it is a¹♭ |
| | In Tenbury–Dublin copy | The page containing this bar is missing. |

It is today usually printed and sung, without sufficient justification, as a¹♮.

Bar 66, beat 4, voice — In Autograph score ♪. ♪

In Tenbury–Dublin copy / RM 16.e.2 copy / *The Songs in Messiah* / Chrysander / Prout / Hamburg copy — ♪.♪

H

'SURELY HE HATH BORNE OUR GRIEFS'
'AND WITH HIS STRIPES'
'ALL WE LIKE SHEEP'

Handel intended these three choruses to be sung as one, without any break. The evidence is:

(a) The second chorus follows the first on the remaining half of the page without either double bar or key signature, merely the change of time signature.

(b) The key signature of 'All we like sheep' is a cancellation signature consisting of one flat and two naturals.

'SURELY HE HATH BORNE OUR GRIEFS'
'AND WITH HIS STRIPES'

In writing these first sections of this three-part choral sequence Handel followed the convention of writing the key signature with one flat less, the fourth flat appearing as an accidental throughout the course of the movement.

'SURELY HE HATH BORNE OUR GRIEFS'

Bar 2,
violin II°

In Autograph score

In Tenbury–Dublin copy
   Hamburg copy
   RM 18.e.2 copy
   Randall and Abell
     printed score

Handel wrote a crotchet too many in this bar. Whilst this mistake in the over-all value was corrected in the MS. copies and the Randall and Abell score the important point, that Handel wanted the third beat to be broken by a rest, was and until now has remained unnoted in all copies and editions.

Bar 2, beat 4,
last
demi-semiquaver,
violin I°

In Autograph score
   Tenbury–Dublin copy   } g''

In Hamburg copy
   RM 18.e.2 copy
   Randall and Abell
     printed score
   and later editors   } f''

Apart from the fact that Handel wrote the note clearly above and separate from the top line of the treble stave, the note g'' creates the drop of a third which is the characteristic of the sequential figure.

Bar 11, beat 3,
violin II°

In the Autograph score Handel omitted the necessary ♮. This omission was corrected by Smith in the Tenbury–Dublin and Hamburg copies.

Bar 11, *beat* 4, *viola*	In the Autograph score Handel omitted the necessary ♮. This error was repeated by Smith in the Tenbury–Dublin and Hamburg copies.

Bar 24, *beats* 1 and 2, *choral tenor*

In Autograph score   ♩. ♪

In Tenbury–Dublin copy ⎤
   Hamburg copy   ⎬   ♩ ♩
   RM 18.e.2 copy   ⎥
   Randall and Abell ⎥
     printed score ⎦

Bar 25, *beat* 1, *basso-continuo*

With his use of the one flat less signature convention Handel's figuring of $\frac{6}{5}$ was incorrect. It was not the third but the sixth from the bass which required the flat, so $\frac{6♭}{5}$. With modern key signature practice, however, the 6 does not require a flat.

'AND WITH HIS STRIPES'

Bar 4, *choral soprano and violin* I°

In Autograph score the time values are smudged and unclear.

In Tenbury–Dublin copy ⎤
   Hamburg copy   ⎥
   RM 18.e.2 copy   ⎬   ♩. ♩
   Randall and Abell ⎥
     printed score ⎥
   Chrysander   ⎦

In Prout   ♩   ♩

In this bar in the Autograph score the basso-continuo clearly consists of two minims but the choral soprano and the violin I° which are smudged

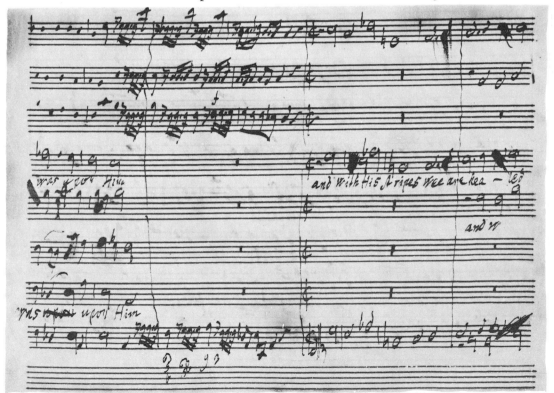

could be regarded either as a dotted minim and a crotchet or as two minims. As the violin is in unison with the voice and the *bassetto* is but an indication of what voice and violin are doing, all three should agree. Yet the Tenbury–Dublin, RM 18.e.2 and Hamburg manuscripts as well as the Randall and Abell printed score (1767) and the Handelgesellschaft (1901), and many others published between those dates, have perpetuated the discrepancy between the even notes in the *bassetti* on the one hand, and the dotted soprano and violin parts on the other. In the early Egerton score, however, violin, voice and continuo all have ♩.♩

Did Handel alter the soprano and violin and omit to alter the *bassetto*, or, writing the voice and violin parts first, did he smudge out the dot and turn the crotchet into a minim? The remainder of the chorus suggests the latter, for in all but one of the numerous statements of the subject the comparable bar consists of two minims.

Bars 19–21, violins and viola

In the Tenbury–Dublin copy Handel here added a few notes when he inserted the *ripieno* instructions.

Bar 71, beat 2, choral alto

In Autograph score
Dublin copy
Hamburg copy
RM 18.e.2 copy
Randall and Abell
  printed score

There is evidence that Handel preferred the upper note.

Bar 76, beat 2, choral bass

In fugal choruses it was Handel's custom to write the words of the complete sentence only at its first appearance. Thereafter he indicated repetition of the whole or part of the sentence by writing the first of the words to be repeated under its appropriate note. In bar 76 under the second minim in the bass he wrote 'and'. I suggest that this was in error for 'are' because 'are healed' seems musically more in character.

'ALL WE LIKE SHEEP'

Bar 24, beat 4, basso-continuo

In Autograph score
RM 18.e.2 copy
Randall and Abell
  printed score

} g and b♮

In Tenbury–Dublin copy
Hamburg copy } f and g

In the Autograph score Handel first wrote these two quavers on f and g; he then altered them to g and b♮ and to make the alteration clear wrote the letter names below the notes. The Tenbury–Dublin copy and the Hamburg copy gives the notes as they stood before Handel altered them.

Bar 63,
last quaver,
basso-continuo
Also Bar 64,
2nd quaver,
basso-continuo

In Autograph score
RM 18.e.2 copy } d

In Hamburg copy — f

In Autograph score — g

In Tenbury–Dublin copy
Hamburg copy
RM 18.e.2 copy
Randall and Abell
   printed score } d

These two points need to be considered together. Handel first wrote the basso-continuo from beat 3 of bar 63 to beat 2 of bar 64

He then altered it to

Again, the notes as they stood before Handel altered them have been copied and repeated.

Bar 64,
5th quaver,
choral tenor

In Autograph score — c¹
But Handel wrote carelessly and the note over-flowed and filled the whole of the b¹ space below.

In Dublin copy
Hamburg copy } b
A copyist's error; c¹ is obviously correct.

Bar 65, beat 4,
choral alto

In Autograph score
Dublin copy
Hamburg copy
RM 18.e.2
Randall and Abell
   printed score }

'ALL THEY THAT SEE HIM'

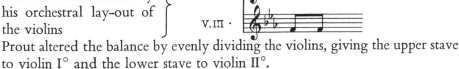

Handel gave a clear indication of tonal balance by his orchestral lay-out of the violins }

Prout altered the balance by evenly dividing the violins, giving the upper stave to violin I° and the lower stave to violin II°.

Appendix C
Bar 10, beat 2

Handel's time group ♪♫♩.♫ obviously is subject to the dotted note convention (see Chapter 5) and therefore is to be played ♪♪♫♩.♫ .

'HE TRUSTED IN GOD'

Bar 2,
choral bass
Bar 7,
choral tenor

In Autograph score
RM 18.e.2 copy
Randall and Abell
printed score
} 'might deliver'

In Tenbury–Dublin copy — was first 'might' and later altered to 'would' in every instance except Bar 37, choral tenor, where it is still 'might'

In Hamburg copy — 'would deliver'

In the Autograph score under the final statement in the bass Handel wrote 'would deliver'

Bar 8, beats 1
and 2,
choral bass

In Autograph score
In Tenbury–Dublin copy
Hamburg copy
Randall and Abell
printed score
RM 18.e.2 copy

At bar 8 in order to save himself the trouble of writing out the notes in the orchestral staves Handel wrote the instruction to the copyist 'Ut Cant, ut Alt, ut Tenor' over the violin I°, violin II° and viola staves respectively; the last actual notes written by him are the viola e'♭ tied over the bar lines of bars 7 and 8 and the following quaver d¹. This poses two problems, for in bars 3 and 4 Handel wrote the choral bass and the basso-continuo as follows:

Choral bass

Basso-continuo

It will be seen that Handel sustained the instrument through the vocal rest and, by a passing note, turned the following vocal quaver into two orchestral semiquavers. Smith when copying the Tenbury–Dublin copy interpreted Handel's 'ut' indications literally from bar 8, and wrote the instrumental parts with the vocal rests and unadorned quavers. But it is reasonable to assume that Handel intended the basso-continuo and viola staves as he wrote them in the opening bars to serve as a model for the orchestral parts for the remainder of the chorus. This is supported by the violin I° in bars 52 and 53, and the *bassetti* in bars 12 and 13 which in both cases he wrote out fully with tied notes and semiquavers. Further, the 5 in the ⁶₅ figuring in bars 25 and 31 is of significance in relation to the tied notes.

Bar 8, *choral tenor*	Handel here wrote 'If he delight in Him' in error for 'Let Him deliver Him'.
Bar 14, *last quaver,* *choral tenor*	In Autograph d^{I} In Tenbury–Dublin copy c^{I} Obviously a copyist's error.

Bar 19, *beat 2,*
basso-continuo

In Autograph copy
  RM 18.e.2 copy
  Foundling *fagotto* part
In Tenbury–Dublin copy
  Hamburg copy
  Foundling copy
  Randall and Abell
    printed score

The even quavers reading creates a logical sequence.

Bar 34,
basso-continuo

The basso-continuo in bars 34 and 35, first beat, in the Autograph is indistinct.
Two things only are clear:
  (a) the semiquaver hook across the stem of the second note in bar 34, and
  (b) the dot after the first note in bar 35.
In Tenbury–Dublin copy
  Hamburg copy
  RM 18.e.2 copy
  Randall and Abell
    printed score
  and later editors

But in view of Handel's practice elsewhere, it is reasonable to read these two
groups as

Bars 52–53,
violin I°

Handel knew that his boy trebles would not sing an effective C in alt. (even
if at all); therefore, when writing the choral soprano part he substituted the
note g^{II} for c^{III} on the first quaver of bar 53. However, determined not to
sacrifice the characteristic shape of the *subject*, he wrote the notes for just these

six beats in the violin I° stave thus:

so temporarily cancelling the 'ut' instructions to the copyist that he had written
in bar 8.

Bar 54,
first 3 notes
choral alto

Handel wrote ♩. ♪♩ obviously in error for ♩. ♪♩

219

Appendix C

Bar 59,
choral tenor

In the Autograph there is a note short. Handel wrote only 5 notes for 6 syllables:

In Autograph

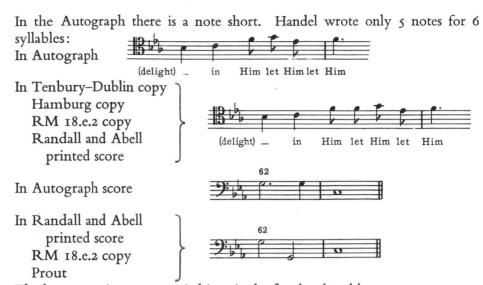

(delight) _ in Him let Him let Him

In Tenbury–Dublin copy
  Hamburg copy
  RM 18.e.2 copy
  Randall and Abell
    printed score

(delight) _ in Him let Him let Him

Bar 62,
choral bass

In Autograph score

In Randall and Abell
    printed score
  RM 18.e.2 copy
  Prout

The basso–continuo was copied in mistake for the choral bass.

'ALL THEY THAT SEE HIM'
'THY REBUKE HATH BROKEN HIS HEART'
'BEHOLD AND SEE IF THERE BE ANY SORROW'
'HE WAS CUT OFF OUT OF THE LAND OF THE LIVING'
'BUT THOU DIDST NOT LEAVE HIS SOUL IN HELL'

Handel wrote these recitatives and airs for tenor voice; in the Autograph score they are written in the tenor C clef. In the margin of 'All they that see Him' in the Autograph score Handel wrote in ink 'Mr. Beard'; in the Tenbury–Dublin copy is written, in addition to 'Mr. Lowe' and 'Mr. Beard', 'Sign^ra Avolio'. In the margin of 'Thy rebuke' in the Autograph score Handel wrote, in ink, 'Sra Avolio'; in the Tenbury–Dublin copy, again in addition to 'Mr. Lowe' and 'Mr. Beard' is written 'Sig^ra Frasi'. There is no trace in the Autograph of any names in the margins either of 'Behold and see' or 'But Thou didst not leave His soul in hell'; in the Tenbury–Dublin copy 'Behold and see', 'He was cut off' and 'But Thou didst not leave' have, in addition to the names of either or both tenors (also, in the case of the last two numbers, 'The Boy') the name 'Sig^ra Frasi'. It is clear, therefore, that all of this solo tenor music was sung on occasion by a soprano.

An examination of the Foundling solo part-books provides evidence that it was the custom at one period for the tenor to sing the first three and the soprano the last two of these numbers; Beard's part-book contains the music of the first three and immediately following 'Behold and see' is written 'Accomp and Song tacet'. The corroborating evidence, the first soprano solo part-book, is unfortunately lost.

In the Hiller 1789 Breitkopf edition all of these numbers are printed in the soprano C clef.

'BEHOLD AND SEE'

<table>
<tr><td>*Bar* 3,
2nd quaver,
basso-continuo</td><td>In Autograph Handel first wrote</td></tr>
</table>

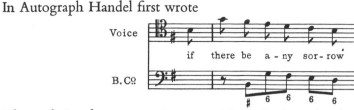

Then, obviously not wanting to anticipate in the voice the effect of the rising sixth in the violin melody of the following *ritornello*, he altered the voice and basso-continuo but forgot to remove the sharp figuring which was now seriously in error.

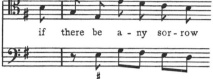

'LIFT UP YOUR HEADS, O YE GATES'

Bar 5, *beat* 3, *violin* II°	In Autograph score Tenbury–Dublin copy Hamburg copy RM 18.e.2 copy	a¹
	In Randall and Abell printed score and later editions	c¹¹

Bars 5–10, *'cello*	The Foundling 'cello part normally incorporates any tenor *bassetti*. Here the Foundling copyist has included the alto *bassetti*. It was obviously a mistake because, using the tenor clef, he has copied the notes exactly as they stood in the Autograph in the alto clef, with the result that the passage is a third too low.

Bars 11, 12, 14, 15, 27, 28, 29	In Autograph score RM 18.e.2 copy	'Who is *this* King of Glory'
	In Tenbury–Dublin copy	Altered in bar 11 from 'the' to 'this'
	In Hamburg copy	Thickened ink looks like an alteration from 'the' to 'this'
	In Randall and Abell printed score	'Who is *the* King of Glory'

Bar 11, *beat* 2, *choral bass*	In Autograph score
	In Tenbury–Dublin copy Hamburg copy RM 18.e.2 copy

The notes of the choral bass and the basso-continuo in this bar are identical and so obviously are the time groups clearly written by Handel as ‖ ♩. ♪♫ ♫ 𝄽 ‖ (the viola, reasonably, agrees with the basso-continuo). The notes of the violin II°

and the choral tenor are identical but there is a discrepancy in the time groups. The choral tenor is | ♪. ♪♪ ♪. ♪♪ ♪ 𝄾 | and with this the violin II° must agree; Handel omitted to dot the third quaver of the violin II°. See also the tenor in bars 14 and 15. The difference between the time groups of the choral bass and tenor on beat two is, however, intentional; cf. the following examples from the Autograph of Handel's concerto in F for two orchestras, based on the same thematic material as this chorus (British Museum RM 20.g.6, folio 47):

Oboe

Bassoon

B.C.°

Note the difference between the oboe and the other two parts in bar 1, beat 2, and between the bassoon and the other two parts in bar 2, beat 2.

Bar 11, beat 2, viola and violin II° and basso-continuo	In Autograph score
	In Tenbury–Dublin copy ⎫
	Hamburg copy ⎬
	RM 18.e.2 copy ⎪
	Randall and Abell ⎪
	printed score ⎭

(See note on bar 11, choral bass.)

Bars 14–15, beat 2, choral tenor

In Autograph score Handel reversed his error of bar 11. He wrote ♪. ♪♪ in violin I° which is doubling the choral tenor and wrote ♪♪ in the choral tenor in error.

Bar 16, beat 2, violin I°	In Autograph score
	In Tenbury–Dublin copy ⎫
	Hamburg copy ⎬
	RM 18.e.2 copy ⎪
	Randall and Abell ⎪
	printed score ⎭

The violin I° is doubling the second soprano which has the dotted group. The even quavers in the violin I° in the Autograph score are obviously in error.

Bar 16, beat 2, violin I°

Handel here wrote even quavers. But as at this point the first violin is in unison with the second soprano there is no reason for a difference in the time group. Handel obviously forgot to add the dot and the semiquaver hook.

Bar 24, the first quaver of beat 4, violin I°

In the Autograph there are two note heads (a' and c'') on the one stem. The thickening of the note stem suggests that Handel first wrote a' and then superimposed c''. The major third a' is already doubled in the viola and tenor, whereas the note c'' completes a well-spaced triad.

Bars 18–60

The pages containing these bars are missing from the Tenbury–Dublin copy.

Bar 36, *last quaver,* *choral tenor*	In Autograph score Hamburg copy RM 18.e.2 copy	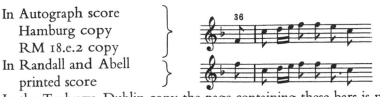
	In Randall and Abell printed score	

In the Tenbury–Dublin copy the page containing these bars is missing.

Bar 43, violin I°,
violin II° and
viola

In Autograph score, after the first crotchet in bar 43 Handel wrote no further notes until bar 52.

except (1) in bar 46 on the violin I° stave only the 3rd beat crotchet c$''$;

(2) from bar 46 beat 3 to the end of bar 48 the notes of the choral alto on the violin II° stave; all but the first note are written an octave higher than the vocal pitch;

(3) bar 47, the first three notes of the choral tenor on the viola stave at the octave above the vocal pitch;

(4) bar 48, the notes of the choral soprano of this bar only on the violin I° stave, written an octave above the vocal pitch; merely to indicate the pitch at which the following bars were to be played.

These indications regarding pitch are equivalent to instructions to the copyist that the orchestra was to double the choral parts.

Bar 44, beats 1 *and 2, choral alto*	In Autograph score Hamburg copy	
	In RM 18.e.2 copy Randall and Abell printed score	

In the Tenbury–Dublin copy the page containing this bar is missing.

Bar 63, *last quaver,* *choral alto* *and tenor*	In Autograph score Tenbury–Dublin copy Hamburg copy RM 18.e.2 copy	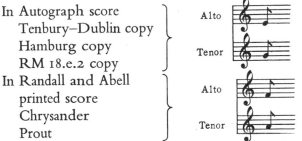
	In Randall and Abell printed score Chrysander Prout	

Writing antiphonally for choir and orchestra Handel clashed C major harmony in the voices against F major harmony in the orchestra. This was obviously in error. Exactly the same thing happened in the fourth semiquaver of bar 19 in 'Surely He hath borne our griefs'. He first wrote

and then altered the alto and tenor notes to f¹ and d¹ respectively in order that they should accord with the violin II° and viola.

Bars 66–67,
choral alto

In Autograph score

After writing in bar 65 the first word 'the' Handel did not write any further words under the alto stave in these bars.

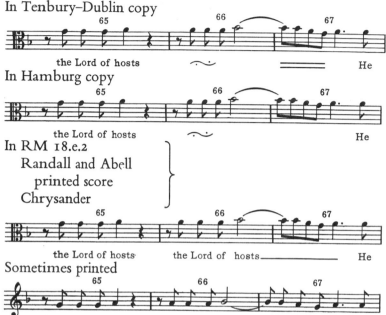

Handel's grouping of the quavers in the first half of bar 67 suggests that the word 'hosts' at the end of bar 66 was to be sustained through the first three and a half beats of bar 67. It was interpreted thus by Smith in the Tenbury–Dublin copy; the sign ⌣ indicates the repetition of a group of words; and a horizontal dash, either single or double, indicates the extension of the previous syllable.

Bars 69–70,
choral bass

In Autograph score
   Tenbury–Dublin copy
   Hamburg copy
In RM 18.e.2 copy
   Randall and Abell
    printed score

Bar 74,
last quaver,
choral alto

In Autograph score
   RM 18.e.2 copy

} f¹

In Tenbury–Dublin copy
   Hamburg copy
   Randall and Abell
    printed score

} a¹

'LET ALL THE ANGELS OF GOD'

Bar 3, *beat* 4,   In Autograph score   Handel first wrote g¹, then altered it to e¹.
choral alto   In Tenbury–Dublin copy   } e¹
                Hamburg copy
           In RM 18.e.2 copy   }
                Randall and Abell   } g¹
                  printed score

In the Autograph score after the 1st beat in bar 9 Handel wrote 'Ut C' and 'Ut A' over the violin I° and violin II° staves respectively; and after the 2nd beat in bar 10 he wrote 'Ut T' over the viola stave. He wrote no further notes on the orchestral staves until the orchestral coda at bar 34,
except (1) just one note on the violin II° stave, bar 10, beat 3, d''';
           (2) just one note in the viola stave, bar 15, beat 3, a¹.
Handel's purpose in writing these two notes was to show his preference for the upper of the two optional octave notes that he had written in the choral alto and tenor.

Bar 10, *beat* 3,   In Autograph score and other MSS. an optional octave d'''.
choral alto

Bar 11, *beat* 2,   Although after the first three notes of bar 10 in the viola stave Handel had
viola   written 'Ut T' as an indication to the copyist to copy the notes of the choral tenor in the viola part he clearly indicated the addition of passing notes to the instrumental parts by the *bassetti*.
In the Autograph:

(C.f. note on 'He trusted in God', bar 8, p. 218.)

Bar 15, *beat* 3,   In Autograph score and other MSS an optional octave a.
choral tenor

Bar 20,   Handel here wrote the words 'And let all angels' in error.
choral alto

Bars 23–24,   In Autograph score
choral alto   RM 18.e.2 copy
                Randall and Abell
                  printed score

In Tenbury–Dublin copy

(wor) - - ship, wor - - - - -

In Hamburg copy   Smith first wrote the word 'him' under the minim, but before writing further he superimposed 'wor-' and a continuation sign under the first notes in bar 24, thus making them agree with the Tenbury–Dublin copy.

Although in the Autograph score bar 23 is much blotted there is no sign of any mark that could be taken for a tie.

The Tenbury–Dublin copy shows signs of having been altered. The paper is roughened by erasure and the writing consequently clumsy.

Bar 27, beat 2,   In Autograph score   An optional upper octave.
1st quaver,   In Tenbury–Dublin copy ⎫
choral tenor   Hamburg copy   ⎬ Only the lower note.
       RM 18.e.2 copy
       Randall and Abell
         printed score ⎭

'THOU ART GONE UP ON HIGH' (ORIGINAL BASS SETTING)

Bar 12, beat 3,   Handel here wrote a quaver in error.
voice

Bar 46, beat 2,   In Autograph score Handel omitted the necessary ♮.
basso-continuo

Bar 77, beat 2,   In Autograph score Handel omitted the necessary ♭.
basso-continuo

'THOU ART GONE UP ON HIGH' (ALTO SETTING)

Bar 52, 3rd note,   Handel here wrote a ♭ against this b¹, presumably in error for a natural as
voice   the key here is A minor. Had he intended the note to be b¹♭, an accidental was unnecessary according to his usage. Moreover the ♭ here weakens the impact of the chromatic harmony of the flattened supertonic on the first beat of the following bar.

'THE LORD GAVE THE WORD'

Bar 6, beat 3,   In Autograph score   ♩. ♩ [*sic*]
viola

    In Tenbury–Dublin copy ⎫
       Hamburg copy   ⎬ ♫
    In RM 18.e.2 copy ⎫
       Randall and Abell   ⎬ ♩. ♪
         printed score ⎭
    In the identical bar 21 Handel wrote   ♩. ♪

	In Autograph score	(musical notation) [sic]
Bar 14, *beat* 1, *viola*	In Tenbury–Dublin copy Hamburg copy RM 18.e.2 copy Randall and Abell printed score	(musical notation)

'HOW BEAUTIFUL ARE THE FEET' (ALTO-DUET AND CHORUS SETTING)

Basso-continuo

Handel indicated the organ as the continuo instrument here by 'org' against the basso-continuo stave. This is the only reference in the Autograph score to the organ.

Bar 52, beat 3, choral alto

In the Autograph the chorus entry is the last note on the page which contains the alto duet written on two separate staves. With the duet still in his mind Handel wrote a different note on each of these two staves for the chorus alto entry. Except for this beat the chorus altos are in unison throughout. There seems no reason why just one single beat should be divided. As the soprano has a', the third of the harmony, it is better for the altos to sing f' unison.

Bar 64, choral soprano

In the Autograph the soprano part is one crotchet short in this bar. Handel wrote only two crotchets, e'' and c''. In view of the disposition of the harmony it is a reasonable assumption that the missing note is c''.

Bar 116, beats 1 and 2, choral soprano

In the Autograph Handel drew a syllable-slur over these two notes, in error.

'HOW BEAUTIFUL ARE THE FEET' (SOPRANO AIR IN G MINOR)

Bars 29–32, voice

In Autograph score

un - to ⎯ the ends of the world ⎯

Handel originally had in mind a different distribution of the words. Neither the slur which he originally wrote over the first two notes in bar 31, nor the three-note slur to which he altered it, agrees with his word-continuation mark from the word 'world' at the beginning of bar 31 to the first note in bar 32. From the beginning Handel had difficulty in setting this air. His first idea for the opening phrase was

How beau-ti-ful are the feet ⎯ of them that preach the gos - pel

'THEIR SOUND IS GONE OUT'

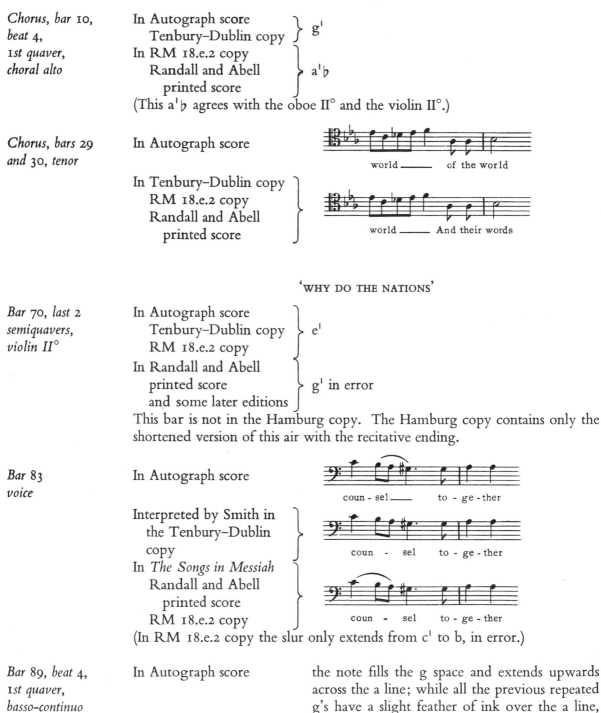

Chorus, bar 10, beat 4, 1st quaver, choral alto

In Autograph score / Tenbury–Dublin copy } g'

In RM 18.e.2 copy / Randall and Abell printed score } a'♭

(This a'♭ agrees with the oboe II° and the violin II°.)

Chorus, bars 29 and 30, *tenor*

In Autograph score

world _____ of the world

In Tenbury–Dublin copy / RM 18.e.2 copy / Randall and Abell printed score

world _____ And their words

'WHY DO THE NATIONS'

Bar 70, *last* 2 *semiquavers, violin II°*

In Autograph score / Tenbury–Dublin copy / RM 18.e.2 copy } e'

In Randall and Abell printed score and some later editions } g' in error

This bar is not in the Hamburg copy. The Hamburg copy contains only the shortened version of this air with the recitative ending.

Bar 83 *voice*

In Autograph score

coun - sel _____ to - ge - ther

Interpreted by Smith in the Tenbury–Dublin copy

coun - sel to - ge - ther

In *The Songs in Messiah* Randall and Abell printed score / RM 18.e.2 copy

coun - sel to - ge - ther

(In RM 18.e.2 copy the slur only extends from c' to b, in error.)

Bar 89, *beat* 4, 1st quaver, *basso-continuo*

In Autograph score

the note fills the g space and extends upwards across the a line; while all the previous repeated g's have a slight feather of ink over the a line, this 7th quaver is very definitely so extended; cf. Handel's notes a on the first beat of bar 90.

In Tenbury–Dublin copy		The note is clearly a.

In RM 18.e.2 copy
  Randall and Abell
    printed score
  and later editions
	}	g

Bar 91,
4th quaver,
basso-continuo

In Autograph score — the note fills the A space and extends upwards across the B line.

In Tenbury–Dublin copy		G

In RM 18.e.2 copy
  Randall and Abell
    printed score
	}	A

Bar 96

In a number of eighteenth-century manuscripts and printed editions (including RM 18.e.2 copy and the Randall and Abell printed score) extending to the present day 'da capo' has been added at the end of this air, but it is not in the Autograph score or the Tenbury–Dublin copy. The words in Handel's writing at the close of his alternative recitative ending and the similarity of the closing bars in both versions indicate that he did not want a 'da capo'.

'LET US BREAK THEIR BONDS ASUNDER'

Bar 8,
choral bass

In Autograph score
  Tenbury–Dublin copy
  Hamburg copy
  RM 18.e.2 copy

In Randall and Abell
  printed score

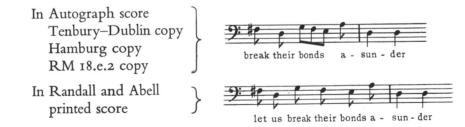

Where voice and instrument are in unison, Handel often failed to copy into the orchestral staves the ties he had written on the choral staves. The Foundling orchestral parts are quite inconsistent, some of the choral ties being copied into the orchestral part and others not. It has generally been assumed that Handel intended whatever he tied in the chorus to be tied in the orchestra. In the Autograph score, however, in some cases, after inserting such ties in the orchestral staves Handel smudged them out; e.g. in this chorus he copied the choral tenor tie in bar 11 into the viola, then smudged it out and, in the many instrumental repetitions of this figure, left the notes untied. Even in the instrumental coda he removed the ties he had written in the violin II° in bar 63 and the violin I° in bar 64. It would seem that in this chorus he wanted the second note of vocal ties to be struck in the orchestra.

Appendix C

Bar 19, beat 3, *basso-continuo*	In Autograph score Tenbury–Dublin copy Hamburg copy	♪. 𝅘𝅥𝅯 *(dotted quaver and semiquaver)*
	In RM 18.e.2 copy Randall and Abell printed score and some later editions	𝅘𝅥𝅮 𝅘𝅥𝅮 *(two even quavers)*

In the Foundling score and 'cello part this is a dotted group but in the Foundling *fagotto* part it consists of even quavers.

Bar 20, beats 2 and 3, *basso-continuo*	In Autograph score Hamburg copy	𝅘𝅥𝅮 𝅘𝅥𝅮 ♪. 𝅘𝅥𝅯
	In Tenbury–Dublin copy	♪. 𝅘𝅥𝅯 ♪. 𝅘𝅥𝅯
	In RM 18.e.2 copy Randall and Abell printed score and some later editions (Cf. bar 19.)	𝅘𝅥𝅮 𝅘𝅥𝅮 𝅘𝅥𝅮 𝅘𝅥𝅮

Bar 20, 2nd semiquaver, violin I°, and Bar 21, beat 1, *basso-continuo*	In Autograph score	Handel omitted the necessary ♯

Bar 25, 4th note, *viola*	In Autograph score RM 18.e.2 copy Randall and Abell printed score	𝅗𝅥. *(dotted minim)*
	In Tenbury–Dublin copy Hamburg copy	𝅗𝅥 𝄾 *(minim and rest)*

Bar 32, beat 1, *violin I°*	In Autograph score Tenbury–Dublin copy Hamburg copy RM 18.e.2	b¹
	In Randall and Abell printed score and some later editions	g¹

Bar 32, beat 2, *choral tenor*	In Autograph score	a crotchet g instead of a rest. Handel was evidently thinking of the bass words in error.

Bar 32, beat 2	The Foundling *fagotto* and 'cello parts have a rest on this beat.

Bar 41, beat 2,
2nd quaver,
viola
	In Autograph score
	  Tenbury–Dublin copy
	  Hamburg copy
	  RM 18.e.2 copy } c¹

This c¹ is clearly a slip of the pen. Handel's placing of the figuring 6 under the second of the three quavers may have been an indication for the playing of a continuo chord on the third beat, but the choral harmony changes in this and the next bar on the first of the three quavers, and the viola is intended to agree with the choral tenor. In the Tenbury–Dublin copy there are no figurings, but in other manuscripts and in the Randall and Abell printed score the figuring 6 is under the first of the three quavers. The correct note d¹ was printed by Arnold and later by both Chrysander and Prout.

Bar 50, 1st note,
choral tenor
	In Autograph score d¹
	In Tenbury–Dublin copy
	  Hamburg copy
	  RM 18.e.2 copy } c¹
	  Randall and Abell
	    printed score

The note c¹ is obviously in error. Note the 5 6 progression in the tenor in bar 49.

In the Autograph Handel first wrote the second quaver as d¹, but then extended the head over the line above and wrote the letter e above the note for the sake of clarity but his e is like a c. Did Smith catch sight of the letter and so write the *first* quaver as c? Above the first note is a thin, hardly recognizable letter d.

Bar 50, *1st quaver,* *viola*	In the Autograph score at the beginning of bar 49 Handel stopped writing the notes in the orchestral staves and wrote a custos on each stave as an 'ut' direction to the copyist. Therefore, as the choral tenor on this quaver is d¹, the viola note is d¹.

        In Tenbury–Dublin copy
          Hamburg copy
          RM 18.e.2 copy   } c¹
          Randall and Abell
            printed score

Obviously the c¹ is in error. Incidentally in RM 18.e.2 the choral tenor note is erroneously also c¹.

The choral tenor in the Autograph score is very clearly d¹. Handel was at some pains to make this bar clear, for having altered the second quaver from d¹ to e¹ he wrote the letter above the note.

Bar 58, beat 1, *2nd quaver,* *violin I°*	In the Autograph the note is clearly d¹¹. But it is a reasonable assumption that Handel intended the violin to reinforce the soprano cadential melody. Further, surely the plain F major harmony sounds better here.

Bar 64,
2nd quaver,
violin I°

In the Autograph score there is in addition to the note f'' a notehead on the a'' leger line. But f'' is a firmly shaped note with the stem attached whereas the a'' is a separate notehead. Further, f'' has musical reason as it maintains both the shape of the figure and the imitation.

'THOU SHALT BREAK THEM'

Bar 38, violin

In Autograph score

In Tenbury–Dublin copy
Hamburg copy
RM 18.e.2 copy

The progression shown in the following composite part made up of bars 37 and 38 of the violin and bar 39 of the voice.

lends some support to the Autograph as against the copies.

Bar 48, voice

In Autograph score
Hamburg copy
RM 18.e.2 copy

In Tenbury–Dublin copy

Bar 63, beat 3

In Autograph score
Tenbury–Dublin copy
The Songs in Messiah

In RM 18.e.2
and later editions

'HALLELUJAH'

Bar 5,
2nd note, tenor

In Autograph score
RM 18.e.2 copy
Hamburg copy
Randall and Abell
    printed score

} is f'♯

His f'♯ was obviously in error for d'; cf. bar 4.

Bars 23–24,
choral tenor (see
also bars 26–27,
choral alto)

In Autograph score

In Tenbury–Dublin copy
Hamburg copy
RM 18.e.2 copy

Hal-le - lu jah Hal-le - lu - jah

In Randall and Abell
printed score
and later editions

Hal-le-lu - jah Hal - le - lu - jah

Bar 29, choral soprano first note

In Autograph score
(See page 95)

Handel wrote an optional octave (note-head only).

Bar 43, first note, choral bass

In Autograph a trill over this minim e . This trill, in Handel's own hand, is the only choral trill in the Autograph.

Bar 46, beat 3, choral alto

In Autograph score
  Hamburg copy
  RM 18.e.2 copy
In Randall and Abell
  printed score

In the Tenbury–Dublin copy there is a notehead for the upper octave but only in pencil.

In the Autograph score the upper d'' is in the viola part.

Bars 76–77, the four unison notes

In Autograph **score**

At this point in the Autograph the only words in Handel's hand are 'And he' in abbreviation of 'And he shall reign'. Written under the bass stave they also stand, according to Handel's usage, for the upper voices. The words 'and Lord of Lords' under the tenor stave and some indecipherable words under the alto stave are smudged out and 'And he shall reign' substituted. The tenor and alto words appear to be in Smith's hand.

233

In Tenbury–Dublin copy
RM 18.e.2 copy } Under all three voices, 'And he shall reign'

In Hamburg copy   Under the bass, 'And he shall reign'; under the tenor and alto, only the word 'and'.

Obviously, when writing the Hamburg copy, Smith did not know whether to write 'And he shall reign' as indicated by Handel's 'And he' or 'And Lord of Lords'.

In Randall and Abell
printed score } 'And he shall reign'

In the Tenbury–Dublin copy there is a loose sheet of paper signed by Otto Goldschmidt. Referring to this point he writes, 'In the score in Smith's handwriting which I possess the 3 unison d's have the words 'And Lord of Lords' substituted in Handel's writing for 'And he shall reign' which are run through with ink'. The statement 'in Handel's writing' can neither be verified nor denied because the whereabouts of the Goldschmidt copy is unknown.

Bar 79, beat 1, choral alto In Autograph score and other MSS.   an optional octave note

Bar 79, beat 2, choral alto

In Autograph score
Tenbury–Dublin copy
Hamburg copy }

In RM 18.e.2 copy
Randall and Abell
printed score }

On four other occasions Handel first wrote the fifth of the harmony for this note and then altered it to the third; in bar 46 in the choral alto, viola and violin II° and in the soprano in bar 49. Further, in bar 79, he wrote $f''\sharp$ in the violin I° and the 1st trumpet. It would appear, therefore, that he wrote the a' in the choral alto in this bar in error.

Bar 81, beat 3, last semiquaver, violin I°

In Autograph score
Tenbury–Dublin copy
Hamburg copy
RM 18.e.2 copy } d''

This has been printed in some twentieth-century editions as e''. It is interesting that in a secondary eighteenth-century manuscript copy, RM 18.b.10, there is a very clear knife-like erasure of some other note previously written. Part of the 4th line of the stave was also removed and then inked over. Handel intended d'', for the other parts also repeat the notes of the harmony:

In the next bar at a similar point Handel writes e'' in the violin I°, but there the violin II° is also moving through a passing note:

Bar 84, beat 3, choral alto

In Autograph score

Handel omitted to write a note for the third beat. Obviously he intended f'♯.

Bar 86, beat 4, and bar 87, beat 2, basso-continuo

In Autograph score
Tenbury–Dublin copy
Hamburg copy
In RM 18.e.2 copy
Randall and Abell
    printed score
and some later editions

'I KNOW THAT MY REDEEMER LIVETH'

Bars 43–45, voice

In Autograph score
Tenbury–Dublin copy
Hamburg copy

43   44   45

liv - eth   and   that   He — shall   stand

In RM 18.e.2 copy
The Songs in Messiah

liv - eth and that He   shall   stand

In Autograph score
Tenbury–Dublin copy
Hamburg copy

Bar 51, violin I°

In RM 18.e.2 copy
Randall and Abell
    printed score
and later editions

Bars 57–59, voice

In Autograph score
Tenbury–Dublin copy
Hamburg copy

57   58   59

liv - eth and that He   shall   stand at the

In *The Songs in Messiah*
RM 18.e.2 copy

liv - eth and that__ He shall stand__ at the

In Goldschmidt copy
(as a correction)

liv - eth and He shall stand_____ at the

Bar 64, beat 3,
voice

In Autograph score
Tenbury–Dublin copy
Hamburg copy
RM 18.e.2 copy

In *The Songs in Messiah*

Bar 125–129,
voice

In Autograph score
Tenbury–Dublin copy
Hamburg copy

the first_____ fruits of them that sleep__

In RM 18.e.2 copy
The Songs in Messiah
Goldschmidt copy

the first fruits of them that sleep__

Bars 133–137,
voice

In Autograph score
Hamburg copy

the first_____ fruits of_ them that sleep

In Tenbury–Dublin copy

the first_____ fruits___ of them that sleep

In *The Songs in Messiah*
RM 18.e.2 copy

the first_____ fruits of them___ that sleep

Bar 147, *voice*   In Autograph score
Tenbury–Dublin copy
Hamburg copy
In *The Songs in Messiah*
and sometimes
printed later

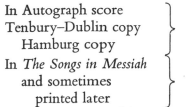

Later editions would seem to have taken this bar from Randall and Abell or *The Songs in Messiah* where, because the violin begins an instrumental episode on the third beat of this bar, continuing on the vocal stave, Handel's minim was printed as a crotchet.

Bars 149–153, *voice*   In Autograph score

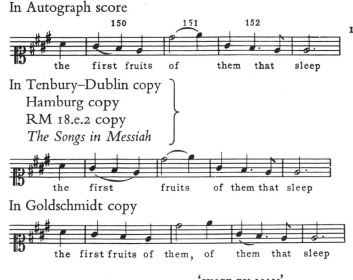

'SINCE BY MAN'

Professor Donald Tovey once declared that Handel 'never wrote a line of unaccompanied choral music'.[2]   There is, however, a considerable body of evidence in support of the opinion that true *a capella* singing was the invention of the Baroque, that it resulted from the sensitivity of the composers of that period to instrumental and vocal colour; this in spite of the instrumental technique that was imposed upon vocal music.

These conflicting opinions apart, the facts remain that Handel wrote rests in the basso-continuo in the *grave* sections of the 'Since by man' sequence, and that in the same sections the Foundling orchestral continuo parts are marked *tacet*, the No. 7 'cello part having the words '*Senza Stromenti* Since by Man Came death'.

[1] N.B. In bar 152 Handel wrote three notes for two syllables but omitted to indicate the grouping.
[2] *Essays in Musical Analysis*, vol v, page 73.

'EVEN SO IN CHRIST SHALL ALL BE MADE ALIVE'

Bars 28–31,
choral bass

In Autograph score (and other principal MSS. and the Randall and Abell printed score)

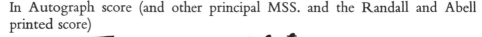

shall all_____ be made a - live

In Prout vocal score

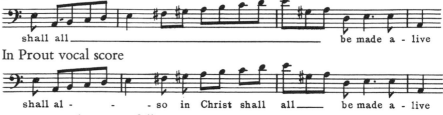

shall al - - - so in Christ shall all___ be made a - live

N.B.—But the Prout full score is correct.

'THE TRUMPET SHALL SOUND'

Bars 3–6,
all parts

In Autograph score
Tenbury–Dublin copy
Hamburg copy

Bars 3–5,
inclusive

In RM 18.e.2 copy
Randall and Abell
  printed score

Bar 6

In RM 18.e.2 copy
Randall and Abell
  printed score

Bar 8, beginning
4th quaver,
basso-continuo

In the Foundling *fagotto* and 'cello parts there are 12 bars' rest from here. It is extremely unlikely, however, that in performance Handel allowed the trumpet to be supported by the harpsichord alone, without string or wind basses. In other works, when he wanted other than the normal practice he gave clear detailed instructions in the basso-continuo. There is no instruction at this point in the *Messiah* Autograph or other important copies.

Bar 22, beats 2,
and 3, violin I°

In Autograph score
Tenbury–Dublin copy
Hamburg copy
In RM 18.e.2 copy
Randall and Abell
  printed score
Some later editions

Bars 38–40,
voice

In Autograph score
Tenbury–Dublin copy
Hamburg copy

rais'd_____ in - cor - rup - ti - ble

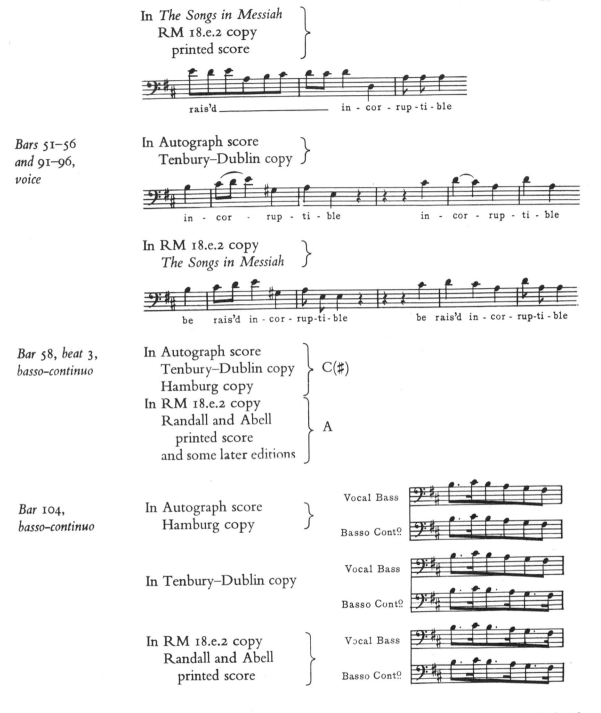

Bars 51–56
and 91–96,
voice

Bar 58, beat 3,
basso-continuo

Bar 104,
basso-continuo

Bars 112–118,
*violin II° and
viola*

In the Tenbury–Dublin copy and in many of the other copies which I have
collated, Handel's notes were copied a bar late, then variously altered by
copyists and editors in order to rectify the resulting incorrect harmony. This

mistake, which was repeated in the first printed *Messiah* music (both the Walsh edition of *Songs in Messiah* and the Randall and Abell full score), has persisted and is to be found in the Chrysander–Handelgesellschaft, the Prout–Novello and the Fischer (New York 1950) editions of the full score.

The following music examples show

(a) four different versions of bar 114 and three of bar 118 and

(b) that the copyists of the RM 18.e.2, RM 18.b.10 Marsh–Matthews and Sterndale Bennett Manuscripts began correctly on the third beat of bar 112, but instead of continuing with Handel's minim on beats one and two of bar 113 wrote rests for these two beats and so fell into the oft-repeated error of writing Handel's violin II° and viola parts a bar late.

The Autograph, Granville, Hamburg, Townley-Hall and Coke manuscripts

The Randall and Abell and the Arnold printed editions

The Chrysander–Handelgesellschaft

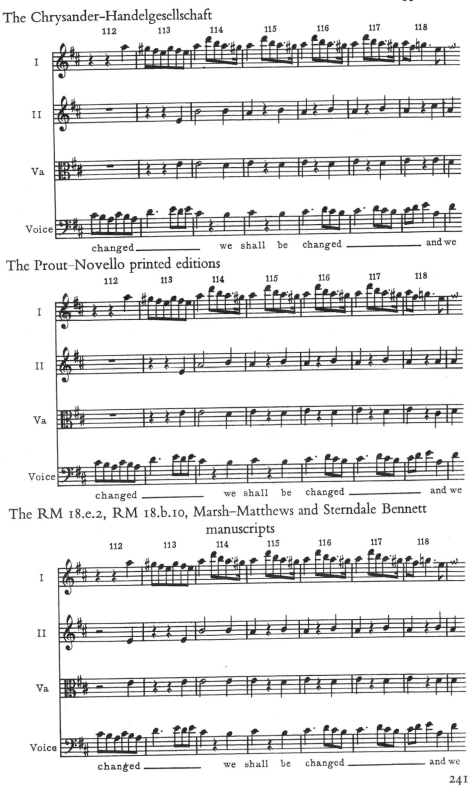

I, II, Va, Voice

changed _____ we shall be changed _____ and we

The Prout–Novello printed editions

changed _____ we shall be changed _____ and we

The RM 18.e.2, RM 18.b.10, Marsh–Matthews and Sterndale Bennett manuscripts

changed _____ we shall be changed _____ and we

Appendix C

Bar 146, *last quaver,* *violin II°*	In Autograph score	c'' (♯)
	In Tenbury–Dublin copy Hamburg copy RM 18.e.2 copy Randall and Abell printed score	a'

In the comparable bar 6 Handel wrote a'.

Bars 155–156, *violin II°*

In Autograph score

Handel wrote the last three notes as e'' and f''♯, obviously a third too high. He wrote the violin II° notes on the same stave as the viola in the alto clef; and this led to his mistaking a leger line (which continued unbroken through 4 bars) for the top line of the stave. This is not to be wondered at, for in order to save a fresh page he crushed 3½ bars into the space of one inch in the margin.

Bar 169, *basso-continuo*

In Autograph score
Tenbury–Dublin copy
Hamburg copy — | 𝅘𝅥. |

In RM 18.e.2 copy
Randell and Abell
    printed score
and some later editions — | 𝅘𝅥 𝄾 |

Bar 194, *basso-continuo*

In Autograph score
Tenbury–Dublin copy
Hamburg copy — | 𝅘𝅥 𝅘𝅥 𝅘𝅥 |

In RM 18.e.2 copy
Randall and Abell
    printed score
and some later editions — | 𝅘𝅥. 𝅘𝅥𝅮𝅘𝅥 |

Bar 211

In Autograph score
Tenbury–Dublin copy
Hamburg copy — *Adagio*

In RM 18.e.2 copy
Randall and Abell
    printed score
and some later editions — There is no indication.

Bar 213, the *double bar line*

In Autograph score — *da capo*

In Tenbury–Dublin copy — *da capo* in Smith's hand, altered by Handel to *dal segno*

Handel first intended a full *da capo*, for immediately following the last vocal note of the middle section he wrote a treble G clef on the vocal stave and wrote the first two notes of the instrumental introduction; but after Smith had completed the Tenbury–Dublin copy Handel evidently changed his mind and decided to take up the repeat from the voice at bar 29. Therefore, in the Tenbury–Dublin copy at this point, in order to make clear his intentions, he wrote the first word of the text 'The', added the necessary note (writing first the note F below the bass stave, in error for d, thinking that the stave was in the treble clef, then altered it to d) and under Smith's *da capo* wrote *dal segno*. The sign was added over the second note of the voice in bar 29.

'THEN SHALL BE BROUGHT TO PASS'

In the Autograph score this recitative has a signature of one flat. It is in the key of B♭ major. It is the only recitative in *Messiah* remaining firmly in one key to which Handel applied the signature convention of one flat less. In the following duet in E♭ major he wrote all three flats in the signature. It is of interest that within the course of one volume, the Randall and Abell printed score, this recitative occurs with the convention signature of one flat in the appendix, and in its true signature of two flats in the body of the score.

'O DEATH WHERE IS THY STING'

A possible cut from bar 5 to bar 23 (6–22 inclusive) is indicated (a) by Handel's own alteration of 'O death' to 'O grave' in bar 5 in the alto stave in the Autograph score.

and (b) by the alternative version of bar 5 written by Handel in the Tenbury–Dublin copy to link up with bar 23:

In Autograph score 　Tenbury–Dublin copy 　*The Songs in Messiah* 　Randall and Abell 　printed score 　(appendix)	the uncut version of 41 bars
In Hamburg copy 　Randall and Abell 　printed score 　(body of score)	the cut version of 24 bars

*Bar 29
(bar 12, cut
version)*

In Autograph score

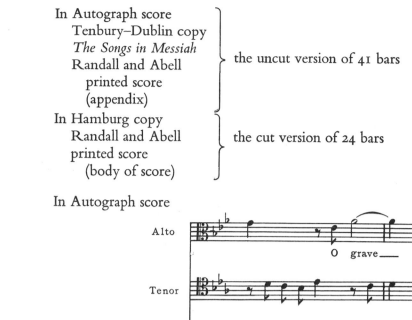

In Tenbury–Dublin **copy**

The position in the bar of the alto note for 'grave' in relation to the tenor, the size of the alto note a¹♭ (clearly a filled-in minim), and the unusually high position of the crotchet rest in the alto stave all indicate that this bar was first copied in the Tenbury–Dublin copy exactly as it is written in the Autograph score and later altered.

*Bar 33, 2nd note
(cut version bar
16), alto*

In Autograph score 　Tenbury–Dublin copy 　RM 18.e.2 copy	a¹ uninflected
In *The Songs in Messiah*	a¹♮
In Hamburg copy	b¹♭

Handel did not write a natural against the note a¹ but obviously he intended the note to be a¹ ♮.

'BUT THANKS BE TO GOD'

Bar 8, beat 3, *note a,* *basso-continuo*	In Autograph score	Handel omitted to insert the necessary ♮ The choral bass is much altered in this bar.

Bar 34, *last quaver,* *choral tenor*

In Autograph score
Tenbury–Dublin copy } d'
Hamburg copy

In RM 18.e.2 copy
Randall and Abell } b♭
  printed score

Apart from supplying a 3rd to the choral harmony, and agreeing with the viola part, the note d makes musical sense by repetition of the descending d c progression in the next bar.

Bar 37, *2nd note,* *choral soprano*

In Autograph score   c''

In Tenbury–Dublin copy
  Hamburg copy
  RM 18.e.2 copy   } b'♭
  Randall and Abell
    printed score

Bar 37, beat 2, *note a,' violin II°* *and choral tenor*	In Autograph score	Handel omitted to insert the necessary ♮

'IF GOD BE FOR US'

Bars 25–27, *voice* — In Autograph score

In Tenbury–Dublin copy
  Hamburg copy
  RM 18.e.2 copy
  The Songs in Messiah

These bars were first written in the Tenbury–Dublin copy exactly as in the Autograph score and later altered.

Bars 37–39, *voice* — In Autograph score

In Tenbury–Dublin copy
  Hamburg copy
  RM 18.e.2 copy
  The Songs in Messiah

Bar 69,
basso-continuo
	In Autograph score
	  Tenbury–Dublin copy
	  Hamburg copy
		} ♩ 𝄽 𝄽

	In RM 18.e.2 copy
	  Randall and Abell
	    printed score
	  and some later editions
		} ♩ 𝄽 ♩

In the Tenbury–Dublin copy the 3rd beat was first written as a note, later altered to a rest.

Bar 71,
2nd note,
violins
	In Autograph score
	  and other MSS.
	and *The Songs in*
	  Messiah
		} e''♭

	Sometimes printed	f''

Bar 72, beat 2,
violin
	In Autograph score
	  Tenbury–Dublin copy
	  Hamburg copy
	  RM 18.e.2 copy
		} No ornament

	In *The Songs in Messiah*	A trill

Bar 89, *voice*	In Autograph score Tenbury–Dublin copy	}

	In Hamburg copy
	  RM 18.e.2 copy
	  The Songs in Messiah
		}

Bars 101 and 103,
violins
	In Autograph score
	  Tenbury–Dublin copy
	  RM 18.e.2 copy
		}

	In Hamburg copy	[*sic*]
	In *The Songs in Messiah*	

Handel did not write a dotted group in any of the other comparable bars in the air. *The Songs in Messiah* taken by itself is not conclusive evidence that the dotted groups in the Autograph were in error. Further, Handel troubled to write the dotted group over two beats and in two bars.

This is the only occasion when both voice and violins move together in quavers and Handel might have written as he did in order to avoid a struck second (in two cases a minor second) on a weak part of the beat.

In the Hamburg copy the time value of the second note is obviously in error.

Bar 104, beat 1, *basso-continuo*	In the Autograph score Handel omitted to insert the necessary ♭.

Bar 115, beat 2,
violins

In Autograph score
   Tenbury–Dublin copy   g¹
   Hamburg copy

In RM 18.e.2 copy
   The Songs in Messiah   b¹♮
   Randall and Abell
   and later editions

The b¹♮ is obviously in error. The original *motif* ends on g¹. Moreover, the interval of the descending fifth runs through the whole air. Cf. bars 76, 124–5, 127–8, and 142.

Bar 147,
voice

In Autograph score

In Tenbury–Dublin copy
Hamburg copy
RM 18.e.2 copy
The Songs in Messiah

Handel wrote the dot but not the semiquaver beam to the following note. It could be argued that, as he introduced the dotted figure in bars 86–89 as a contrast to the even quavers of the previous bars, he wanted the same contrast here; therefore, that his omission to make the second note a semiquaver was in error. On the other hand, in bars 86–89 the dotted figure is developed into a rhythmic sequence whereas bar 147 is a single cadential bar, in reality a completion of the evenly flowing figure that begins at bar 134; in which case the dot is in error. Cf. the air 'Their land brought forth frogs' from *Israel in Egypt*, where, in bars 25–28 and 65–67, the music consisting of sequential repetitions unbroken by any sustained notes, he uses the dotted figure; in contrast to bars 75–79 where a minim is tied to the first note of the following bar, and the bar consists entirely of even quavers.

Bar 161, 2nd
and 3rd notes,
voice

In Autograph score
   Tenbury–Dublin copy
   Hamburg copy
RM 18.e.2 copy
   The Songs in Messiah

In Mozart–Hiller

Sometimes printed

Bar 162,
voice

In Autograph score
   Tenbury–Dublin copy
   Hamburg copy
   Chrysander

In RM 18.e.2 copy
   The Songs in Messiah
   Prout

In *The Songs in Messiah* and the Randall and Abell printed score the voice and the violin share the same stave in this bar; the voice takes the first two beats as a minim and the violin enters on the third beat. The voice and violin are on different staves in RM 18.e.2 but the voice is still a minim minus the dot: | 𝅗𝅥 𝄾 |

'WORTHY IS THE LAMB THAT WAS SLAIN'

Bar 2, beats 3 and 4, viola

In Autograph score
   Tenbury–Dublin copy   } f¹♯
   Hamburg copy
In Randall and Abell
   printed score   } a¹
   and some later
   editions
In RM 18.e.2 copy   g¹ in error

Bar 21, last quaver, 2nd trumpet

In the Autograph Handel wrote e¹¹, but it is more likely that he intended the trumpet to agree with the choral tenor's f¹♯.

Bars 26–28, choral bass

In the Tenbury–Dublin copy Smith omitted to write the words under the tenor stave. In the empty space Handel wrote other words:

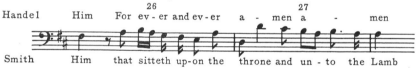

This word alteration may have some bearing upon the additional cadential amen written by Handel in the Tenbury–Dublin copy. In this copy 'Blessing, Honour' finishes halfway down folio 132 recto, and the 'Amen' chorus begins on folio 132 verso. In the blank space on folio 132 recto Handel wrote:

The word alteration in bars 26–28 might easily have indicated a cut from bar 28 to the beginning of the 'Amen' chorus, or a cut to the above four-note cadence on some occasion when the singing of the 'Amen' chorus was impracticable.

Sir William Cusins in *Handel's Messiah: an examination of the original and some contemporary MSS* (1874) wrote, 'In the [Tenbury–]Dublin Copy Handel made an arrangement doing away entirely with the "Amen" chorus. He altered the subject of the *larghetto* so' (see Tenbury–Dublin example above).

These alterations, however, do not support the view (to be found in Schoelcher's *The Life of Handel*) that the 'Hallelujah' chorus was intended as the final chorus in the oratorio, and that the 'Amen' chorus was an afterthought. In the Autograph Handel finished writing 'Blessing and honour' literally at the end of a folio recto, and began the 'Amen' at the beginning of the same folio verso.

Bar 33,
4th note,
choral soprano

In Autograph score

In Tenbury–Dublin copy
  Hamburg copy,
  RM 18.e.2. copy
} there is not any trace of the notehead

Handel would appear to have been hearing mentally the alto theme played by the 2nd violin at the upper octave. Later, in bar 35, he gave the soprano an ascending scale of A with the climax on the upper octave. He then emphasized this in bar 36 by giving the tenors the descending scale of A, beginning on the upper octave. He was still obsessed with the a'' however, for in bar 42, fourth beat, he first wrote the soprano entry at the upper octave, beginning on a''.

Bar 39, beat 4

In Autograph score a possible cut is indicated from this point to bar 53, beat 4. In the Tenbury–Dublin, Hamburg and RM 18.e.2 copies there is no sign of a cut. In the Autograph score on the trumpet and timpani staves at bar 39 is pencilled

Trumpet

Timpani

Bar 50, beat 4,
last semiquaver
violin I°

In Autograph score
  Tenbury–Dublin copy }

In the Hamburg copy the last note is not clearly written. There is not a leger line either through or under the note but the note is well above the stave, not resting on the top line.

In RM 18.e.2 copy
  Randall and Abell
    printed score
  and some later editions }

Handel clearly intended b'', for the sopranos on this beat sing

Bar 56, beat 3,
2nd quaver,
viola

In Autograph score
  Tenbury–Dublin copy
  Hamburg copy
} f'♯

In Randall and Abell
    printed score
  and some later editions
} a'

Bar 57,
4th quaver
choral bass

In Autograph score
  Other MSS.
  Randall and Abell
    printed score
  Chrysander
} d

Sometimes printed   d'

I

Bar 57, beat 1,   In Autograph score
second quaver,   Tenbury–Dublin copy   }   f'♯
viola   Hamburg copy
          In RM 18.e.2 copy
            Randall and Abell   }   d'
              printed score
            and later editions

Bars 65–66,   In Autograph score
choral alto

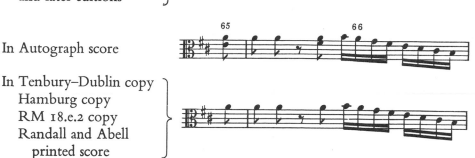

     In Tenbury–Dublin copy
        Hamburg copy
        RM 18.e.2 copy
        Randall and Abell
        printed score

The note a¹ would appear to be Handel's second thought; he rejected his first idea of repeating the rising 4th figure (cf. bars 64–65), possibly in order to strengthen the choral harmony.

'AMEN' CHORUS

For easy reference, the 'Amen' section of 'Worthy is the Lamb' is barred as a separate chorus.

Bar 5, beat 3,   Handel's first idea for bars 4–5 was in the Autograph score
choral bass

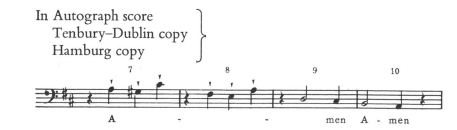

This is the reason for the smudged syllable 'men' on the 3rd beat of bar 5 in the Autograph that has been copied in error in some later editions.

Bar 9,   In the Autograph the first syllable of the Amen beginning in bar 7 is continued
choral tenor   through and beyond bar 9. It is sometimes printed or performed with a con-
       cluding syllable 'men' on the second f♯ in bar 9, a new 'Amen' beginning on
       the following g♯. It must be remembered that the singing of repeated notes
       to the same vowel was an ordinary part of vocal technique in this period.

Bars 7–10,   In Autograph score
choral bass   Tenbury–Dublin copy
            Hamburg copy

In RM 18.e.2 copy } the syllable distribution is the same as in the
Randall and Abell } Autograph but the staccato marks are omitted
printed score }

Sometimes printed

A - men,   A - men,   A - men, A - men.

Bar 11, beat 4,   Handel here wrote the choral alto and tenor notes on the *bassetti* stave but
basso-continuo   omitted to write the tenor note, 4th beat, c'♯.

Bar 31,   In Autograph score
choral alto

In Tenbury–Dublin copy ⎫
Hamburg copy   ⎬
RM 18.e.2 copy   ⎬
Randall and Abell   ⎬
printed score   ⎭

The position of the dot and the general appearance of the two notes suggests
that f' was Handel's first thought and that it was later changed to a'.

Bar 32, beats 2,   In Autograph score   ⎫
3 and 4,   Tenbury–Dublin copy ⎬ staccato marks over these notes
choral soprano

In Hamburg copy   ⎫
RM 18.e.2 copy   ⎬ these notes are without staccato marks
Randall and Abell   ⎬
printed score   ⎭

Bar 38,   In Autograph score
choral alto

A - men A -   men

In Tenbury–Dublin copy ⎫
Hamburg copy   ⎬
RM 18.e.2 copy   ⎬
Randall and Abell   ⎬
printed score   ⎭

A -   men

Bar 38, beat 3,   In Autograph score   e'
1st quaver,   In Tenbury–Dublin copy ⎫
viola   Hamburg copy   ⎬
RM 18.e.2 copy   ⎬
Randall and Abell   ⎬ c'♯
printed score   ⎬
and some later   ⎬
editions   ⎭

Bars 38–39,
choral tenor

In Autograph score

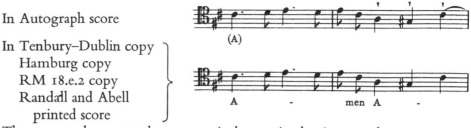

In Tenbury–Dublin copy
  Hamburg copy
  RM 18.e.2 copy
  Randall and Abell
    printed score

The separate beams to the quavers in bar 39 in the Autograph score suggest that Handel omitted the syllable 'men' in bar 39 in error.

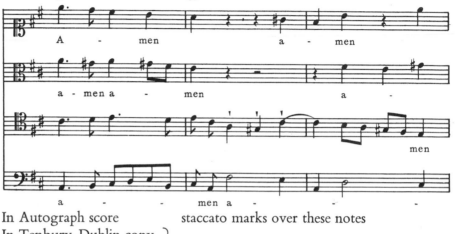

Bar 39, beats 2,
3 and 4,
choral tenor

In Autograph score   staccato marks over these notes

In Tenbury–Dublin copy
  Hamburg copy   these notes are without staccato marks
  RM 18.e.2 copy

In RM 18.e.2 there are dashes only in the tenor part, and only in bars 13 and 17. There are no dashes elsewhere. In the Randall and Abell printed score there are no dashes in the bass either in bars 7–8 or elsewhere. N.B., although dashes in the tenor in bar 13 there are slurs in the tenor in bars 17 and 19 and in the alto in bars 18 and 19. The slurs are unquestionably in error.

Bar 41,
violin I°

In Autograph score
  Randall and Abell
    printed score
In Tenbury–Dublin copy
  Hamburg copy
  RM 18.e.2 copy

The MS. copies are in error; the violin I° is here doubling the soprano and the soprano part is syncopated.

Bar 54, beats 2,
3 and 4, choral
bass

In Autograph score
  Tenbury–Dublin copy   } staccato marks over these notes

In Hamburg copy
  RM 18.e.2 copy   } these notes are without staccato marks

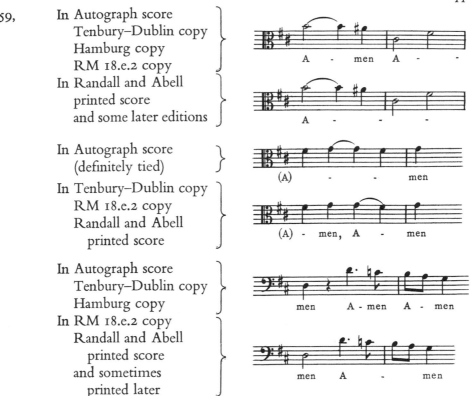

Bars 58 and 59, *choral alto*	In Autograph score Tenbury–Dublin copy Hamburg copy RM 18.e.2 copy
	In Randall and Abell printed score and some later editions
Bar 67, *choral alto*	In Autograph score (definitely tied)
	In Tenbury–Dublin copy RM 18.e.2 copy Randall and Abell printed score
Bars 67–68, *choral bass*	In Autograph score Tenbury–Dublin copy Hamburg copy
	In RM 18.e.2 copy Randall and Abell printed score and sometimes printed later

Once again forgetting Handel's practice of resting the voice on a second beat against a sustained continuo, Smith has copied Handel's continuo in mistake for the choral bass. Cf. 'He trusted in God', bar 8, choral bass.

Bar 81, *choral tenor*	In Autograph score Tenbury–Dublin copy Hamburg copy
	In RM 18.e.2 copy Randall and Abell printed score

In the Autograph score Handel did not write the word under the tenor stave; but his grouping of the notes is a clear indication of his intended syllable distribution.

'BUT WHO MAY ABIDE' (ORIGINAL BASS SETTING)

Bar 116,
final vocal
cadence

The final vocal cadence of the original (all in $\frac{3}{8}$) bass setting of 'But who may abide' was first copied into the Tenbury–Dublin copy as Handel wrote it in the Autograph score. It was later altered to

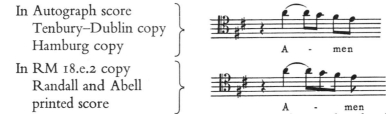

There is a very faint trace of these alternative lower notes in the Autograph, so faint as to be almost invisible to the naked eye, and, moreover, in pencil; there is no evidence of by whom or when they were inserted. In his facsimile, Chrysander shows this bar with both endings in equal type as though given as equal alternatives in the Autograph.

In the Tenbury–Dublin copy Handel's crotchet note a from the Autograph was written nearer to the bar line and then erased (but not completely); the note a, as shown in the above music example, has been added in pencil.

'REJOICE GREATLY' (ORIGINAL $\frac{12}{8}$ SETTING)

Bar 92

When Handel decided to make a cut from bar 44 to this point, it was necessary for him to alter this bar because of the change in key relationships from B♭ major-G minor to F major-G minor.

'WHY DO THE NATIONS'

In an alternative shortened version of this air Handel replaced the music from bar 39 to the end with a recitative. The Foundling copy contains only the shortened setting. Therefore, the Foundling bassoon part, made for that setting, ends in bar 39.

'WHY DO THE NATIONS' (RECITATIVE ENDING)

Last note,
basso-continuo

In repairs to the page of the original manuscript, this note head has been obliterated, but it appears in other contemporary manuscript copies.

APPENDIX D
EXTRACTS FROM THE MINUTES OF THE
GENERAL COMMITTEE OF THE FOUNDLING HOSPITAL

2nd May 1750

That the thanks of this Committee be given to George Frederick Handel Esq. for his performing in the Chapel yesterday of the Oratorio called *Messiah* to a very numerous audience, who expressed the greatest satisfaction at the excellency thereof, and of his great benevolence in promoting this charity; which the Chairman did.

(Page 114 of No. 3 Minute book of the General Committee)

13th June 1750

. . . And that the money received for the last Performance of the Oratorio, called *Messiah*, in the Chapel of the Hospital, amounted to Three hundred and Fourteen pounds Nine shillings & sixpence. And that the Treasurer had also paid Thirty five pounds, for the Performers in the said Performance; and had given Mr. Handel's Servants Three Guineas, for their Attendance on both performances.

The Secretary acquainted the Committee, that Mr. Gates the Master of the Children of the King's Chapel, having received, by Mr. Handel's order, Seven Guineas for their Performance, in the Chapel of this Hospital on the 1st and 15th May last, had brought to the Secretary Five pounds Nineteen shillings thereof, chusing only to be reimbursed the One Pound Eight shillings he paid for the Two Days Coach hire for the said Children to and from the Hospital, which the Secretary paid the Treasurer as the Benefaction of the said Mr. Gates to this Hospital.

ORDERED

That the Secretary do return the Thanks of this Committee to Mr. Gates for the same, and sign a Copy of this Minute for that purpose.

29th May 1754

The Treasurer reported, that the Net Money arising from the Performance of the Oratorio of the *Messiah* in the Chapel of this Hospital the 15th Instant, amounted to the sum of £607.17.6 . . . To wit . . .

For 1219 Tickets, and by Cash received	£666	15	0
Paid for Musicians, Constables, etc. as by the following Account	58	17	6
	£607	17	6

		£	s	d
Messrs.	Brown	£1	1	0
	Collet		15	0
	Freek		15	0
	Claudio		10	0
	Scarpettini		10	0
	Wood		10	0
	Wood Junr.		10	0
Violins	Jackson		10	0
	Abbington		10	0
	Dunn		10	0
	Stockton		10	0
	Nicholson		10	0
	Neal		8	0
	Davis		8	0
	Rash		8	0
	Smith		8	0
Tenors	Warner		8	0
	Warner Junr.		8	0
	Rawlins		8	0
	Ebelin		8	0
Violoncelli	Gillier		10	6
	Haron		10	6
	Hebden		10	6
Contra Bassi	Dietrich		15	0
	Thompson		15	0
Bassoons	Baumgarden		10	0
	Jarvis		8	0
	Goodman		8	0
	Dyke		8	0
Hautbois	Eyford		10	0
	Teede		10	0
	Vincent		10	0
	Simpson		8	0
Trumpets	Adcock		10	6
	Willis		8	0
Horns and	Fr. Smith		10	6
Kettledrums	Frova		10	6
	Miller		10	6
	Carried up	£19	8	6

		£	s	d
	Brought forward	£19	8	6
	Christ.° Smith Org.	—	—	—
	Beard	—	—	—
	Frasi		6	6 0
	Galli		4	14 6
	Passesini		4	14 6
	Wass		1	11 6
	Boys		3	3 0
	Baildon			10 6
	Barrow			10 6
Singers	Cheriton			10 6
	Ladd			10 6
	Baildon Junr.			10 6
	Vandenon			10 6
	Champness			10 6
	Courtney			10 6
	Wilder			10 6
	Dupee			10 6
	Walz			10 6
	Cox			10 6
	Legg			10 6
	Le Blanc		1	1 0
	Gundal			10 6
Servants	Prince			10 6
	Lee			10 6
	Shepherd			10 6
	Musick Porters		1	1 0
		£50	18	6
Presented Mr. Ch. Smith			5	5 0
		£56	3	6
To the Constables			2	2 0
Organ Blowers 4/-				
Porterage of Tickets 8/-				12 0
Total		£58	17	6

25th June 1754

Mr. Fauquier reported, That Mr. White being ill he had waited on Mr. Handel in pursuance of a Minute of the 5th instant: And that Mr. Handel approved of the Committee's appointing Mr. Smith organist to the Chapel to conduct his Musical Compositions; but that, on account of his health, he excused himself from giving any further instructions relating to the Performances.

27th April 1758

Singers at the Performance of the Oratorio at the Foundling Hospital

Sigra. Frasi	£6	6	0
Miss Frederick	4	4	0
Miss Young	3	3	0
Mr. Beard	–	–	–
Mr. Champness	1	11	6
Mr. Wass	1	1	0
6 Boys	4	14	6
Baildon	1	1	0
Barrow	1	1	0
Champness		10	6
Baildon Jnr.		10	6
Ladd		10	6
Cox		10	6
Munck		10	6
Reinhold		10	6
Walz		10	6
Courtney		10	6
Kurz		10	6
	£27	16	6
	£55	11	0

Servants

John Duberg Mr. Handel's man	£1	1	0
Evens		10	6
Condel		10	6
Green		10	6
Mason		10	6
Musick Porters	1	11	6
	£4	14	6
Singers	27	16	6
Orchestra	17	15	0
	£50	6	0
Mr. Smith	5	5	0
May 2nd 1758	£55	11	0

Received of Saml. Wilkinson the Sum of Fifty Five Pounds Eleven Shillings for the performers of the Oratorio 27 April 1758 in full of all Demands

by me
Christopher Smith

To the Constables for their attendance	3	3	0
	£58	14	0

A list of the Performers—*Messiah* on Thursday April 27th 1758.

	Messrs. Brown	.	.	. £1 1 0		Gillier	.	.	10 6
	Collet	.	.	15 0	Violoncelli	Haron	.	.	10 6
	Freeke	.	.	15 0		Hebden	.	.	10 6
	Frowd	.	.	15 0					
	Claudis	.	.	10 0	Contra Bassi	Dietrich	.	.	15 0
Violins	Wood	.	.	10 0		Sworms	.	.	10 0
	Wood Junr.	.	.	10 0					
	Demier	.	.	10 0	Trumpets	Adcock	.	.	10 6
	Abbington	.	.	10 0		Willis	.	.	10 6
	Grosman	.	.	10 0					
	Jackson	.	.	10 0	Horns	Frova	.	.	10 6
	Nicholson	.	.	10 0		Miller	.	.	10 6
	Nash	.	.	8 0	Tympani	Fr. Smith	.	.	10 6
Violas	Warner	.	.	8 0					
	Stockton	.	.	8 0					£5 9 0
						Brought over	.	12 6 0
	Eyford	.	.	10 6					
Oboes	Teede	.	.	10 6		In all	.	. £17 15 0
	Vincent	.	.	10 0					
	Weichsel	.	.	8 0					
	Miller	.	.	10 6					
Bassoons	Baumgarden	.	.	10 6					
	Goodman	.	.	8 0					
	Owen	.	.	8 0					
				£12 6 0					

18th April 1759[1]

That the advertisement for the Oratorio be published four times a week in each of the Daily papers, and that Mr. Smith's name be inserted in the room of Mr. Handel's.

[1] This was immediately after Handel's death

APPENDIX E
METRONOME RATINGS

THIS table is an accurate calculation of the relation between length of pendulum and the number of beats per minute.

Inches		M.M. rate	Nearest whole number as used in music Crotchets per minute
5	equals	167·8	168
6		153·1	153
7		141·8	142
8		132·6	133
9		125·0	125
10		118·7	119
10½		115·8	116
11		113·1	113
12		108·2	108
14		100·2	100
15		96·85	97
16		93·78	94
17		90·99	91
18		88·53	89
19		86·06	86
20		83·89	84
21		81·87	82
24		76·58	77
26		73·57	74
27		72·18	72
30		68·48	68
39		60·06	60

COMPARATIVE TABLE OF TEMPI

	Crotch		John Clarke	Rim-bault	Elvey Surman	Chrys-ander Per-forming	Prout	Cooper-smith
	Piano arrange-ment	Monthly magazine letter						
Overture, *Grave*	♪=14″(100)	♪=10½″(116)	𝅗𝅥=50	♪=84	𝅗𝅥=50	𝅗𝅥=58	𝅗𝅥=60	𝅗𝅥=60
Overture, *Allegro moderato*	𝅗𝅥=11″(113)		𝅗𝅥=108	𝅗𝅥=126	𝅗𝅥=108	—	𝅗𝅥=116	𝅗𝅥=116
'Comfort ye'			♪=58	♪=60	♪=58	♩=60	♪=72	♪=80
'Every valley'		♪=1′7″(86)	♩=92	♩=72	♩=92	♩=84	♩=80	♩=88
'And the glory'	♩=15″(97)	♩=1′0″(108)	♩=108	♩=116	♩=108	♩=116	♩=100	♩=116
'Thus saith the Lord'			—	♪=120	—	—	♩=76	—
'But who may abide'								
larghetto			♪=72	♪=76	♪=72	—	♪=88	♪=88
prestissimo		𝅗𝅥=24″(77)	𝅗𝅥=88	𝅗𝅥=144	𝅗𝅥=88	—	𝅗𝅥=138	𝅗𝅥=138
'And He shall purify'	♪=9″(125)		♩=72	♩=60	♩=72	—	♩=72	♩=84
'O Thou that tellest'	♪=10″(119)		♩.=50	♪=120	♩.=50	♪=120	♪=138	♪=126
'For behold, darkness'			♪=72	♪=76	♪=72	♪=76	♪=72	♪=80
'The people that walked'			♩=84	♩=66	♩=84	♩=69	♩=72	♩=72
'For unto us'	♪=8″(133)		♩=92	♩=66	♩=92	♩=72	♩=76	♩=80
Pastoral Symphony	♪=18″(89)		♩=80[1]	♪=104	♪=80	♪=54[2]	♪=132	♪=104
'And lo!'			♪=88	♪=92	♪=88	♪=69	♩=56	♪=69
'And suddenly'			♪=100	♪=108	♪=100	♩=84	♩=72	♩=84
'Glory to God'	♪=9″(125)		♩=84	—	♩=84	♩=84	♩=80	♩=88
'Rejoice greatly'			♩=108	𝅗𝅥=96	—	♩=100	♩=88	♩=96
'He shall feed His flock'			♩=80	♩=104	♩=80	♩.=58	♪=112	♪=120
'His yoke is easy'	♪=9″(125)		♩=88	♩=66	♩=88	♩=84	♩=69	♩=80
'Behold the Lamb'	♪=26″(74)		♩=80	♩=84	♩=80	♩=54	♩=80	♩=88
'He was despised'		♪=3′3″(60)	♪=56	♪=60	♪=56	♪=60	♪=72	♪=88
'Surely'	♪=26″(74)		♪=92	—	♪=92	♪=80	♪=72	♪=80
'And with His stripes'	𝅗𝅥=20″(84)	𝅗𝅥=1′2″(100)	𝅗𝅥=100	𝅗𝅥=80	𝅗𝅥=100	𝅗𝅥=69	𝅗𝅥=80	𝅗𝅥=88
'All we like sheep'	♪=6″(153)		♩=100	♩=88	♩=100	♩=92	♩=92	♩=92
'All we like sheep', *Adagio*	♪=20″(84)		♩=58	—	♩=58	♩=88	♩=60	♩=66
'All they that see Him'			♪=88	♪=63	♪=88	—	♪=80	♪=80
'He trusted in God'	♩=21″(82)	♩=1′5″(91)	♩=88	♩=69	♩=88	♩=88	♩=80	♩=88
'Thy rebuke'			—	♪=56	—	♪=58	—	—
'Behold and see'			♩=50(2)	♪=56	♩=50	♩=50	♪=66	♪=66
'But Thou didst not leave'			♪=84	♪=92	♪=84	♩=66	♪=108	♪=108
'Lift up your heads'	♩=26″(74)		♩=92	♩=76	♩=92	♩=84	♩=76	♩=80

[1] ? a misprint. In another copy of the Clarks – Jones edition in my possession the Pastoral Symphony is given ♪=80.

[2] ? a misprint.

	Crotch		John Clarke	Rim-bault	Elvey Surman	Chrys-ander Per-forming	Prout	Cooper-smith
	Piano arrange-ment	Monthly magazine letter						
'Let all the Angels'	𝅗𝅥=26″(74)		𝅗𝅥=92	𝅗𝅥=80	𝅗𝅥=92	—	𝅗𝅥=72	𝅗𝅥=88
'Thou art gone up'			𝅗𝅥=108	𝅗𝅥=100	𝅗𝅥=108	—	𝅗𝅥=84	𝅗𝅥=84
'The Lord gave the word'	♪=8″(133)		𝅗𝅥=76	𝅗𝅥=58	𝅗𝅥=76	𝅗𝅥=92	𝅗𝅥=80	𝅗𝅥=80
'How beautiful' (Air G minor)			♪=80	♪=96	♪=80	♩.=58	♪=104	♪=108
'Their sound is gone out' (Chorus)	♪=8″(133)		𝅗𝅥=76	𝅗𝅥=88	𝅗𝅥=76	—	𝅗𝅥=88	𝅗𝅥=88
'How beautiful' (Alto duet)			—	—	—	—	—	𝅗𝅥=92
'Break forth into joy' (Chorus)	𝅗𝅥=16″(94)		—	—	—	—	—	𝅗𝅥=92
'Their sound' (Tenor arioso)		♪=1′4″(94)	—	—	—	𝅗𝅥=60	—	𝅗𝅥=72
'Why do the nations'			♩=132	♩=120	♩=132	♩=116	♩=112	♩=126
'Let us break'	♪=7″(142)	♪=6″(153)	♩=104	♩=92	♩=104	—	♩=76	♩=88
'Thou shalt break them'			♩=92	♩=108	♩=92	—	♩=84	♩=84
'Hallelujah'	♪=7″(142)		♩=76	—	♩=76	♩=88	♩=72	♩=92
'I know that my Redeemer'			♩=54	♩=60	♩=54	♩=63	♩=72	♩=76
'Since by man'	♪=27″(72)	♪=2′6″(68)	♪=80	♩=50	♪=80[1]	♩=63	♩=60	♩=60
'By man came also'	𝅗𝅥=18″(89)		♩=96	♩=84	♩=96	♩=96	♩=84	♩=92
'For as in Adam'			—	—	♩=80[1]	♩=63	—	♩=60
'Even so in Christ'			—	—	♩=96	♩=100	—	♩=96
'Behold I tell you a mystery'			—	—	—	𝅗𝅥=69	—	—
'The trumpet shall sound'			𝅗𝅥=92	𝅗𝅥=104	𝅗𝅥=92	𝅗𝅥=92	𝅗𝅥=80	𝅗𝅥=84
'O Death, where is thy sting'	♪=12″(108)	♪=6″(153)	♪=96	♪=100	♪=66	—	𝅗𝅥=69	𝅗𝅥=69
'But thanks be to God'	♪=10″(119)		𝅗𝅥=88	𝅗𝅥=72	𝅗𝅥=88	—	𝅗𝅥=69	𝅗𝅥=69
'If God be for us'			𝅗𝅥=92	𝅗𝅥=104	𝅗𝅥=92[1]	—	𝅗𝅥=88	𝅗𝅥=88
'Worthy is the Lamb', largo	♪=39″(60)	♪=2′6″(68)	♪=60	♪=50	♪=60	𝅗𝅥=66	𝅗𝅥=60	𝅗𝅥=60
andante	♪=14″(100)		♪=100	♪=84	♪=100	𝅗𝅥=76	♪=120	𝅗𝅥=84
larghetto	♪=10″(119)	♪=7″(142)	♪=80	♪=72	♪=80	𝅗𝅥=84	𝅗𝅥=72	𝅗𝅥=76
'Amen'	𝅗𝅥=24″(77)		𝅗𝅥=92	𝅗𝅥=84	𝅗𝅥=92	𝅗𝅥=112	𝅗𝅥=84	𝅗𝅥=92
'How beautiful', (Alto C minor air)								♪=108
'But lo,' (Arioso)								𝅗𝅥=69
'Rejoice greatly' 12/8								♩.=96
'Thou art gone up' (Soprano)								𝅗𝅥=84
'Thou art gone up' (Guadagni)								𝅗𝅥=84
'But who may abide' (Bass)								♪=88

[1] ? a misprint.

SUMMARY IN TERMS OF SPEED

Overture
Grave

Rblt.	Crot. Cl. Elv.	Crot. Chrys.	Prt. Cpsmth.
♪=84	♪=100(♩=50)	♪=116	♪=120(♩=60)

Allegro moderato

Crot.	Prt. Cpsmth.	Rblt.	Cl. Elv.
♩=56	♩=58	♩=63	♩=108

'Comfort ye'

Cl. Elv.	Rblt.	Prt.	Cpsmth.	Chrys.
♪=58	♪=60	♪=72	♪=80	♪=120(♩=60)

'Every valley'

Crot.	Rblt.	Prt,	Chrys.	Cpsmth.	Cl. Elv.
♩=44(♪=86)	♩=72	♩=80	♩=84	♩=88	♩=92

'And the glory'

Crot.	Prt.	Crot. Cl. Elv.	Rblt. Chrys. Cpsmth.
♩=96	♩=100	♩=108	♩=116

'But who may abide'
Larghetto

Cl. Elv.	Rblt.	Prt. Cpsmth.
♪=72	♪=76	♪=88

Prestissimo

Prt.	Rblt.	Crot.	Cl. Elv.
♩=69	♩=72	♩=76	♩=88

'And He shall purify'

Rblt.	Crot.	Cl. Elv. Prt.	Cpsmth.
♩=60	♩=63	♩=72	♩=84

'O Thou that tellest'

Crot. Rblt. Chrys.	Cpsmth.	Prt.	Cl. Elv.
♪=120	♪=126	♪=138	♪=150

'For behold, darkness'

Cl. Elv. Prt.	Rblt. Chrys.	Cpsmth.
♪=72	♪=76	♪=80

'The people that walked'

Rblt.	Chrys.	Prt. Cpsmth.	Cl. Elv.
♩=66	♩=69	♩=72	♩=84

'For unto us'

Crot. Rblt.	Chrys.	Prt.	Cpsmth.	Cl. Elv.
♩=66	♩=72	♩=76	♩=80	♩=92

Pastoral Symphony

Cl. Elv.	Crot.	Rblt. Cpsmth.	Prt.	Chrys.
♪=80	♪=88	♪=104	♪=132	♪=162(♩.[1]=54)

'And lo!' (*accompagnato*)

Cl. Elv.	Rblt.	Prt.	Chrys. Cpsmth.
♪=88	♪=92	♪=112	♪=138

'And suddenly'

Cl. Elv.	Rblt.	Prt.	Chrys. Cpsmth.
♩=50	♩=54	♩=72	♩=84

'Glory to God'

Crot.	Prt.	Cl. Elv. Chrys.	Cpsmth.
♩=63	♩=80	♩=84	♩=88

'Rejoice' (4/4)

Prt.	Rblt. Cpsmth.	Chrys.	Cl.
♩=88	♩=96	♩=100	♩=108

'He shall feed His flock'

Cl. Elv.	Rblt.	Prt.	Cpsmth.	Chrys.
♪=80	♪=104	♪=112	♪=120	♪=174(♩.=58)

'His yoke is easy'

Crot.	Rblt.	Prt.	Cpsmth.	Chrys.	Cl. Elv.
♩=63	♩=66	♩=69	♩=80	♩=84	♩=88

[1] ? a misprint.

	Crot.	Cl. Elv. Prt.	Rblt.	Cpsmth.	Chrys.
'Behold the lamb'	♪=72	♪=80	♪=84	♪=88	♪=108
	Cl. Elv.	Crot. Rblt.	Prt.	Cpsmth.	Chrys.
'He was despised'	♪=56	♪=60	♪=72	♪=88	♪=120(♩=60)
	Crot. Prt.	Chrys. Cpsmth.	Cl. Elv.		
'Surely'	♪=72	♪=80	♪=92		
	Chrys.	Rblt. Prt. Crot.	Cpsmth.	Crot. Cl. Elv.	
'And with His stripes'	𝅗𝅥=69	𝅗𝅥=80	𝅗𝅥=84	𝅗𝅥=88	𝅗𝅥=100
	Crot.	Rblt.	Chrys. Prt. Cpsmth	Cl. Elv.	
'All we like sheep'	♩=76	♩=88	♩=92	♩=100	
	Rblt.	Prt. Cpsmth.	Cl. Elv.		
'All they that see Him'	♪=63	♪=80	♪=88		
	Rblt.	Prt. Crot.	Cl. Elv. Chrys. Cpsmth.	Crot.	
'He trusted in God'	𝅗𝅥=69	𝅗𝅥=80	𝅗𝅥=88	𝅗𝅥=92	
	Rblt.	Chrys.			
'Thy rebuke'	♪=56	𝅗𝅥=58			
	Rblt.	Prt. Cpsmth.	Cl. Elv. Chrys.		
'Behold and see'	♪=56	♪=66	♪=100(𝅗𝅥=50)		
	Cl. Elv.	Rblt.	Prt. Cpsmth	Chrys.	
'But thou didst not leave'	♪=84	♪=92	♪=108	♪=132	
	Crot.	Rblt. Prt.	Cpsmth.	Chrys.	Elv. Cl.
'Lift up your heads'	𝅗𝅥=72	𝅗𝅥=76	𝅗𝅥=80	𝅗𝅥=84	𝅗𝅥=92
	Prt. Crot.		Rblt.	Cpsmth.	Cl. Elv.
'Let all the angels'	𝅗𝅥=72		𝅗𝅥=80	𝅗𝅥=88	𝅗𝅥=92
	Prt. Cpsmth.		Rblt.	Cl. Elv.	
'Thou art gone up'	𝅗𝅥=84		𝅗𝅥=100	𝅗𝅥=108	
	Rblt.	Crot.	Cl. Elv.	Prt. Cpsmth.	Chrys.
The Lord gave the word'	𝅗𝅥=58	𝅗𝅥=66	𝅗𝅥=76	𝅗𝅥=80	𝅗𝅥=92
	Cl. Elv.	Rblt.	Prt.	Cpsmth.	Chrys.
'How beautiful' (air)	♪=80	♪=96	♪=104	♪=108	♪=176
'Their sound is gone out' (chorus)	Crot. 𝅗𝅥=66	Cl. Elv. 𝅗𝅥—76	Rblt. Prt. Cpsmth. 𝅗𝅥=88		
'How beautiful' (alto duet and chorus)	Crot. 𝅗𝅥=92	Cpsmth. 𝅗𝅥=92			
'Their sound is gone out' (arioso)	Crot. ♪=92	Chrys. ♪=120	Cpsmth. ♪=144(𝅗𝅥=72)		
	Prt.	Chrys.	Rblt.	Cpsmth.	Cl. Elv.
'Why do the nations'	𝅗𝅥=112	𝅗𝅥=116	𝅗𝅥=120	𝅗𝅥=126	𝅗𝅥=132
	Crot.	Crot. Prt.	Cpsmth.	Rblt.	Cl. El.
'Let us break'	𝅗𝅥=69	𝅗𝅥=76	𝅗𝅥=88	𝅗𝅥=92	𝅗𝅥=104

'Thou shalt break them'	*Prt. Cpsmth.* 𝅗𝅥=84	*Cl. Elv.* 𝅗𝅥=92	*Rblt.* 𝅗𝅥=108		
'Hallelujah'	*Crot.* 𝅗𝅥=69	*Prt.* 𝅗𝅥=72	*Cl. Elv.* 𝅗𝅥=76	*Chrys.* 𝅗𝅥=88	*Cpsmth.* 𝅗𝅥=92
'I know that my Redeemer liveth'	*Cl. Elv.* 𝅗𝅥=54	*Rblt.* 𝅗𝅥=60	*Chrys.* 𝅗𝅥=63	*Prt.* 𝅗𝅥=72	*Cpsmth.* 𝅗𝅥=76

'Since by man' and **'As in Adam'**

Crot. ♪=69	*Crot.* ♪=72	*Cl.* ♪=80	*Rblt.* ♪=100(𝅗𝅥=50)	*Prt. Cpsmth.* ♪=120(𝅗𝅥=60)
Chrys. ♪=126(𝅗𝅥=63)	*Elv.* ♪=160(𝅗𝅥=80)			

'By man came also'	*Rblt. Prt. Crot.* 𝅗𝅥=84	*Crot.* 𝅗𝅥=88	*Cpsmth* 𝅗𝅥=92	*Cl. Elv. Chrys.* 𝅗𝅥=96
'Even so in Christ'	*Chrys.* 𝅗𝅥=100[1]	*Cpsmth.* 𝅗𝅥=96[1]		

'The trumpet shall sound'	*Prt.* 𝅗𝅥=80	*Cpsmth.* 𝅗𝅥=84	*Cl. Elv. Chrys.* 𝅗𝅥=92	*Rblt.* 𝅗𝅥=104

'O Death'	*Elv.* ♪=66	*Cl.* ♪=96	*Rblt.* ♪=100	*Crot.* ♪=108	*Prt. Cpsmth.* ♪=138 *Crot.* ♪=152
'But thanks be to God'	*Crot.* ♪=120	*Prt. Cpsmth.* ♪=138	*Rblt.* ♪=144	*Cl. Elv.* ♪=176	
'If God is for us'	*Prt. Cpsmth.* 𝅗𝅥=88	*Cl. Elv.* 𝅗𝅥=92	*Rblt.* 𝅗𝅥=104		

'Worthy is the Lamb' *(largo)*

Crot. Elv. Cl. ♪=60	*Crot.* ♪=69	*Rblt.* ♪=100(𝅗𝅥=50)	*Prt. Cpsmth.* ♪=120(𝅗𝅥=60)	*Chrys.* ♪=132(𝅗𝅥=66)

(andante)

Rblt. ♪=84	*Crot. Cl. Elv.* ♪=100	*Prt.* ♪=120	*Chrys.* ♪=152(𝅗𝅥=76)	*Cpsmth.* ♪=168(𝅗𝅥=84)

(larghetto)

Cl. Elv. ♪=80	*Crot.* ♪=120	*Crot.* ♪=138	*Rblt. Prt.* ♪=144	*Cpsmth.* ♪=152(𝅗𝅥=76)	*Chrys.* ♪=168(𝅗𝅥=84)

'Amen'	*Crot.* 𝅗𝅥=76	*Rblt. Prt.* 𝅗𝅥=84	*Cl. Elv. Cpsmth.* 𝅗𝅥=92	*Chrys.* 𝅗𝅥=112

[1] These two editions alone give a tempo differing from that of 'By man came also'

IRISH MANUSCRIPTS CONTENTS—I

Townley Hall	Marsh–Matthews	Mann 'Dublin'
GLORY TO GOD Chorus	GLORY TO GOD Chorus	GLORY TO GOD Chorus
	ALTERNATIVE I REJOICE GREATLY (page 93) The $\frac{12}{8}$ setting. Complete. THEN SHALL THE EYES OF THE BLIND (page 99) At the soprano pitch as in the Autograph score and with the voice part written in the soprano C clef. HE SHALL FEED HIS FLOCK (page 100) Soprano solo as in the Autograph score. Both stanzas in B♮ major with the voice part written in the soprano C clef.	
ALTERNATIVE II REJOICE GREATLY The $\frac{12}{8}$ setting. Shortened version.	REJOICE GREATLY (page 105)[1] The $\frac{12}{8}$ setting. Shortened version.	*ALTERNATIVE III* REJOICE GREATLY The $\frac{12}{8}$ setting. Shortened version.
THEN SHALL THE EYES OF THE BLIND Transposed down for alto with the voice part written in the alto C clef.	THEN SHALL THE EYES (on verso of half sheet between pages 110 and 111) Transposed down for alto with the voice part written in the alto C clef.	THEN SHALL THE EYES OF THE BLIND Transposed down for alto with the voice part written in the alto C clef.
HE SHALL FEED HIS FLOCK Alto solo. Both stanzas transposed down into F major, with the voice part written in the alto C clef.	HE SHALL FEED HIS FLOCK Alto solo. Both stanzas transposed down into F major, with the voice part written in the also C clef.	HE SHALL FEED HIS FLOCK Alto solo. Both stanzas transposed down into F major, with the voice part written in the alto C clef.
	ALTERNATIVE IV REJOICE GREATLY (page 117) The $\frac{4}{4}$ setting as in the Tenbury-Dublin copy, but in Handel's own hand. THEN SHALL THE EYES OF THE BLIND Transposed down for alto with the voice part written in the alto C clef. HE SHALL FEED HIS FLOCK 'Duet' version. First stanza in F major, second stanza in B♮ major with the voice part in alto and soprano C clefs respectively.	
HIS YOKE IS EASY Chorus	HIS YOKE IS EASY (page 133) Chorus	HIS YOKE IS EASY Chorus

[1] At this point in the manuscript is written 'turn back to page 99 for the recit. 'Then shall the eyes of the blind, etc.,' and then on page 100 is written the song 'He shall feed His flock'.

IRISH MANUSCRIPTS CONTENTS—II

Townley Hall	Marsh–Matthews	Mann 'Dublin'
THE LORD GAVE THE WORD Chorus	THE LORD GAVE THE WORD Chorus	THE LORD GAVE THE WORD Chorus
	ALTERNATIVE I HOW BEAUTIFUL ARE THE FEET (Romans X, 15 and 18) Soprano *da capo* air in G minor with the middle section set to the text 'Their sound is gone out' followed by a *dal segno* repeat. WHY DO THE NATIONS The original complete air of 96 bars.	
HOW BEAUTIFUL ARE THE FEET (Isaiah LII, 7 and 9) Alto-duet and chorus setting. This text does not include 'Their sound is gone out'. Verse 9 reads 'Break forth into joy'. This is the text of the choral section.	**ALTERNATIVE II** HOW BEAUTIFUL ARE THE FEET (Isaiah LII, 7 and 9) Alto-duet and chorus setting. As I have indicated Handel here set a different text. It does not include 'Their sound is gone out'. Verse 9 reads 'Break forth into joy'. This is the text of the choral section.	HOW BEAUTIFUL ARE THE FEET (Isaiah LII, 7 and 9) Alto-duet and chorus setting. This text does not include 'Their sound is gone out'. Verse 9 reads 'Break forth into joy'. This is the text of the choral section.
THEIR SOUND IS GONE OUT An arioso for tenor.	THEIR SOUND IS GONE OUT An arioso for tenor with, in this manuscript, an indication for a reprise of the choral section of the previous number.[1]	THEIR SOUND IS GONE OUT An arioso for tenor.
WHY DO THE NATIONS The shortened version with the recitative ending. In all 45 bars in length.	WHY DO THE NATIONS The shortened version with the recitative ending. In all 45 bars in length.	WHY DO THE NATIONS The shortened version with the recitative ending. In all 45 bars in length.
LET US BREAK Chorus	LET US BREAK Chorus	LET US BREAK Chorus

[1] The impact of this reprise upon my article 'A Messiah Problem' in *Music and Letters*, Volume 36 No. 4, that dealt with the half-close and full close versions of the alto duet and chorus settings of 'How beautiful' and the possibility of a *da capo*, is discussed on page 000.

A Short Bibliography

BIOGRAPHY

Memoirs of the Life of the Late George Frederic Handel, John Mainwaring, London 1760.
The Life of Handel, Victor Schoelcher (translated), London 1857.
G. F. Handel (3 vols.), Friedrich Chrysander, Leipzig 1858–67.
Georg-Friedrich Händel, Fritz Volbach (2nd edition), Berlin 1907.
Handel, R. A. Streatfield (with an introduction by J. Merrill Knapp, New York, 1964), London 1909.
Beethoven and Handel, Romain Rolland (translated), London 1916.
Handel, Percy M. Young, London 1947.
George Frideric Handel, Newman Flower (revised edition), London 1959.
George Frideric Handel, James S. Hall (revised and enlarged edition, 1963), London 1961.
Handel, Stanley Sadie, London 1962.

MANUSCRIPTS

Händel: Seine Lebensumstände, Herder (Adrastea, Vol. 3), Leipzig 1802.
Für Freunde der Tonkunst (Vols. I-IV), J. F. Rochlitz, Leipzig 1830–32.
Handel's Messiah. An Examination of the Original and Some Contemporary MSS., W. G. Cusins, London 1874.
The Mutilation of a Masterpiece, W. H. Cummings (Royal Musical Association, Vol. VII), London 1880.
Handel's Messiah: Discovery of the Original Word-book, Dublin, 1742, J. C. Culwick, Dublin 1891.
Handel's Messiah: the Oratorio and its History, J. Allanson Benson, London 1923.
Handel's Messiah, H. Watkins Shaw, London 1965.
Concerning Handel, William C. Smith, London 1948.
Messiah, Julian Herbage, London 1948.
'The Messiah: Handel's Second Thoughts,' Julian Herbage (*Musical Times*, October 1948).
Handel's Messiah, Robert M. Myers, New York 1948.
'*Messiah* Restored,' John Tobin (*Musical Times*, April 1950).
The Catalogue of the *Messiah* exhibition in the British Museum, London 1951.
'A *Messiah* Problem,' John Tobin (*Music and Letters*, October 1955).
Handel's Messiah, J. P. Larsen, London 1957.
'John Matthews Manuscript of *Messiah*,' H. Watkins Shaw (*Music and Letters*, April 1958).

THE ORATORIOS

Handel's Sacred Oratorios, T. Heptinstall, London 1799.
Händel's biblische Oratorien, Friedrich Chrysander, Hamburg 1897.
Geschichte des Oratoriums, A. Schering, Leipzig 1911.
The Oratorios of Handel, Percy M. Young, London 1949.
Handel: A Symposium, Ed. Gerald Abraham, London 1954.
Die Chorfuge in Händel's Werken, Georg-Friedrich Wieber, Frankfurt/Main 1958.
Handel's Dramatic Oratorios and Masques, Winton Dean, London, 1959.
Georg Friedrich Händel: Thema und 20 Variationen, Walter Siegmund-Schülze, Halle (Saale) 1965.

THE ORCHESTRA

The Orchestra of Bach and Handel, E. Prout (Royal Musical Association, Vol. XII), London 1885.
'Handel's Wind Parts to the *Messiah*,' E. Prout (*Monthly Musical Record*, Vol. XXIV), London 1894.
'Mozart, Handel and Johann Adam Hiller,' J. S. Shedlock (*Musical Times*, August 1918).
'The *Messiah* Accompaniments,' Thomas Armstrong (*Music and Letters*, Vol. IX), London 1928.
History of the Trumpet of Bach and Handel, W. Menke (tr. Gerald Abraham), London 1934.

European Musical Instruments, Francis W. Galpin, London 1937.

'Handel's Horn and Trombone Parts,' W. F. H. Blandford (*Musical Times*, Vol. LXXX), London 1939.

The Orchestra in the XVIII Century, Adam Carse, Cambridge 1940.

Musical Instruments Through the Ages, Ed. Anthony Baines, London 1961.

INFLUENCES

'Graun's Passion Oratorio and Handel's knowledge of it,' E. Prout (*Monthly Musical Record*, Vol. XXIV), London 1894.

The Indebtedness of Handel to Works by Other Composers, Sedley Taylor, Cambridge 1906.

Handel and His Orbit, P. Robinson, London 1908.

ACCOMPANIMENT

Singe, Spiel- und Generalbass-Übungen, G. Ph. Telemann (Ed. Max Seiffert, Kassell 1920), Hamburg 1733/4.

Versuch über die wahre Art das Clavier zu spielen, C. P. E. Bach (tr. into English by William J. Mitchell, London 1949), 1753, 1762.

Figured Bass Playing, J. Raymond Tobin, London 1909.

Die Anfang des Basso Continuo und seiner Bezifferung, Max Schneider, Leipzig 1918.

The Art of Accompaniment from a Thorough Bass, F. T. Arnold, London 1931.

The Cadence in 18th Century Recitative, Sven Hostrup Hansell (*The Musical Quarterly*, Vol. LIV No. 2), New York, 1968.

The Harpsichord, Eta Harich-Schneider, St. Louis, U.S.A., 1945.

Early Keyboard Instruments, Philip James.

PERFORMANCE

Der Harmonische Gottesdienst, Georg Ph. Telemann (Ed. Gustave Fock, Kassell 1953), Hamburg 1725.

Observations on the Florid Song, Pier Francesco Tosi (tr. Galliard), London 1743.

Versuch einer Gründlichen Violinschule, Leopold Mozart (tr. Editha Knocker, London 1951), Augsburg 1756.

An Essay on Musical Expression, Charles Avison, London 1775.

Versuch einer Anweisung die Flute traversiere zu spielen, Johann Joachim Quantz (Facsimile Ed. by Hans-Peter Schmitz, Kassel 1953), Berlin 1789.

Die Lehre von der vocalen Ornamentik, Hugo Goldschmidt, 1907.

Die Verzierung der Sologesänge im Händels Messias, M. Seiffert (Sammelbände der Internationalen Musikgesellschaft, Vol. VIII), 1907.

Die Ornamentik der Musik, Adolf Beyschlag, Leipzig 1908.

'Über Chrysanders Bearbeitung des Händel'schen *Messias* und über die Musikpraxis zur Zeit Händels,' A. Beyschlag (*Die Musik Jg.*), 1910–11.

The Interpretation of Music of the XVII and XVIIIth Centurie, Arnold Dolmetsch, London 1916.

Gesangskunst der Kastraten, Franz Haböck, Vienna 1923.

Aufführungspraxis, Robert Haas, Potsdam 1931.

Aufführungspraxis Alter Musik, A. Schering 1931.

Origins of Musical Time and Expression, Rosamond Harding, London 1938.

Music in the Baroque Era, Manfred F. Bukofzer, New York 1947.

The Interpretation of Music, Thurston Dart, London 1953.

Bach's Ornaments, Walter Emery, London 1954.

The Interpretation of Early Music, Robert Donington, London 1963.

Schule des Generalbasspiels, Hermann Keller, Kassell 1950 (translated London 1966).

MISCELLANEOUS

An Account of the Musical Performances in Westminster Abbey and the Pantheon in 1784, Charles Burney, London 1785.

'The Granville Collection of Handel Manuscripts,' R. A. Streatfield (*Musical Antiquary*, Vol. II, 1911).

'The English influences on Handel,' E. J. Dent (*Monthly Musical Record*, Vol. LXI), London· 1931.

'Handel Lacunae,' J. M. Coopersmith (*Musical Quarterly*), New York 1938.

The Letters and Writings of George Frideric Handel, E. Müller, London 1935.

Bach and Handel: The Consummation of the Baroque in Music, Archibald T. Davison, Cambridge, Mass. 1951.

Musical Year Book, Vol. VII, pp. 358 ff, 460 ff. Ed. Max Hinrichsen.

'Goethe and Handel,' Stanley Godman (The English Goethe Society, Vol. XXIII), London 1954.

Handel: A Documentary Biography, O. E. Deutsch, London 1955.

The Castrati in Opera, Angus Heriot, London 1956.

Händel-Jahrbuch, Ed. Walther Siegmund-Schülze, Leipzig 1957.

Handel. A Descriptive Catalogue of the Early Editions, William C. Smith, London 1960.

Händel Bibliographie, Konrad Sasse, Leipzig 1963 (Supplement 1967).

A Handelian's Notebook, William C. Smith, London 1965.

Handel and His Autographs, A. Hyatt King, London 1967.

Watermarks in Paper in the XVII and XVIII Centuries, W. A. Churchill, Amsterdam 1935.

Music in the Baroque Era, Manfred F. Bukofzer, New York 1947.

Acknowledgments

I ACKNOWLEDGE my indebtedness:

To Her Majesty the Queen for gracious permission to use photographic reproductions of the Autograph score of *Messiah* and other Handel autographs in the Royal Music Library before its gift to the nation, and afterwards to the Trustees of the British Museum; to the Warden and Fellows of St. Michael's College, Tenbury, Worcestershire, for the reproductions from the Dublin copy; to the Director of the Hamburg State and University Library for the reproduction from the Schoelcher copy;

To Mr. C. B. Oldham, formerly Principal Keeper of Printed Books, British Museum; to Mr. A. Hyatt King, Superintendent in charge of the Music Room, British Museum; to Dr. Bertram Schofield, formerly Keeper of Manuscripts, British Museum; to the Warden, Fellows, and Hon. Librarian, Mr. H. Watkins Shaw (and the immediate past Warden, the Rev. Noel, Kemp-Welch) of St. Michael's College, Tenbury; to the Provost and Fellows of King's College, Cambridge; to the Director, Fitzwilliam Museum, Cambridge; to the Governors of the Thomas Coram Foundation (lately the Foundling Hospital); to the Board of Trinity College, Dublin; to the Director (Dr. H. Tiemann), his Adviser (Dr. E. Zimmerman) and the Superintendent of the Music Department (Dr. K. W. A. Richter) of the State and University Library, Hamburg; to the Governors and Guardians of the Archbishop Marsh Library, Dublin; to Mr. Gerald Coke, the late R. Sterndale Bennett, and the late Sir Newman Flower for their ready co-operation in making available the manuscripts and other material essential to my research;

To Mr. William C. Smith, for his generous assistance in supplying data from his vast fund of Handelian research, as well as for giving access to his Handel collection, which now forms part of the Gerald Coke collection;

To Mr. C. L. Cudworth, Librarian of the University Music School, Cambridge, for his assistance in endeavouring to establish the authorship of the ornamentation in the Barrett-Lennard MS. score in the Fitzwilliam Museum;

To Dr. Ernest Stacy Griffith, Dean of the School of International Service, American University; Dr. Harold Spivacke, Director of the Music Section, Library of Congress, Washington D.C., and Mr. John F. Fleming, New York, for information regarding the Goldschmidt copy;

To Professor Widdis, Librarian of the Royal College of Surgeons in Ireland, and Dr. Bethel Solomons, for information regarding the music in Mercer's Hospital, Dublin;

To the Librarian of Trinity College, Dublin, to Mr. Desmond FitzGerald, and to the City Librarian, Dublin, for information regarding further copies of the 1742 Word-book;

To my brother, the late J. Raymond Tobin, the late Robert Elkin, and Mr. Denis Brearley, for the sacrifice of much precious time in critically reading endless typescripts, considering evidence, and assisting me to arrive at conclusions;

To Mr. Frederick C. Brown, Secretary of the Thomas Coram Foundation, for his assistance in the search for and the rediscovery of an important piece of evidence in the archives of the Foundation;

To the late Dr. H. Lowery, for converting Crotch's tempo measurements into M.M. rates with mathematical accuracy;

To Dr. Konrad Sasse, Director of the Handel Museum Halle (Saale), for permission to reproduce the portrait of Handel in the frontispiece;

To Miss Maureen Garnham and Miss Doris Cawdron for much invaluable assistance;

To the London Choral Society for its performance of my reconstruction of Handel's *Messiah* in St. Paul's Cathedral on 18th March 1950, the preparation for which was the *fons et origo* of my research; also to all the artists, vocal and instrumental, not forgetting that maker of superb harpsichords, Mr. Thomas Goff, for enabling me to put my research to the test of performance;

To Miss Joan Bernard, in particular for her work on the German translation, and for unearthing the eighteenth-century MS. of the harpsichord-conducting score of *Messiah*, and in general for her untiring assistance over some eight years in the research for the preparation of the score, assistance without which the work could hardly have been completed;

And finally to my wife, for her understanding and encouragement throughout the whole period of my research.

Index